WINTHROP'S BOSTON

JOHN WINTHROP
1588-1649

(The American Antiquarian Society Portrait)

WINTHROP'S
BOSTON

PORTRAIT OF A PURITAN TOWN
1630-1649

by

DARRETT B. RUTMAN

PUBLISHED FOR THE
Institute of Early American History and Culture
AT WILLIAMSBURG, VIRGINIA
By The University of North Carolina Press · *Chapel Hill*

For Anita

PREFACE

Toward the end of the seventeenth century Lawrence Hammond, a prominent freeman of Charlestown, jotted in his journal a current joke concerning an exciseman, "a Hectoring Debauchee, Residt in Boston," who chanced to meet "an Honest, Ingenious Countryman" while traveling.

"What Newes Countryman?" the exciseman asked.

"I know none," the other answered.

"I'll tell you som."

"What is it?"

"The Devil is Dead."

"How!" the countryman exclaimed. "I believe not that."

"Yes," said the exciseman, "he is dead for certaine."

"Well then," said the countryman, "if he be dead, he hath left many fatherless Children in Boston."

The story is, as all such stories are, apocryphal. Yet it indicates a truism which is particularly pertinent to the present work: What is said of Boston is not necessarily true of all New England.

The nature of this book is that of an extended essay—an analytical and interpretive study dealing with its subject from a limited point of view. Its broad purpose is to assess the nature of the difference between the ideal which lay behind the Winthrop migration of 1630 and the reality of the settled community as reflected in institutional development; its method has been to utilize John Winthrop and the town of Boston as protagonists, the man because he was avowedly the mainspring of the 1630 movement, the town because it was most clearly associated with Winthrop, and, while it originally embraced all the attributes of other Massachusetts communities, it was subsequently most affected by the impact of the commonwealth's turn to trade and commerce. There is, however, no attempt to imply that the tendencies and institutional developments observed in Boston can be unvaryingly applied to other towns, or to the commonwealth and section as a whole; only the thought that perhaps such an application can be made, that in Boston general currents were merely exaggerated by the town's peculiar situation, and that certainly the finite study of additional communities is necessary before generalizations can be expressed with any certainty.

The hallmark of institutions being constant change, particularly in these early years, the story is presented in the form of a narrative. It begins with Winthrop aboard the *Arbella* and proceeds through 1649, the year of the Governor's death, the separate but interrelated developments in government, church, land, and commerce being woven together in a rough chronological system. Too, the story is cast in the form of a tragedy, the steady decline of what are discerned as Winthropian ideals and their eventual defeat in the light of the developments in the town and to a lesser extent the commonwealth (for while the focus is Boston, events elsewhere are introduced when they play a role in the evolution of the town and its institutions, or reflect such evolution). One could easily reverse the tone to applaud and even glorify those tendencies, antipathetical to Winthrop's ideals, which would ultimately emerge as facets of an American character. Yet every historian is at least entitled and at most obliged to have a point of view. Winthrop's vision, impractical as it may have been, was as majestic as his faith in God, and one cannot avoid feeling a little saddened by its fate, even though that fate involved progress toward the present.

Boston was a dynamic community made up eventually of thousands of individuals, each with his or her own driving motives and aspirations. Wherever accepted generalizations could not be applied to the evolution of the town and to the doings of these thousands, the generalities have given way—with regard to the idea of a pre-existing notion as to church polity among the initial settlers, for example; to town government, which was far more than a mere agency of the commonwealth; to the existence of a specific "Puritan Mind." Indeed, the adjective "Puritan," together with the arguments surrounding it, have seemed inapplicable to Boston in any meaningful way, the total community being fragmented from almost the very beginning and, being made up of ordinary people, neither wholeheartedly humanistic nor frigidly glacial, neither entirely emotional nor entirely rational. Although I have spent little space arguing these specific points, it will be obvious where my conclusions differ from other commentators on the subject of New England and New England Puritanism. I have set them down unvarnished and without apology for their deviation from what have become in the last few decades standard interpretations, having drawn them from a close study of a wide range of material—rather than from any one preselected and limited area, as, for example, the writings of the ministers when dealing with the church.

All quotations have been modernized to the extent of expanding standard abbreviations and contractions, changing the characters thorn "y" to "th" and, where they have been used interchangeably, "v" to "u" and "i" to "j." Superscript letters have been reduced to line. Numerals sometimes recorded in Roman style, have been changed to our more customary form, while abbreviations *li, s,* and *d* have been used consistently for pounds, shillings, and pence. All dates in the text are given Old Style except the years, which have been modernized to make January 1 New Year's Day. To transpose the days of the month to New Style, add ten days. Where applicable, both Old and New Style dates are given in the notes.

An appended note on sources has been used to supply the bibliographical necessities and to sketch the methods used. The author's indebtedness to other historians is acknowledged there. It remains only to thank those persons who have directly facilitated the preparation of the book: Mr. James Morton Smith, Editor of Publications of the Institute of Early American History and Culture and his staff; *The William and Mary Quarterly,* which kindly consented to the inclusion of portions of two of the author's articles, "God's Bridge Falling Down: 'Another Approach' to New England Puritanism Assayed," and "Governor Winthrop's Garden Crop: The Significance of Agriculture in the Early Commerce of Massachusetts Bay"; the American Council of Learned Societies and the University of Minnesota, whose grants-in-aid of research enabled the writer to explore the manuscript depositories in and around Boston; and the writer's graduate students in early American history at the University of Minnesota, particularly Mr. Robert F. Scholz, whose arduous labors in gathering together the extant papers of John Cotton were of incalculable assistance. Finally, the author wishes to acknowledge the assistance of the many librarians and manuscript curators who have so kindly aided his work. Some are anonymous—the librarian who left her Monday wash in Winthrop, Massachusetts, to come to the public library to assist an inquiring stranger. (It was her day off and only she knew where the manuscript collection was stored.) Others are too numerous to mention by name: the staffs of the Walter Library of the University of Minnesota; the Alderman Library of the University of Virginia, where the work was begun; the library of the Minnesota Historical Society; the Boston Athenaeum; the Bostonian Society Library. Individuals stand out, however: Mr. Zoltán Haraszti, now Keeper Emeritus of Rare Books of the Boston Public Library, and his successor, Mr. John Alden; Mr. Clifford K. Shipton, Director of the American Antiquarian Society; Mr. Richard Walden Hale of the Massachusetts Archives, together with Mr. Leo Flaherty, Curator, and his charming wife; Mr. Clarkson A. Collins III, Librarian of the Rhode Island Historical Society; Mr. Robert W. Hill of the New York Public Library; Miss Marion Charlotte Reed of the New England Historic Genealogical Society; above all, Mr. Stephen T. Riley of the Massachusetts Historical Society and his staff, whose friendliness and efficiency contributed so much to a pleasant and fruitful summer, and most particularly Mr. John D. Cushing of the Society, whose assistance far exceeded normal courtesy and merits far more than normal thanks.

The University of Minnesota   D.B.R.

CONTENTS

LIST OF MAPS AND
ILLUSTRATIONS

*Maps and line graphs rendered from the author's sketches by
the Cartographic Laboratory, the University of Minnesota*

WINTHROP'S BOSTON

I

"A CITTY UPON A HILL"

THE MIND of any period or people of the past is an indescribable thing, for it is a conglomerate of the ever-changing desires, prejudices, and standards of the incoherent many as well as of the vociferous few. The writings of the leading figures will echo basic assumptions which, at the given moment, guide to a degree the conduct of the generality; but the compilation of assumptions does not constitute a description of the mind. What is written or said in one place at one time may not reflect another place or another time, although the difference be only a year or a score of miles. Certainly this is true with regard to the mind of the people called Puritans who sailed from England in 1630 intending to settle somewhere in the area of Massachusetts Bay. What the laymen and ministers who led them wrote before or after their migration will tell the present little about the total movement, for it was only the great who wrote, and even their thoughts were subject to change as their condition changed, first from old England to New, then as time progressed.

The mind of one man at one place and time is clear to us, however: that of John Winthrop, lawyer, manor lord of Groton in Suffolk, England, first governor of the Massachusetts Bay commonwealth, he whom the "Cheife undertakers" of the migration would not do without, "the wellfare of the Plantation" depending "upon his goeinge" with them to the New World.[1] En route across the Atlantic on the *Arbella,* the flagship of the 1630 migration—poised, as it were, between two worlds—Winthrop prepared a lay sermon, "A Modell of Christian Charity," which he delivered

1. "Perticular Considerations in the case of J:W: [1629]," in Massachusetts Historical Society, *Winthrop Papers,* 5 vols. (Boston, 1929-47), II, 133, hereafter cited as *Winthrop Papers.*

to his fellow passengers. In one phrase of the peroration he
summed up his thought: "Wee shall be as a Citty upon a Hill."[2]

Winthrop's expression was much more than a literary conceit
borrowed from the Gospel of Matthew. It reflected the core of his
thinking about the society he and his fellows intended to establish.
It would be a "city," first, in the literal, physical sense, for the
leaders of the Winthrop fleet—eleven ships carrying some seven
hundred passengers—anticipated settling in one centralized community.[3] Within the community each settler would have his
house and garden; beyond it would be the fields which the generality would cultivate and on which they would graze their cattle,
and the larger farms granted to the more wealthy and prominent
as their due, or for services rendered the group, or in return for
their investment in the enterprise—large enclaves in the wilderness
worked by servants. But the community would be the center, the
seat of the church, the place of government, a fortified refuge
should the Indians prove hostile or foreign enemies make an
appearance.

It would be a city, secondly, in the sense of a "city of God."
Man would serve God here in all the ways that God demanded He
be served. A meetinghouse where God's word in all its purity
could be heard would bulk large, and men would worship God as
He would have them worship. But far more: Men would serve
their fellow men in this city as God would have them serve; men
would fit into a society of men in such a way that the society would
redound to God's credit, add luster to His crown.

The idea of a godly society predominated in Winthrop's
thoughts as he crossed the Atlantic, his *Arbella* discourse being devoted to it rather than to other aspects of the city. And this was
natural. For while Winthrop and his fellows of 1630 were coming from a society where ideas of Christian brotherhood and right
conduct were expounded from every pulpit, where "the whole

2. Matt. 5:14; "A Modell of Christian Charity," *Winthrop Papers*, II, 282-
95. Except where otherwise noted, all quotations in this chapter are from the
"Modell."

3. In the absence of a direct statement, the intent of the leadership to settle a
single community must be assumed from the evidence of what happened. For
elaboration, see Appendix I.

society of man" was constantly being claimed for God,[4] it was nevertheless a crass, cruel society marked by fundamental social, political, and particularly economic changes in which emerging individualism, having disrupted the social unity of the past, was proceeding to extol and enrich the greater individual at the expense of the lesser. Some men during the century antedating Winthrop had already come to the conclusion that change at the expense of brotherhood was wrong. The commonweal movement had risen, eschewing the idea that a man could seek his profit without thought of others or limitations by church or state: "If the possessioners would consider themselves to be but stewards and not lords over their possessions," Robert Crowley had written in the mid-sixteenth century, "this oppression would soon be redressed. But so long as this persuasion sticketh in their minds: It is mine own, who should warn me to do with mine own as myself listeth? it shall not be possible to have any redress at all."[5] During the years between Crowley and Winthrop the state had intervened with a succession of statutes regulating the economy and providing for the impotent poor; the church had preached of morals and conscience and the cause of the community above private gain. But the laws remained, to 1629, largely ineffectual; the pulpit was too often ignored. "Conscience," a contemporary wrote, "is a pretty thing to carry to church but he that useth it in a fair market or shop may die a beggar."[6]

To Winthrop, England in 1622 had been "this sinfull lande."[7] And the sin he wrote of was social in nature. Two years later, in a list of "common grevances groaninge for reformation" drawn up in consultation with others, he had listed some of the causes of his dissatisfaction. Among them were those referring to the condition of the church—"the daylye encrease of the multitudes of papistes," "scandalous and dombe ministers," the "suspension and silenceing of many painfull learned ministers for not conformitie in some poynts of ceremonies." But most of Winthrop's complaints re-

4. Charles H. and Katherine George, *The Protestant Mind of the English Reformation, 1570-1640* (Princeton, 1961), 183.
5. Quoted in Stanley T. Bindoff, *Tudor England* (Harmondsworth, Eng., 1950), 131.
6. Quoted in Wallace Notestein, *The English People on the Eve of Colonization, 1603-1630* (New York, 1954), 22.
7. Winthrop to Thomas Fones, Jan. 29, 1621/22, *Winthrop Papers*, I, 268.

ferred to lay affairs: "the common scarcitie of woode and tymber," the necessity of reforming the system for "mendinge of hie wayes," "horse stealeinge," inequitable taxation, "the greate delayes in swetes of lawe" and "the undoeinge of many poore familyes" through the actions of "the multitude of Atturnies in the Courtes" and the "multitude and lewdnesse of Baylyfs," "the pittifull complainte of the orphanes fatherlesse and many poore creditors," the "intollerably burdened" farmer subjected to abuses by the "clerke of the market."[8]

Subsequently, as he prepared to leave England in 1629, he was more pointed. God, he wrote, had given "the sons of men" the whole earth that it might "be tilld and improved by them"; he had commanded them "to encrease and multiply and replenish the earth and subdue it . . . that man may enjoye the fruit of the earth, and God may have his due glory from the Creature." But pointing to the vagrants and beggars of England's countryside and cities, the malpractices of the market, the ponderous legal machinery with which he was so familiar, the extremes of rich and poor, he asked where "is the happinesse we should rest in?" "In the civill state"? "What means then the bleating of so many oppressed with wronge, that drink wormwood, for righteousnesse? why doe so many seely sheep that seeke shelter at the judgment seates returne without their fleeces? why meet we so many wandering ghostes in shape of men, so many spectacles of misery in all our streetes, our houses full of victuals, and our entryes of hunger-starved Christians? our shoppes full of riche wares, and under our stalles lye our own fleshe in nakednesse." "Our people perish for want of sustenance and imployment," he went on; "many others live miserably and not to the honor of so bountifull a housekeeper as the lord of heaven and earth is . . . : all our townes complain of the burden of poore people and strive by all menes to ridde any such as they have, and to keepe of[f] such as would come to them." To him, commerce was corrupt. He could not cite a single case "wherein a man may looke for recompence sutable to his expence of tyme and industrye, except falshood be admitted to equall the ballance." Agriculture in England was uneconomic: "If we should

8. Winthrop, "Common Grevances Groaninge for Reformation," *ca*. Feb.-Mar., 1623/24, *ibid.*, 295ff.

imploye our children in that waye now, their worke would soon eate up their stocks." Redress? It "might be had in these thinges by the magistrate, [but it] dothe not conclude that it shalbe."[9]

Winthrop himself was not personally oppressed in this society. Indeed, he was a comparatively well-to-do member of the English gentry. But his sensibilities were moved by the England about him. He dreamed of a better society, and sought the New World to make it a reality. The "Modell of Christian Charity" was his exposition of the nature of the new society he wished to establish in New England.[10]

In common with Christianity from its inception, Winthrop had of necessity to reconcile status, property, and God. He was too much a part of the seventeenth century to abandon any one of the three. God was, to him, the supreme, omnipotent, and omnipresent Prince of Heaven, the creator of all for His own purposes; God it was who had sent His son to live among men, humbly and without riches, appealing more to the poor in possessions and heart than to the wealthy and vain and promising in effect that the lowest on earth should be the highest in heaven.

Yet society, as it existed, was distinguished by its divisions into rich and poor, high and low; property existed, and the divisions of society rested largely upon its possession or lack. The mental image of God the creator and Christ who preached of rich men and eyes of needles had to be reconciled to the very real picture of property and status. Hence Winthrop began his discourse by establishing the God-ordained nature of social stratification and the ownership of property: "God Almightie in his most holy and wise providence hath soe disposed of the Condition of mankinde, as in

9. Winthrop, "General Observations [For the Plantation of New England, 1629]," and Winthrop to [?], 1629, *ibid.*, II, 115, 122-23.

10. In the absence of a major modern work on Winthrop, his own writings constitute his best biography; hence, because it is so replete with quotations, Robert C. Winthrop's *Life and Letters of John Winthrop* ..., 2 vols. (Boston, 1864-67), is the most adequate. Highly suggestive, however, is Edmund S. Morgan, *The Puritan Dilemma: The Story of John Winthrop* (Boston and Toronto, 1958). Winthrop's political and to a lesser extent social thought have been the subject of occasional commentary, most notably by Stanley Gray, "The Political Thought of John Winthrop," *New England Quarterly*, 3 (1930), 681-705, and George L. Mosse, *The Holy Pretence: A Study in Christianity and Reasons of State from William Perkins to John Winthrop* (Oxford, 1957), chap. 6.

all times some must be rich some poore, some highe and eminent in power and dignitie; others meane and in subjeccion." He had done so for a number of reasons: because His glory is made manifest in the creation of variety; because He can display His power over the wicked rich by restraining them from eating up the poor, and over the wicked poor by preventing them from rising up against their superiors; because He would have a setting in which His saints could display themselves, the sainted rich by their love, mercy, gentleness, the sainted poor by their faith, patience, obedience; and finally, He had arranged mankind in orders so that all men might have need of one another. The conclusion Winthrop desired was easily and logically drawn from such a godly and purposeful arrangement: No man is made more honorable or rich out of respect of himself, but for the purposes of God; God therefore has a first call upon his property.

Yet all too obviously there was a misuse of property and position in Winthrop's England and in the world at large, for the rich regularly ate the sustenance of the poor and, on occasion, the poor rose up against the rich. In the lore of Christianity and the Protestant theology of the churches of England, Winthrop found the solution. Man, living in the light of God, would have that perfect love toward God and mankind which would result in a godly use of property. Adam, before the fall, had such love, but Adam had wrenched himself and his posterity from his creator. As a consequence, love for one's brother was corrupted: "Every man is borne with this principle in him, to love and seeke himselfe onely." In this condition he would remain "till Christ comes and takes possession of the soule," gathering together the scattered bones of "perfect old man Adam" and infusing a new principle, "Love to God and our brother."

Looking out over the passengers aboard the *Arbella*, seeing in his mind's eye the men and women aboard the *Ambrose, Talbot, William and Francis*, and the other vessels of the fleet—men and women gathered together through the efforts of himself and his friends—Winthrop thought of the settlers as either actually or potentially infused with this regenerating principle. "Wee are a Company professing our selves fellow members of Christ," he wrote; before, in England, we were scattered, "absent from eache

other many miles, and had our imploymentes as farre distant."
But having embarked on this voyage "wee ought to account our
selves knitt together by this bond of love, and live in the exercise
of it." Status and property would then assume their proper position as godly gifts, given for God's purposes. Specifically, Winthrop asked charity of the settlers—the giving of one's abundance
in ordinary times, and the giving even beyond one's means on
extraordinary occasions. He would have them temper the spirit
of commerce with mercy, giving where it was necessary, lending
only where feasible in terms of the capability of the recipient to
repay, forgiving a debt when the debtor could not pay.

Winthrop's vision of Christian "love" involved more than mere
mercy and charity, however. It embodied his desire for form,
unity, and stability in society. Without Christian love, he wrote,
society could never be perfect. Men would strive after their own
good without thought of the well-being either of their fellows in
the society or of the society as a whole. The community resulting
from such individuality would be no more than an association of
independent objects "as disportionate and as much disordering as
soe many contrary quallities or elements." On the other hand,
Christian love pervading the society would serve as the "ligament"
binding the individual members to the one body. Individuality
would remain, but "all the partes of this body being thus united"
would be "soe contiguous in a speciall relacion as they must needes
partake of each others strength and infirmity, joy, and sorrowe,
weale and woe." "This sensiblenes and Sympathy of each others
Condicions will necessarily infuse into each parte a native desire and
endeavour, to strengthen defend preserve and comfort the other."
Implicitly, each member of the body would have its place and duty
in the total structure, some to serve, others to be served, some to
rule, others to be ruled, all happily accepting their place and work
for the benefit of all. Winthrop's simile was man's mouth, which
"is at all the paines to receive, and mince the foode which serves
for the nourishment of all the other partes of the body, yet it hath
noe cause to complaine; for . . . the other partes send backe by secret
passages a due proporcion of the same nourishment in a better
forme for the strengthening and comforteing the mouthe."

"Goe forth, every man that goeth, with a publick spirit,

looking not on your owne things onely," John Cotton, the eminent
minister of Boston, England, had exhorted the *Arbella*'s passengers
in his farewell sermon.[11]   Winthrop, describing the individual's
duty in the model society, echoed him: "The care of the publique
must oversway all private respects."   "Wee must love brotherly
without dissimulation, wee must love one another with a pure
heart fervently wee must beare one anothers burthens, wee must
not looke onely on our owne things, but allsoe on the things of our
brethren."   Conscience tells us this, Winthrop preached, but so too
does necessity, for recall that we are going to a strange, forbidding
land where dangers and difficulties will constantly beset us.   "Wee
must be knitt together in this work as one man, wee must entertaine
each other in brotherly affeccion, wee must be willing to abridge
our selves of superfluities, for the supply of others necessities, wee
must uphold a familiar Commerce together in all meekeness, gentlenes, patience and liberallitie, we must delight in each other, make
others Conditions our owne[,] rejoyce together, mourne together,
labour, and suffer together."   And, finally, the settlers were to do
these things not by command of the magistrate (the law having
proved futile in England when it sought to impose itself on the
spirit) but by virtue of the godly nature of that love which joined
them together.   Whatever coercion Winthrop would invoke would
not be man's, but God's.   We have a covenant with Him, he said;
we have accepted the obligation to live in such a way that ourselves
and our posterity might be better preserved from the common corruptions of the world; if we should fail and embrace this present
world, pursue carnal intentions, the Lord will break out in wrath
against us.

     In his discourse, Winthrop did not deal with the nature of gov-
ernment and church, though perhaps these subjects had been contemplated to some extent by the leaders while still in England.[12]
Yet his view of the nature of government is implicit both in his
discussion of men rich and poor, "highe and eminent in power and
dignitie; others meane and in subjeccion," and in his comment about
the covenant binding the settlers with God.   The first thought took
cognizance of the natural disparity between men which Winthrop,

11. John Cotton, *Gods Promise to His Plantation* ... (London, 1630), 19.
12. Arthur Tyndal to Winthrop, Nov. 10, 1629, *Winthrop Papers*, II, 166.

as the master of Groton, could not help accepting and which the English pulpit constantly pronounced as God's will, minister William Perkins, for example, writing that "God hath appointed that in every societie one person should be above or under another; not making all equall, as though the bodie should be all head and nothing else."[13] Reacting against conditions in England, however, Winthrop could not allow natural disparities to go untempered: Power was not a right of the mighty but a godly duty to deal in "love mercy, gentlenes, temperance" with those in subjection.

The second thought pertaining to government in the "Modell" reflected the pervasive contemporary view of the nature of the state which held that man in society selected the forms and personnel of government by way of a compact, and then bound himself to that government. In the western world, this idea of contract—or compact, or covenant—was ancient, but it was particularly relevant for the religious polemicists of the sixteenth and seventeenth centuries. The French *Vindiciae Contra Tyrannos*, establishing a philosophic basis for Protestants to rebel against a Catholic king, argued for the sovereignty of the people and the contracts which a people, as a people of God, made with God that "it will be and will remain the people of God" and with its ruler "to obey the king truly while he rules truly."[14] Protestant England wrote of the "covenant and bargaine" inherent in the coronation of the king by which "the people is bound and sworne to doe their allegance to their Kings, so the Kings are also solemnly sworne to maintaine and defend true Religion, the estate of Justice, the peace and tranquillity of their subjects, and the right and priviledges (which are nothing but the Lawes) of the Realme."[15] Richard Hooker, in his *Ecclesiastical Polity*, would have kings hold "their right to the power of dominion, with dependency upon the whole entire body politic over which they rule as kings," though he attempted to avoid the tendency toward revolutionary doctrine by confirming

13. William Perkins, *The Works of That Famous and Worthie Minister of Christ*, 3 vols. (London, 1612-13), I, 755.

14. Quoted in Sir Ernest Barker, *Church, State and Education* (Ann Arbor, 1957), 87-88. On the impact of the *Vindiciae* in England see J. H. Salmon, *The French Religious Wars in English Political Thought* (Oxford, 1959), *passim*.

15. Thomas Beard, *The Theatre of God's Judgements* ..., 3d ed. (London, 1648), 10.

the divine nature of kings once established. "God creating mankind did endue it naturally with full power to guide itselv, in what kind of societies soever it should choose to live," yet those on whom power "is bestowed even at men's discretion, they likewise do hold it by divine right," for "albeit God do neither appoint the thing nor assign the person; nevertheless when men have established both, who doth doubt but that sundry duties and offices depending thereupon are prescribed in the word of God." Therefore, Hooker concluded, "we by the law of God stand bound meekly to acknowledge them for God's lieutenants."[16]

From the aura of his times and from the Gospel—for he cited only the Gospels as his authority—Winthrop derived his own idea of the covenant. He spoke of the settlers having "entered into Covenant" with the Lord by virtue of their having committed themselves to His protection on the voyage and in the land where they were going. The covenant, though, was in the simplest of terms: their agreement to be God's people, to live in a godly fashion —that fashion which Winthrop had already outlined in terms of Christian love—in return for which "the Lord will be our God and delight to dwell among us." Having said this, he needed to say nothing more about government, for the divisions of rich and poor, rulers and ruled, were ordained by God. Consequently, in his city, the natural leaders—the wealthy, the gentlemen—would rule in the interest of the people, seeking "their welfare in all things,"[17] and the people would accept the government of these natural leaders out of their own God-ordained duty to "faithe patience, obedience."

Only subsequently would Winthrop elaborate on the covenant between the rulers and ruled. Fifteen years later, to the Massachusetts General Court and through it to the populace, he was to define the covenant in terms of "the oath you have taken of us"— the oath of fidelity required of all inhabitants by that time—"which is to this purpose, that we shall govern you and judge your causes by the rules of God's laws and our own, according to our best skill."

16. Richard Hooker, *Of the Laws of Ecclesiastical Polity*, Bk. VIII [1648], chap. 2, par. 5-6, 9, as reprinted in *The Works of ... Mr. Richard Hooker*, 7th ed. (Oxford, 1887).

17. Thomas Hutchinson, comp., *A Collection of Original Papers Relative to the History of the Colony of Massachusetts-Bay* (Boston, 1769), 100.

But the governors were not self-appointed; they were, rather, God-appointed through the people. "It is yourselves," he said, "who have called us to this office, and being called by you, we have our authority from God, in a way of ordinance, such as hath the image of God eminently stamped upon it, the contempt and violation whereof hath been vindicated with examples of divine vengeance."[18]

In contemplating the nature of the church, Winthrop also undoubtedly derived his ideas from the aura of his times, most notably from the assumptions of the churches of England. His terminology in the "Modell of Christian Charity" was that of English Calvinism. He saw the effects of the difficult economic and social adjustment in England in terms of the depravity of man. His own social attitudes and those he would have the settlers adopt were phrased in terms of the regeneration of man. He reflected faithfully the utter dependence of man upon God in effecting this regeneration, quoting the Apostle John in describing his Christian love, the ligament of the new society. "Love cometh of god and every one that loveth is borne of god, soe that this love is the fruite of the new birthe, and none can have it but the new Creature."

Yet Winthrop expressed social ideas in theological terms only because there were no other terms available to him, not because they formed the basis of his thought. He was not bound by the logic of the theology he expressed; indeed, he regularly violated that logic. His equating of Christian love with "new birthe," for example, echoed basic Calvinism and its relegation of man to the status of "an empty vessel" awaiting God's pleasure in filling it, a mute, inactive recipient of God's free grace. But there is no indication that Winthrop in his *Arbella* discourse was directing his words to a particular body of love-infused saints within the total number of settlers, nor was there a thought in the "Modell" or elsewhere in Winthrop's writings of the impossibility of creating a society bound by Christian love when the persons embarked on the attempt included (as they must have included) regenerates and reprobates, saints and sinners. There is, then, the paradox in the "Modell"

18. James Kendall Hosmer, ed., [*John*] *Winthrop's Journal "History of New England," 1630-1649*, 2 vols. (N.Y., 1908), II, 237-39; hereafter cited as *Winthrop's Journal*.

of anticipating a society of saints and sinners held together by a quality available only to the saints.

The paradox, though it does not disappear, becomes at least explicable on realizing the confused, chaotic, and contradictory thought of the English churches from which Winthrop was emerging. There was the England of the Thirty-Nine Articles of Faith, a reiteration of basic Calvinism, but there was also the England which had drifted away from Calvin to pronounce that "despite the fact that man cannot will himself into salvation [or into Winthrop's Christian love], nonetheless he does possess the capacity to cooperate with and consent to God's will to save him."[19] There was the England, too, which had gone even further, exceeding the limitations on ministerial activity inherent in Calvinism by actively soliciting conversion, as when Hugh Peter prayed for the Queen that "the light of Goshen might shine into her soul, and that she might not perish in the day of Christ" or reported his activity at St. Sepulchre in London: "There was six or seven thousand Hearers, and the circumstances fit for such good work" that "above an hundred every week were persuaded from sin to Christ."[20] As one modern study expresses it, "the very activities of an intensely proselytizing and evangelical church, as early [English] Protestantism was, are directly contradictory, in terms of simple logic, to strict predestinarian doctrine. Indeed, the whole literature of English Protestantism is a product of ministerial enthusiasm which seems constantly to be overstepping the limits which logically it has set for itself."[21] In this climate, is it too much to expect that Winthrop should pay homage to God's free grace and proceed illogically to the optimistic view of man's ability to rise above his depraved nature by himself and form a godly society on earth? For in the last analysis, the "Modell of Christian Charity" is an optimistic document. All the men and women of the migration were considered to be capable of that Christian love for brothers and for the community necessary to the creation of a godly city. Christians all, the settlers were "to worke upon their heartes, by

19. George and George, *Protestant Mind of the English Reformation,* 64-65, quoting Bishop Lancelot Andrewes.

20. Quoted in Raymond Phineas Stearns, *The Strenuous Puritan: Hugh Peter,* *1598-1660* (Urbana, 1954), 36, 44.

21. George and George, *Protestant Mind of the English Reformation,* 58.

prayer meditacion continuall exercise . . . till Christ be formed in them and they in him all in eache other knitt together by this bond of love."

In still another area—that of church polity—English thought was confused. On the one hand, the religious establishment constituted a national church embracing the total population of England; it was, too, an authoritarian church, pyramidally organized from the peak of earthly authority (the king) downward through archbishops, bishops, and priests to the lowly communicant. On the other hand, however, theory held that original authority rested in the individual congregations within the church and was merely delegated upward. Richard Hooker, in constructing a philosophic basis for the episcopal hierarchy, had written of "the whole body of the Church being the first original subject of all mandatory and coercive power within itself." That the churches in England had granted power to a higher body and even a single man (as had the people of England with regard to the state) did not diminish the validity of the concept of original power residing at the bottom, and Hooker could even envision the congregations drawing power back to themselves in extreme cases. Theory also held that there were in reality two churches, one visible, one invisible. Hooker, concerned as he was with the visible institutional church of all Englishmen, nevertheless recognized the true saints of the invisible church as well, "that Church of Christ, which we properly term his body mystical" and which resides within the body of the institutional church but cannot be "sensibly discerned by any man," only by God. William Perkins, too, spoke of the church as a "mixt . . . companie of men . . . true beleevers and hypocrites mingled together," the believers being the invisible church known to God, the totality being the visible church of man. James Ussher, on the other side of many doctrinal fences from Perkins, similarly acknowledged the outer church but stressed that true membership was confined to those who "are by the Spirit and Faith secretly and inseparably conjoyned unto Christ their head." And along with some other English Protestants, he strained the logical barrier—that God, not man, identifies His saints—to advise the godly to shun the ungodly, "to renounce all fellowship with sin and sinners" and keep company with "one another in faith and love . . . in the society of the Saints."[22] The espousal of the communion of the elect was the antithesis of the principle of a national church.

As Winthrop and his companions sailed, English religious thought was—as it had been for long, and would be for longer yet —in the throes of a reconciliation of its innate contradictions. Orthodox Anglicanism was being hammered out, and with it dissent. The process was agonizing, the intellectual air electric with clashing doctrines, the disputations of the clerics in print and pulpit a thunderous discord. The forms and practices of worship were in constant dispute as many, frequently the most ardent and zealous of the churchmen, called for a wiping away of the last vestiges of Catholicism and a return to the verities of the primitive church of the first centuries after Christ. The mingling of godly and ungodly within the church, at times under the spiritual care of ministers who were themselves ungodly, was for some churchmen a most heinous error. Such clerics stressed the communion of the elect at the expense of the national church and sought, by excluding the palpably ungodly, to form a rough correlation between the visible and invisible churches. They tended, moreover, to accent the congregational nature of the churches. Finding in their studies of the New Testament and the "fathers" of the church that the primitive church had been congregationally organized, they considered the hierarchy of prelates found in England an aberration from Christ's pure structure and, going beyond Hooker's theoretic congregationalism, they argued for a return of actual authority to the English congregations. Here and there extremists renounced the English churches entirely, declared them "false and counterfeit," and set about establishing separatist congregations, voluntarily covenanting together to live as a people of God under ministers of their own choosing (rather than ministers set over them by a bishop), free to discipline their own membership, and admitting to communion and to the baptism of their children only those who, "so far as men in charity could judge," were "justified, sanctified, and entitled to the

22. Hooker, *Ecclesiastical Polity*, Bk. VIII, chap. 6, par. 3; Bk. III [1594], chap. 1, par. 2; Perkins, *Works*, III, 16; James Ussher, *A Body of Divinitie or The Summe and Substance of Christian Religion . . .*, 5th ed. (London, 1658), 188, 191.

promises of salvation, and life eternal."[23] Their course was a dangerous one, for separation was anathema to the English mind and such "schismatics" were subject to persecution. But their number was small. More normally the dissenting ministers remained within the national church as nonconformists, accepting the establishment with all its errors in the hopes of an ultimate reformation, all the while using casuistry and taking advantage of the relative laxness of the hierarchy prior to the late 1620's and early 1630's to purify their services and, in some cases, profess in varying degrees and ways a vague and ill-defined congregationalism devoid of separatist connotations.

Winthrop and the leaders of the 1630 migration emerged from that area of England most affected by the dissenting zeal—London and the eastern counties from Kent to Lincoln; they were themselves zealous in their desire to cleave to God and undoubtedly familiar to an extent with the various arguments put forth by their ardent ministers. But as a group they do not appear as advocates of any precise synthesis.[24] They sailed as English Protestants and went out of their way to say so in *The Humble Request* to the congregations of England written and published as they departed. Belief was not leading them to separate from the English church, they wrote; the church was, rather, "our deare Mother," and they drew a parallel between themselves sailing to the New World to establish another church and the primitive church of Philippi "which was a colonie from *Rome*."[25] Winthrop's own writings reflect not that he had chosen between the contradictions in English religious thought, but the contradictions themselves. The very act of leaving sinful England to found a godly city was an expression of the idea of the communion of the elect; but the joining together of the godly and ungodly in the attempt (even with undertones of the

23. *A True Confession of the Faith, and Humble Acknowledgment of the Alegeance, Which Wee Hir Majesties Subjects, Falsely Called Brownists, Doo Hould [towards] God, and Yield to Hir Majestie* (n.p., 1596), as reprinted in Williston Walker, ed., *The Creeds and Platforms of Congregationalism*, Pilgrim Press ed. (Boston, 1960), 51; John Robinson, quoted in Edmund S. Morgan, *Visible Saints: The History of a Puritan Idea* (N. Y., 1963), 57.

24. See below, chap. 3, pp. 47-48, and Appendix II.

25. *The Humble Request of His Majesties Loyall Subjects, the Governour and the Company Late Gone for New England; to the Rest of Their Brethren in and of the Church of England* (London, 1630), as reprinted in *Winthrop Papers*, II, 232.

ungodly being capable of conversion from sin to the good life) implied the idea of a universal church. The contradiction between the two went unresolved.

In the New World, however, resolution would be forced upon Winthrop and his followers. There they would be faced with the necessity of forming churches as centers for new communities without an existing prelacy to which the congregations could delegate power; they would find churches at Plymouth and Salem composed of the professedly godly and organized on a congregational basis. There, too, the newcomers would drift into the same practices, drawing upon the knowledge of congregational theory which they brought from England and using Salem and Plymouth as models. Yet the drift was not without difficulties, indicating that the practices they were to adopt were not implicit in Winthrop's "Citty upon a Hill." Indeed, Winthrop's initial contact with the congregational practices of Salem was seemingly something of a surprise. On first landing, he and some of his companions appeared at the Salem church seeking communion for themselves and the baptism of a child born at sea. They came, as they would to any church in England, to take advantage of the facilities held out to all. But Salem refused to accept them inasmuch as the church there had come to hold that the seals of the church (baptism and communion) should be offered only to covenanted members and those recommended by a similarly organized congregation. One or more of the Winthrop group was disturbed enough by the incident to report it to the Reverend John Cotton in England, prompting that worthy divine to write a critical letter to the Salem minister about the church's practices.[26]

Subsequently the leaders and ministers among the settlers found themselves divided over church polity. Samuel Fuller, who, together with others from Plymouth and Salem, was free with his advice as to the form of church organization which the newcomers should adopt, wrote of holding long wearisome conferences with the ministers and lay leaders of the Bay. "Opposers" of the

26. The child was William Coddington's. *A Sermon Preached by the Reverend, Mr. John Cotton, Teacher of the First Church in Boston in New England. Deliver'd at Salem,* [*June*] *1636* ... (Boston, 1713), 1-2; John Cotton to Samuel Skelton, Oct. 2, 1630, in Thaddeus Mason Harris, *Memorials of the First Church in Dorchester* (Boston, 1830), 53-57.

Plymouth-Salem way "there is not wanting, and satan is busy," he reported to Governor William Bradford at Plymouth. The Reverend John Warham argued for a church organization in line with contemporary English practice, a universal church consisting "of a mixed people,—godly, and openly ungodly." Some of the leaders of the Winthrop fleet apparently insisted that the Reverend George Phillips should minister to them by virtue of his English ordination rather than a congregational call, for Phillips told Fuller during a private conference "that if they will have him stand minister, by that calling which he received from the prelates in England, he will leave them." (Years later Cotton Mather was to write that Phillips was, from the standpoint of what would become New England orthodoxy, "better acquainted with the true *church-discipline* than most of the ministers that came with him into the country.") The Reverend John Wilson, on the other hand, seemed more amenable in this regard, for he was to accept the call of the church gathered at Charlestown "with this protestation by all, that it was only as a sign of election and confirmation, not of any intent that [he] should renounce his ministery he received in England."[27]

That Winthrop and his compatriots sailed without a precise idea of the nature of the church they were to erect should not be surprising. The Winthrop migration was a lay movement, not clerical. "Able and sufficient Ministers" were sought after to journey with the settlers, for religion was an integral part of life.[28] But notably few ministers were willing to hazard themselves in the venture in 1629 and 1630. Only later would they come, and then eagerly, seeking sanctuary from Archbishop William Laud's attempt to create a Church of England out of the diverse churches of England.

As a lay movement, the ideals of 1630 were lay ideals, social, rather than religious, though to the extent that the church was a part of the social organization, it too would be reformed. Win-

27. Samuel Fuller to William Bradford, June 28, 1630, Mass. Hist. Soc., *Collections*, 1st Ser., 3 (1794), 75; Cotton Mather, *Magnalia Christi Americana; or, the Ecclesiastical History of New-England . . .*, 2 vols. (Hartford, 1853), I, 377; *Winthrop's Journal*, I, 51.

28. John Winthrop and others to [?], Oct. 27, 1629, *Winthrop Papers*, II, 163-64.

throp quite obviously did not subscribe to all the practices of the
English church. His 1624 catalogue of "common grevances groaninge for reformation" included criticisms of the establishment, particularly the conduct of that part of the ministry which was corrupted by impoverishment and intent upon the pursuit of security
in this world rather than the next; he preferred a simplicity of
religious service, yet he conformed to the forms and practices of
England, considering that "ceremonyes ar by our ch[urch] of
England holden to be but thinges indifferent."[29] His great pecu-
liarity, however, was his intensity, his literal application to society
of the Biblical injunction to "love thy neighbor as thyself." Time
after time this intensity—and its origin in the pulpit pronounce-
ments and polemic literature of Protestant England—appears in
his writings. As to "the estate of our Churche and Com[mon]-
w[ealth]," he wrote just prior to the migration, "let the grones
and fears of Godes people give a silent answer: If our condition be
good, why doe his Embassadours [the ministers] turne their mes-
sages into complaintes and threatninges? why doe they so constantly denounce wrathe and judgment against us? why doe they
pray so muche for healinge if we be not sicke?"[30] And on the
Arbella, summing up the duties of the citizen in the godly society,
he preached, "Whatsoever wee did or ought to have done when wee
lived in England, the same must wee doe and more allsoe where
wee goe: That which the most in theire Churches mainteine as a
truthe in profession onely, wee must bring into familiar and constant practise."

One can call Winthrop a "Puritan," but not in the sense of
his holding to a logical edifice of theology and polity. He was a
Puritan only in the most limited of senses—that of Perry Miller
when he writes of "the Augustinian strain of piety" which leads
men to that futile search for a road to bring them face to face with
truth, God; of Alan Simpson and James F. Maclear when they
write of Puritanism as a "blind thrust," an "unbelievable intensity"
of feeling toward God and fellow man, "deep emotional longings
for personal encounter and direct communion with God"; and of

29. "Common Grevances," *ibid.*, I, 295ff, 305; Christopher Hill, *Economic
Problems of the Church: From Archbishop Whitgift to the Long Parliament*
(Oxford, 1956), chap. 9.
30. Winthrop to [?], 1629, *Winthrop Papers*, II, 121.

William Perkins when he described "Puritans and Presitions" as "those that most indeavour to get and keepe the puritie of heart in a good conscience."[31] Similarly, one can term Winthrop's errand to the New World "religious" in but the simplest sense of the word. His was a blind thrust into the wilderness, undertaken precipitously—there is no evidence of his preparing to remove prior to 1629—and without elaborate planning. Fear lay behind the movement to America, fear of the successes of Catholicism in the Counter Reformation then in progress. But more important as a motivating factor was what can be termed Winthrop's "social conscience"—his concern for the generality of an England which to him was growing "wearye of her Inhabitantes, so as man which is the most pretious of all Creatures, is heere more vile and base, then the earthe they treade upon"—and his vision of a new society, perhaps one which in God's good time the rest of the world would emulate, a setting in which salvation would be more readily obtainable for himself and all who desired to live in Christ's shadow.[32] In the broadest sense of the word, too, one can call Winthrop a "utopian" as he crossed the Atlantic aboard the *Arbella,* a dreamer of heaven on earth; he would have Christian love pervade the new society, while holding that "to love and live beloved is the soules paradice, both heare and in heaven."

Ironically, however, Winthrop was doomed to failure, in large measure by the very land he chose for his venture. Reacting to the contemporary English scene, he envisioned a society in which men would subordinate themselves to their brothers' and the community's good, but he sought to erect that society in a land where opportunity for individual profit lay ready to every hand. And Winthrop's optimism that man could overcome his own nature—so illogical in view of his apparent Calvinism—was to prove sadly misplaced. Speaking aboard the *Arbella,* his was but one small voice, one mind, among hundreds; his dream was not necessarily that of the whole number of settlers, nor of those who would

31. Perry Miller, *The New England Mind: The Seventeenth Century,* Beacon Press ed. (Boston, 1961), 3ff; Alan Simpson, *Puritanism in Old and New England* (Chicago, 1955), 21, and *passim;* James Fulton Maclear, " 'The Heart of New England Rent': The Mystical Element in Early Puritan History," *Mississippi Valley Historical Review,* 42 (1956), 623; Perkins, *Works,* III, 15.
32. "General Observations," *Winthrop Papers,* II, 114.

arrive in the commonwealth in the years ahead. On the contrary, to judge by actions in the New World, his was the exceptional mind. In America, the acquisitive instincts of the contemporary Englishman would rush to the surface, overwhelming Winthrop's communal ideal; conflicting minds would fragment the society which Winthrop would have perfectly united in thought, speech, judgment, and, above all, God's holy love. Institutions—defined as the various postures the community assumes in undertaking specific functions—would initially display the marks of Winthrop's ideal, but their evolution would reflect other minds and the new land. The process of disruption would begin immediately upon landing. Within two months a stunned Winthrop would write of Satan bending "his forces against us . . . so that I thinke heere are some persons who never shewed so much wickednesse in England as they have doone heer." Within five years another would comment that in leaving England men of pure hearts had "made an ill change, even from the snare to the pitt."[33] Within twenty years, Winthrop—who had rejected the vision of modern man he had seen in England and sought the refuge of a secular monastery (for that is what his "Citty upon a Hill" sums up to)—would be dead, and his commonwealth would be distinctly modern.

33. Winthrop to Margaret Winthrop, July 23, 1630, and Nathaniel Ward to John Winthrop, Jr., Dec. 24, [1635], *ibid.*, 303, III, 216.

II

SHAWMUT

"SALEM, WHERE WE LANDED, pleased us not," wrote Thomas Dudley, describing the arrival of the Winthrop fleet in June 1630.[1] But the Deputy Governor of the Massachusetts Bay Company did not elaborate. Perhaps the Cape Ann peninsula, where the parent company of the Massachusetts Bay venture had already established a commercial outpost under the government of John Endecott, was too constricted for the settlement envisioned by the newcomers, or too rockbound. Or perhaps the conditions in Salem at their coming dissuaded them, for Dudley wrote that "we found the Colony in a sad and unexpected condition," eighty or more of the old settlers having died during the previous winter, "many of those alive weak and sick" and "all the corn and bread amongst them all hardly sufficient to feed them a fortnight."[2]

But if we do not know exactly why the newcomers left Salem, Dudley's words still imply that Cape Ann had been the site selected in England for their settlement, the leaders of the Winthrop fleet probably anticipating establishing their town near Salem or even merging with the settlers already there. Rejecting Cape Ann, they were forced to look for an alternative location. In the course of the search Winthrop's "Citty upon a Hill" in the first sense of the phrase—that of a centralized community—would disappear, the men and women of the fleet dispersing into scattered towns. One of them would be Boston.

The search began five days after the *Arbella* arrived off Salem.[3]

1. Dudley to Lady Bridget, Countess of Lincoln, Mar. 12, 1630/31, in Alexander Young, comp., *Chronicles of the First Planters of the Colony of Massachusetts Bay, from 1623 to 1636* (Boston, 1846), 312.
2. *Ibid.*, 311.
3. Documentary material relative to the activities of the settlers during the first year and the actual settlement of Boston is extremely scarce. Winthrop

From descriptive letters and pamphlets which circulated in England, the leaders had a firm knowledge of the coast. But the men of Salem seem to have been consulted too, during the few days prior to June 17 when the first of two exploratory parties set out from the fleet. Winthrop himself led this group, traveling by boat into Massachusetts Bay and what would become Boston Harbor or, as they termed it, Boston Bay. One can easily visualize the scene: The pinnace twisting and turning among the islands dotting the harbor; a half-dozen odd sailors, roughly clad and rough in their language, working the vessel, watching the strange waters for rocks and obstructions; three or four quiet, earnest men from the fleet sitting together in the thwarts, staring eagerly at the shoreline. Now and again one of them would point out a cove breaking the pattern of beach and sandy-colored cliff or gesture toward the rolling hills encircling the harbor at a distance. Here and there along the shore or on islands lived scattered Englishmen and women, the residue of earlier attempts to settle the area—a few fishermen on Nantasket, the bar-like peninsula guarding the entrance to the harbor; the widow Thompson; Samuel Maverick at Winnisimmet on the north shore of the harbor; the Reverend William Blackston on the hilly, tadpole-shaped peninsula which the Indians called "Shawmut"; an isolated party from Salem occupying the Charlestown peninsula. The explorers sailed past all of these and, rounding Shawmut, found two rivers flowing into the harbor, one from the southwest (the Charles), the other from the north-

himself was far too busy to keep a full account, although one can partially construct a chronology from the entries in *Winthrop's Journal*, I. His extant letters to England tell little. Thomas Dudley's lengthy letter of Mar. 1631 to Lady Bridget in Young, comp., *Chronicles of the First Planters*, 303-41, and the letters dispatched to Plymouth in 1630 by Samuel Fuller and others, included in "Governor [William] Bradford's Letter Book," Mass. Hist. Soc., *Collections*, 1st Ser., 3 (1794), 27-76, afford the fullest accounts. John Noble and John F. Cronin, eds., *Records of the Court of Assistants of the Colony of the Massachusetts Bay, 1630-1692*, 3 vols. (Boston, 1901-28), hereafter cited as *Assistants' Records*, begins early enough to be helpful. The memoirs of Captain Roger Clap reprinted by Young (pp. 345-67) are valuable, particularly for the Dorchester settlers. On Dudley see Augustine Jones, *The Life and Work of Thomas Dudley, the Second Governor of Massachusetts* (Boston and N.Y., 1899); [Cotton Mather], "The Life of Mr. Thomas Dudley, Several Times Governor of Massachusetts Colony, in New England," Mass. Hist. Soc., *Proceedings*, 1st Ser., 11 (1871), 207-22. Michael J. Canavan, "Isaac Johnson, Esquire, The Founder of Boston," Colonial Society of Massachusetts, *Publications*, 27 (1932), 272-85, is helpful on both Johnson and the Reverend William Blackston.

west (the Mystic). On the latter, six miles upstream they discovered what they were looking for: broad acres, much of the land already cleared by Indian burnings, fresh-water streams, a site for their community. Retracing their voyage, the party spent the night with Maverick and returned to the ships at Salem on June 18.

Although Winthrop recommended the Mystic River location, the other leaders of the migration did not accept his report. Instead, it precipitated an argument which was to drag on for more than a year. Deputy Governor Dudley seems to have started it. An enigmatic man, as pious as Winthrop and as deeply religious, he had none of Winthrop's gentleness or moderation. On the contrary, he was proud and overbearing, irascible and argumentative. The orphaned son of an English soldier, he had been brought up on the fringes of good society in England—page in the household of the Earl of Northampton, clerk to a judge, protégé of Lord Saye and Sele, steward for the Earl of Lincoln, handling the lands and rents of that young lord. Thus he knew authority and high position but had possessed little of either. In his election as deputy governor of the company as it prepared to leave England and in his continued officeholding in New England, he was to have and relish both.

Initially, nothing other than Dudley's newborn sense of the prerogatives of his office seems to have been involved in his argument with Winthrop, the Deputy merely insisting that another expedition be dispatched "to approve or dislike" the "judgement" of the first. Winthrop agreed, and the second exploration, which Dudley apparently led, departed for the Bay area. Upon returning the group reported the existence of another site "three leagues up Charles river," and Dudley became its advocate against Winthrop.[4] For over a week the dispute between the two went on. Then, as the fleet had almost all arrived at Salem and the passengers were anxious to disembark, a compromise was arranged by which the settlers and their equipment and supplies would be put ashore at a point equidistant from the two proposed sites and a temporary camp set up. The spot chosen was the narrow Charlestown peninsula separating the mouths of the Charles and Mystic

4. Dudley to Lady Bridget, Young, comp., *Chronicles of the First Planters*, 312.

rivers, where, the year before, a Salem group had constructed a house and a few wigwams. The final decision on the location of the settlement was left for later.

Winthrop's settlers were not the first newcomers in the Bay area that year. Even as the Governor was first exploring Mystic River, one hundred and forty men and women arrived aboard the *Mary and John,* dispatched under the patronage of the Reverend John White of Dorchester, England, an early advocate of New England settlement. (His Dorchester Associates had planted a fishing settlement on Cape Ann—a precursor to Salem —in 1624.) White's settlers were only loosely affiliated with those of the Winthrop fleet and apparently intended to settle apart from the larger group. Entering the Bay, they sent out their own exploring party, and while Winthrop's settlers waited at Salem for a decision about where to locate, the *Mary and John*'s passengers moved onto a peninsula south of Shawmut—"Mattapan" to the Indians, Dorchester to its new inhabitants. The leaders of the Winthrop group sought early to embrace the Dorchester people in their central community, inaugurating talks with the leaders at Dorchester. At one point an agreement seems to have been reached, for on June 28 Samuel Fuller of Plymouth reported home that "they of Matapan purpose to go and plant" with the Winthrop settlers.[5] But events were to preclude the merger.

By the end of the first week of July the ships of the Winthrop fleet had disgorged the last of the settlers at Charlestown. A sprawling tent community quickly sprang up, the generality housing themselves as best they could. Winthrop "and the rest of the gentlemen" found quarters better fitted to their stations, buying from its Salem owners the house built earlier on the peninsula. For the moment it became "the governor's house," the seat of authority and the meeting place of the Court of Assistants—

5. Fuller to Bradford, June 28, 1630, Mass. Hist. Soc., *Collections*, 1st Ser., 3 (1794), 74. Eighty settlers aboard the ship *Lyon*, mentioned in Appendix I, were in the same relationship to those of the Winthrop fleet as the *Mary and John* settlers. They made land at Salem, however, and apparently merged with the larger group immediately. "Diverse Christians" from Leicester, together with forty persons from Manchester (mentioned in Isaac Johnson to John Winthrop, Dec. 17, 1629, *Winthrop Papers*, II, 178) might have constituted a third such group but they do not seem to have made the journey.

the governing body. Here the leaders resumed their discussion
of the permanent location of their community.

Two factors interrupted their considerations. Weakened after
the long confinement at sea, unaccustomed to the available food
and the climate with its extremes of heat in the day and cold at
night, careless and ignorant of sanitation, and foolishly crowded
together on a limited site, the settlers fell prey to disease. The
bloody flux broke out among them, then scurvy.[6] Filth and refuse accumulated in the camp, and the epidemic grew in proportion. The doctors from older settlements and those who had come
with the fleet were powerless to help them. "The sad news here
is, that many are sick, and many are dead," Doctor Fuller wrote
to the governor of Plymouth. "I here but lose time and long to
be at home: I can do them no good, for I want drugs, and things
fitting to work with."[7] But bad as it was, the disease only set the
stage. A rumor spread from a late-arriving ship that the French
were preparing to launch an attack on the infant settlement.
Hastily the leaders met, "forced to change counsel."[8] The settlers were too weak to fortify their temporary location, too weak
even to drag the ordnance they had brought from England up
from the beach where the sailors had unloaded it. The only
solution—the one to answer both problems of defense and disease
—was to disperse.

From late July through August and September, conforming
to this decision, small groups left the Charlestown encampment,
each under one or two of the most prominent leaders. A body led
by Sir Richard Saltonstall and including the Reverend Mr. Phillips
was apparently the first to leave, settling during the last week of
July at Watertown, a mile above Dudley's projected location on
the Charles.[9] Another group, led by William Pynchon, went out

6. J. Franklin Jameson, ed., [Edward] Johnson's Wonder-Working Providence, 1628-1651 (N. Y., 1910), 65-66, hereafter cited as Johnson's Wonder-
Working Providence; Samuel Danforth, An Almanack ... (Cambridge, Mass.,
1648), under date of June; Earnest Caulfield, "Some Common Diseases of
Colonial Children," Col. Soc. Mass., Publications, 35(1951), 44-45.

7. Fuller to Bradford, Aug. 2, 1630, Mass. Hist. Soc., Collections, 1st Ser., 3
(1794), 76.

8. Dudley to Lady Bridget, Young, comp., Chronicles of the First Planters,
313.

9. Cf. Fuller and Edward Winslow to Bradford, July 26, 1630, Mass. Hist.

to found Roxbury. By the end of September the newcomers were scattered in seven towns: Watertown, Roxbury, Dorchester (whose settlers had never come into the Charlestown camp), Medford on the site first proposed by Winthrop, Saugus to the north of the Bay, Charlestown where some few of the settlers remained under Increase Nowell, and Shawmut peninsula directly across the Charles River from Charlestown—Boston.

Boston's was an inauspicious beginning. The name itself had been selected earlier for the central community, commemorative of Boston in old England whose minister, John Cotton, had delivered the farewell sermon to the settlers.[10] But no interest had been displayed in Shawmut peninsula by the various exploring parties. It was too small for the settlement Winthrop and his companions were contemplating, and being directly on the harbor, too open to shipborne attack. From the Charlestown camp, the most conspicuous features of the peninsula were the three peaks of what would be known eventually as Beacon Hill; hence the settlers first called the peninsula "Tramount" or "Trimountain," but no more than a few adventuresome souls crossed the narrows to explore. Even in the dispersal from Charlestown, no one single group under an established leader occupied the peninsula. Settlement came to Shawmut slowly as a succession of small bands moved out of the camp and across the Charles.

The first movement was prompted by the Reverend Mr. Blackston, the Anglican minister living in self-imposed isolation on the southern slope of Beacon Hill since the mid-1620's. In England, Blackston had been a longtime friend of Isaac Johnson, one of the most prominent figures among the leaders of the settlers. (His wife, Arbella, sister of the Earl of Lincoln, had given her name to the flagship.) When Johnson arrived in the Massachusetts Bay area, Blackston hastened to greet his old friend, opening his house on Shawmut to him. Others from the Charlestown camp were attracted to the peninsula by Johnson's presence there, and by September 7 there were enough people to warrant

---

Soc., *Collections*, 1st Ser., 3 (1794), 75, and Mather, *Magnalia Christi Americana*, I, 375.
    10. Dudley to Lady Bridget, Young, comp., *Chronicles of the First Planters*, 313.

a proper name, Tramount giving way to "Boston" by order of the Court of Assistants. By the end of the month it was one of the two largest settlements, the other being Watertown. Johnson died on September 30, but by then Blackston had extended his invitation to Winthrop, Dudley, minister John Wilson, and others among the leaders. Winthrop's movement to Shawmut attracted still more people from the Charlestown camp, and by mid-October the town had a population of perhaps 150. By then, too, the government, following the Governor and Deputy Governor, had been transferred from Charlestown and the public munitions had been carried across the river. In another month a regular ferry connected the two peninsulas. By December 26, the church originally gathered in Charlestown had moved and become the First Church of Boston.

The assignment of the name Boston to the town building on Shawmut did not signify that the peninsula was to be the central community, though that concept was still in the minds of some—in that of Deputy Governor Dudley in particular. To him, the dispersal of the settlers into numerous towns was neither desirable nor permanent, only a temporary expedient. "Help it we could not," he wrote from Blackston's house on Shawmut, "wanting ability to remove to any place fit to build a town upon, and the time too short to deliberate any longer."[11] But for the moment, as the settlers labored to erect shelters for the winter, all discussion about a permanent location lapsed.

In November and December, probably through the instigation of Dudley, talk was resumed, first at Boston among the leaders living at Blackston's, then in a series of meetings held at Roxbury and Watertown. On December 6, at Roxbury, Winthrop, Dudley, and the other leaders tentatively agreed to build a fortified town in the area between Roxbury and Boston; a week later, however, the committee appointed to plan the new community rejected the site on the grounds that it lacked running water and, more important, "the most part of the people had built already, and would not be able to build again," a tacit acceptance of the fact that the dispersal had made a centralized community impossible to achieve.

11. *Ibid.*, 314.

Although Winthrop and the others could accept the fact that their plans had gone awry and proceed upon this assumption in organizing local government and soliciting additional ministers for the towns,[12] Dudley could not. Late in December the leaders met again, this time at Watertown, and accepted Dudley's original location on the Charles River as the eventual central city. A sudden uprooting of the settlers from the homes they had built was to be avoided, however, and instead of ordering a general reassembling—which by this time none but Dudley apparently wanted—the leaders merely agreed to build their own houses in the new town the following spring and to winter there the next year. John Endecott, well established at Salem, was the only one of the leaders planning to stay in the settlements to remain outside the agreement. The example of the leaders, in addition to the collecting of all the ordnance and munitions and the compulsory settling of all new arrivals there would, it was thought, attract the settlers of all but Salem into the new community. For want of any other name, since Boston was already being used, they called the community to be built simply "the new town," or Newtown. In the end, "if God would," a fortified, central town would emerge.[13]

The leaders had recognized that the settlers would be reluctant to lose the labor of "six months' building" by moving to the new town.[14] But it was not this factor alone which brought the scheme to nothing. Even though the towns had been founded out of sheer necessity rather than plan, it was there that the communal life which had been disrupted for the individual by his departure from his English community was being rapidly refabricated. Friendships were growing, as were the social and political relationships which, by virtue of their familiarity, lend the individual in society a sense of stability and security. Neither the leaders of the migration who were being accepted as the

12. See below, the appointment of town constables as early as Sept. 28, 1630 (chap. 3, p. 44) and the solicitation of additional ministers from England during the fall and winter of that year (chap. 5, pp. 101-3).

13. Dudley to Lady Bridget, Young, comp., *Chronicles of the First Planters*, 320; *Winthrop's Journal*, I, 54; Emmanuel Downing to John Winthrop, Apr. 30, [1631], *Winthrop Papers*, III, 30-31.

14. Dudley to Lady Bridget, Young, comp., *Chronicles of the First Planters*, 321.

natural leaders of the towns, nor the generality who were coming to feel secure in their leadership would hazard what they had for the sake of centralization.

Nevertheless, in the spring a halfhearted attempt was made to effect the plan. Sometime after March 1631, Dudley moved out of Boston and, with a few servants, went to Newtown and began building. Winthrop, too, sent servants up the Charles and the frame of his house was begun. To improve landing facilities, a creek running from the Charles River into the center of the projected town was widened and deepened. The construction of a stockade to surround the town was set underway. When fire destroyed two houses in Boston, the settlers took note and decreed that no one could build with wooden chimneys or thatch roofs in Newtown. By the end of the summer, Dudley's house was completed and the Deputy turned to "wainscotting and adorning" it.[15] His wife and children came up from Boston to join him. Winthrop's house was also nearing completion and a half-dozen of the Governor's servants moved in to live. In Boston, the settlers—many of them originally from the vicinity of Winthrop's home in old England and bound to him by personal ties, others having adopted him as the natural leader of the community—decided to follow him up the Charles. The town of Boston, so recently founded, was about to be deserted.

Yet it was not to be. Sometime during that summer or fall Dudley had a change of mind. He had, for his own purposes, insisted that the central community be built where he wanted it built. Now that community was coming into existence; his house stood there, the finest in the town. But it was obviously not the community it was intended to be. None of the other leaders except Winthrop had built houses there; none of the scattered towns had been abandoned in its favor. Indeed, there were no more than eight or ten families in the town. These few, however, looked to Dudley for leadership, just as in Boston the inhabitants looked to Winthrop. His new position of personal leadership seems to have become all-important to the Deputy, aggravating with suspicious jealousy the already high regard he had for his own prerogatives. Thus he set about to discourage the inhabitants

15. *Winthrop's Journal,* I, 77.

of Boston when they indicated their desire to follow Winthrop upriver, perhaps fearing that should they come they would continue to look to the Governor for leadership, relegating him to a secondary position. At the same time he insisted that Winthrop abide by the agreement to move to Newtown, since the Governor's presence would enhance Dudley's town by making it the capital. His manipulations failed when the Bostonians appealed to Winthrop, asking him not to leave Shawmut unless they too left. Winthrop readily agreed. He had never been overly fond of Dudley's location; and having abandoned the idea of a single, centralized community as impractical under the circumstances, he gave his loyalty to Boston. In the fall, without consulting either Dudley or the other leaders, he had his servants dismantle the house he had been erecting at Newtown and bring the pieces down to Shawmut.[16] There they were reassembled and his house completed, presumably in time for the arrival of his wife Margaret from England in November.

If Boston's beginnings were inauspicious, so too was the geography of the town's peninsula unsuited for a settlement in which agriculture was at first to be the primary occupation.[17] It was small, roughly two miles long and a mile wide at its most extreme points; it was almost an island, joined to the mainland

16. *Ibid.*, 84.

17. Antiquarians and amateur archaeologists have expended prodigious labors in tracing the shoreline of the old peninsula and identifying its various features. The results are best followed in several Massachusetts journals, most notably Mass. Hist. Soc., *Proceedings* and *Collections*. Of the many descriptive books, note Justin Winsor, ed., *Memorial History of Boston, Including Suffolk County, Massachusetts*, 4 vols. (Boston, 1881-86), I; Nathaniel B. Shurtleff, *A Topographical and Historical Description of Boston* (Boston, 1871); Annie Haven Thwing, *The Crooked and Narrow Streets of the Town of Boston, 1630-1822* (Boston, 1920); the "Gleaner" articles of Nathaniel Ingersoll Bowditch, originally published in the *Boston Daily Transcript* in 1855 and reprinted in the City of Boston, *Report of the Record Commissioners*, V (Boston, 1884); Allen Chamberlain, *Beacon Hill: Its Ancient Pastures and Early Mansions* (Boston and N. Y., 1925); M. A. DeWolfe Howe, *Boston Common; Scenes from Four Centuries* (Cambridge, Mass., 1910); Walter Muir Whitehill, *Boston: A Topographical History* (Cambridge, Mass., 1959). Note, too, Charles Lamb, comp., *Series of Plans of Boston Showing Existing Ways and Owners of Property, 1630-1635- 1640-1645* (Boston, 1905), and Samuel C. Clough's various articles— "Remarks on the Compilation of the Boston Book of Possessions," "Topography of Boston, 1648," "Cotton Hill and Adjacent Estates, 1650-1750," and "Ownership of Certain Land in Boston," Col. Soc. Mass., *Publications*, 27 (1932), 6-21, 21 (1920), 251-54, 20 (1920), 264, 25 (1924) 43-47.

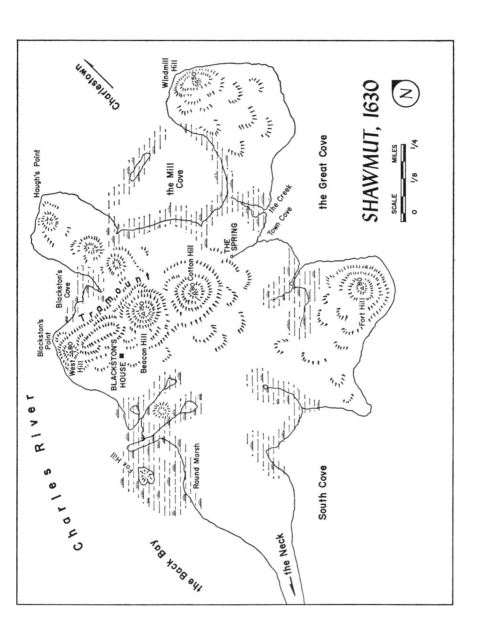

SHAWMUT, 1630

N

SCALE   MILES
0   1/8   1/4

Charles River

the Back Bay

Fox Hill

Round Marsh

the Neck

South Cove

Blackston's Point
West 80 Hill
BLACKSTON'S HOUSE
Beacon Hill
Blackston's Cove

Tramount

150

Cotton Hill 80

Haugh's Point

the Mill Cove

THE SPRING

the Creek
Town Cove

the Great Cove

Fort Hill 80

Windmill Hill 50

Charlestown

by a long neck or causeway so narrow and low-lying that storms swept the waters of the harbor across it. However, Shawmut proper—about seven hundred acres when the area of the Neck was excepted—was high enough, being dominated by three hills. Windmill Hill (to use the earliest common names) rose precipitously from the water at the northern tip to a height of fifty feet, then gently sloped south and west until it submerged in a swamp which separated the northern quarter of the peninsula and made it almost a second island. To the south, Corn or Fort Hill rose steeply from the waterside eighty feet, then trailed off to the south and west. Between the two, forming the backbone of the peninsula, was Beacon Hill or Tramount, a ridge rising in the east-center and stretching westward until it fell into the Charles at Blackston's Point. Three peaks crowned the ridge, the eighty-foot Cotton Hill to the east, West Hill balancing it toward the Charles, and, between them, Beacon Hill proper or "Centry Hill," a mound rising 150 feet, somewhat flattened on top. From its summit, as a contemporary wrote, one might "over-looke all the Ilands which lie before the Bay, and discry such ships as are upon the Sea-coast."[18] Other hills, less significant, were sprinkled along the western shoreline of the peninsula, from Fox Hill rising out of the marshes of the Back Bay, to Haugh's Point opposite Charlestown.

Ultimately, to give himself more room on this constricted peninsula, man would push the hills into the harbor, leaving Beacon Hill only a poor remnant of its former lofty self. He would intervene in the long battle between the hills, fighting for their existence, and the waters of the Bay. For the tide and wind-driven waves had been pounding the eastern face of the peninsula since the glaciers first dumped it there, cutting away the land to create the cliff-faces of Windmill Hill and Fort Hill, gouging deep declivities in the shoreline between hills, most notably South Cove between Fort Hill and the mainland, and "the great cove" between Fort Hill and Windmill Hill, with Town Cove at its head. On the west the waters of the Charles had been at work,

18. William Wood, *New Englands Prospect. A True, Lively, and Experimentall Description of That Part of America, Commonly Called New England . . .* [London, 1634] (Boston, 1865), 42.

carving the Back Bay out of the peninsula, Blackston's Cove and the Mill Cove, then partially filling in with debris washed down from the interior the very indentations it had created. Seeds had found their way into the fill and sprouted, giving rise to the salt marshes which garlanded the whole peninsula, but particularly the Charles River side. Here and there the swamps penetrated the peninsula to form channels by which the waters of the in-numerable springs could find their way into the harbor.

To Anne Pollard, a child of eight when she scrambled from the boat carrying her from Charlestown, this virgin peninsula was admirably suited to berry-picking and hide-and-seek; as an old woman she would still remember its "small hollows and swamps," its "blueberries and other bushes."[19] But the adult mind was more critical in weighing pros and cons, and in the balance Shawmut was found lacking in two of the prime neces-sities of New World life. On the asset side, water was as plenti-ful as the many comments relative to the "sweete and pleasant springs" which dotted the peninsula. Indeed, local tradition, hallowed by three centuries of repetition, has the springs the most important factor in attracting first Johnson, then Winthrop and the settlers to the peninsula. The fact that it was a peninsula allowed the first inhabitants to graze their cattle with a mini-mum of fencing. But wood for building and burning was lacking, for there were few trees on the peninsula, except for an occasional clump toward the Neck. The average family would need fifteen cords of wood a winter according to one computation, the equiva-lent of three-fifths of an acre of standing timber.[20] Hence, wood would have to be brought from the mainland or from the islands in the harbor, a laborious and hazardous undertaking. On at least one occasion the lack almost brought about the abandonment of the town, Winthrop writing his son during the winter of 1637-38 that "we at Boston were almost readye to breake up for want of wood."[21] On the other hand, the absence of woodlands, according to one observer, meant that the settlers would be free of "three great

19. Winsor, ed., *Memorial History of Boston*, I, 521.

20. Ralph H. Brown, *Historical Geography of the United States* (N. Y., 1948), 108.

21. Winthrop to John Winthrop, Jr., Jan. 31, 1637/38, *Winthrop Papers*, IV, 10.

annoyances, of Woolves, Rattle-snakes, and Musketos" which plagued the other towns.[22]   More important was the fact that the land was good, "affording rich Corne-fields, and fruitefull Gardens," and did not require clearing before being put to use. Yet land—the second great lack—was limited within the confines of the peninsula and too much was taken up by the hills and marshes. Only the lower slopes were suitable for gardens and grazing, the crests being unusable. In the swamps, marsh-grass for thatch roofing and fodder abounded, but fodder, too, was insufficient to meet the eventual requirements and the inhabitants were to bring their hay "in Loyters" from the mainland and islands.[23]

It was around one of the springs that Boston's first inhabitants grouped themselves, that which came to the surface just below the looming mass of Cotton Hill and flowed into the harbor through Town Cove.[24] Some few of the newcomers scattered over the peninsula, but the tradition of life in England and the desirability of clinging to each other in the wilderness brought most to build compactly to the south and west of the cove, away from the marsh to the north. In 1630, the lesser people built shacks or huts or wigwams along the shore, anything to tide them over the first hard winter. In these they suffered the climate and disease, for the scurvy which had broken out in Charlestown did not abate at Shawmut until the arrival in February of a ship from England carrying a quantity of lemon juice. With the spring, however, they began building better houses and planting gardens—John Biggs and his wife Mary who had followed Winthrop from Groton to Charlestown, then Boston; John Odlin; Robert and Sarah Walker; John Ruggle and his family; James and Lydia Penniman, and others. The more prominent stayed with Blackston on the Charles River side of the peninsula through the winter and until their servants completed their houses, although Winthrop joined the generality occasionally and "fell to

22. Wood, *New Englands Prospect,* 42.   Nevertheless at least three wolves had been killed on Shawmut by Nov. 1634.   John Winthrop to John Winthrop, Jr., Nov. 6, 1634, *Winthrop Papers,* III, 175.
23. Wood, *New Englands Prospect,* 42.
24. Michael J. Canavan, "Mr. Blackstone's 'Excellent Spring,'" Col. Soc. Mass., *Publications,* 11 (1910), 295-328.

worke with his owne hands" as an encouragement to them.[25] Fire struck the thatch roofs and daubed-wood chimneys, burning Thomas Sharpe's house and that of William Colborne, a deacon of the First Church. But gradually, in 1631 and 1632, the town took form. The first meetinghouse—to serve both public and religious purposes—was built; Samuel and Anne Cole completed their house, and soon had opened part of it for a tavern; William Coddington built the first brick house in the town, an exception to the general wooden construction. Close to the waterside south of the cove, Winthrop's house was erected; Pastor John Wilson's house, built with the aid of servants supplied him by the government, went up slightly above Winthrop's, as did that of James Penn, the "beadle" or marshal of the new commonwealth. The houses formed two rough semi-circles at first, one curving around the head of Town Cove, which served as the earliest landing place, the other immediately to the south around what would become the marketplace.

The shoreline and the hills would guide the direction in which the town would grow in future years—to some 315 houses, a total of over 350 buildings, by 1649.[26] One arm of the town would follow "the high street," originally an Indian path which the settlers appropriated, as it skirted the Tramount, then struck southward to the Neck and across to Roxbury and beyond. Where the road passed "the round marsh" just before the Neck, Deacon Colborne would rebuild following the fire, giving the area its name: Colborne's End. Another arm of the town would cling precariously to the harborside to the north, crossing the swamp which separated the town proper from the "North End," a phrase applied almost from the beginning. Eventually the swamp would be cut across and the "Mill Creek" formed, a spillway whose water power turned the wheels of grist mills; a bridge across the creek would connect the North End with the larger part of the peninsula. Still a third extension of the town would push directly west to form "Sudbury End" between Cotton Hill and the Mill

25. Anon., "Narrative [addressed to Secretary Cooke?] concerning the settlement of New England—1630," Mass. Hist. Soc., *Proceedings*, 1st Ser., 5 (1862), 131.

26. Computed by Samuel C. Clough in Col. Soc. Mass., *Publications*, 21 (1920), 253.

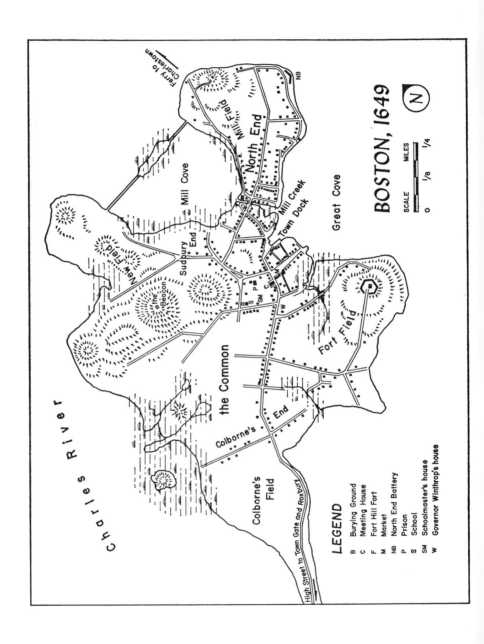

BOSTON, 1649

N

SCALE   MILES

0   1/8   1/4

Charles River

Ferry to
Charlestown

Mill Field

North End

NB

Great Cove

Mill Creek

Mill Cove

Town Dock

Sudbury
End

New Field

The
Beacon

Fort Field

F

the Common

Colborne's
End

Colborne's
Field

High Street to Town Gate and Roxbury

LEGEND

B   Burying Ground
C   Meeting House
F   Fort Hill Fort
M   Market
NB   North End Battery
P   Prison
S   School
SM   Schoolmaster's house
W   Governor Winthrop's house

Cove. But always the center would be where the newcomers first set down: Town Cove where the merchants would hold forth, and the market. Always, too, in these early years, the town would have a gray look about it, the cast of unpainted weather-beaten clapboard and fence.

For the moment, however, the town was but a straggling village—no more than forty houses by the end of 1632—and in common with the other towns of the commonwealth it was tied closely to the soil. Around every house there was a garden patch, in some cases a small orchard as the settlers planted the saplings they had brought with them from England. One by one, too, the various "fields" were being opened to the inhabitants for cultivation, each family being allotted between one and four acres, and new fields being laid out as the population grew. The first was probably that on the gentle southwestern slope of Fort Hill, hence "the Fort Field," followed by "the mylne field" on the North End, "the new field" or "Sentrie field" beyond Sudbury End, and "the field next Roxbury" or "Colborne's Field" far down toward the Neck beyond Colborne's End. Between Tramount and Colborne's End lay Blackston's land which, in 1634, the town purchased for thirty pounds sterling as a common pasture and training field for the militia. The area at hand, however, was not enough to support the growing population of the town and expansion was required. Gradually most of the major islands among the forty-seven in the Bay would come under the town's jurisdiction.[27] Similarly the town would be awarded areas on the mainland for its inhabitants to farm, at Muddy River beyond Roxbury, at Mount Wollaston on the south shore of the Bay, and along the North Shore from Winnisimmet to Pullen Point at the harbor entrance.

The town's future did not lie in the soil, however. It lay in the Bay itself. Nature, which was unkind to Boston's agricultural pursuits, was eminently kind to her trade. Shawmut was not only situated at the center of the new commonwealth, with towns scattered to the north, east, south, and west; it was also the one necessary link in all lines of communication among the

27. "A Topographical and Historical Description of Boston, 1794," Mass. Hist. Soc., *Collections*, 1st Ser., 3 (1794), 295-98.

towns and between the towns and the outside world. Boston Bay
effectively split the settlements of Massachusetts apart, separating
those southeast of the Charles from those north and northeast.
But Shawmut was almost a bridge, the quarter-mile between its
northern point and Charlestown and the half-mile to the North
Shore easily crossed by ferry. The Indian name reflected this
cardinal geographic position—"Shawmut," "where there is a going
by boat," a crossing place.[28] Again, travel by land, though often
undertaken, was difficult; travel by water easy. Shawmut, thrust
out across the mouths of the Charles and Mystic, was in the center
of all traffic between the towns along the Bay and the interior
towns along the rivers, an ideal place for landing goods for trans-
shipment. Complementing this geographic position was the un-
derwater topography of the Bay: deep enough for the largest
vessels from across the sea to anchor near the peninsula, yet shal-
low enough along the shoreline of the Great Cove to allow easy
construction of wharves and piers.

Its site fortuitously selected, its beginning unpropitious—this
was Boston in 1630. Its people were immediately busy building,
fencing, breaking ground, planting, building roads and bridges
and fortifications, for as John Winthrop, Jr., was to write, they
had "all thinges to doe, as in the beginninge of the world." Their
major concern at their arrival was to wrest a subsistence from the
soil. But William Wood, preparing his *New Englands Prospect*,
saw in the geography of the peninsula something more: "the
cheife place for shipping and Merchandize."[29] Few understood
this future.

28. J. Hammond Trumbull in Mass. Hist. Soc., *Proceedings*, 1st Ser., 9
(1867), 376-79. For another view, see "On the Question—What is the meaning
of the Aboriginal Phrase Shawmut?" Mass. Hist. Soc., *Collections*, 2d Ser., 10
(1823), 173-74, in which the author translates it as "fountains of living water,"
or "springs."
29. John Winthrop, Jr., to Mr. Oldenburg, Secretary of the Royal Society,
Nov. 12, 1668, Mass. Hist. Soc., *Proceedings*, 1st Ser., 16 (1879), 236-37; Wood,
New Englands Prospect, 42.

III

THE EMERGENCE OF TOWN GOVERNMENT

As the first settlers moved onto Shawmut in the summer and fall of 1630, there was no preconceived plan of town organization to guide them in forming a body politic. They had only the obvious need to do so, their English traditions, and—closest at hand—the formal provisions of the charter of the Massachusetts Bay Company. In time, however, one other factor, a congregational church polity adopted during the first year, would have a major effect in molding town government.

The charter of the Massachusetts Bay Company had established it as a commercial enterprise empowered to regulate itself and its possessions in the New World through a relatively simple government. The freemen, or stockholders, of the company were to meet together four times a year as "one greate, generall, and solemne Assemblie" to admit additional freemen and to "make, ordeine, and establishe all manner of wholesome and reasonable orders, lawes, statutes, and ordinances, directions, and instructions" for the colony to be established, provided only that such were "not contrarie to the lawes of this our realme of England." Once a year, at the spring meeting of the General Court, the freemen were to elect from among themselves a governor, a deputy governor, and a court of eighteen assistants "to take care for the best disposeing and ordering of the general buysines and affaires of ... the said landes and premisses ... and the government of the people there."[1] The initial design, of course, was that this government should reside in England and deal with the

1. William MacDonald, ed., *Select Charters and Other Documents Illustrative of American History, 1606-1775* (N. Y., 1904), 40-41.

settlers through a subsidiary agency in the colony, as for example, John Endecott's government at Salem prior to the arrival of the Winthrop fleet.

But Winthrop and his companions, gentry in England, had not been willing to hazard themselves, their property, and their status in the New World while control of the venture rested in London. Having decided to leave England for America, they had insisted that "the whole governement together with the Patent for the said plantacion bee ... legally transferred and established to remayne with us and others which shall inhabite" there.[2] The company had agreed, and in 1629 the prospective emigrants had moved into positions of authority in the company structure to prepare for the impending departure. When the Winthrop fleet made land in the New World, a legal, chartered government, its officers having been selected in England, was on hand: Governor Winthrop, Deputy Governor Dudley, and, as assistants, Sir Richard Saltonstall, Roger Ludlow, Edward Rossiter, Increase Nowell, Thomas Sharpe, William Pynchon, Simon Bradstreet, Isaac Johnson, John Endecott, and William Coddington.[3]

Meeting informally at first, then regularly as the Court of Assistants, these men had, at Salem, debated the alternative sites for settlement, finally determining upon Charlestown as a temporary expedient. In the governor's house at Charlestown they had deviated from their plans and, in the face of disease and rumored attack, directed the dispersal into several communities. That they collectively retained control over the dispersal is indicated by an order of September 7, 1630, recalling those settlers who had independently wandered north to set down at the future site of Ipswich and establishing the rule that "noe person shall plant in any place within the lymitts of this Pattent, without leave from the Governor and Assistants, or the major parte of them."[4] But they also assumed individual leadership within the towns, for the settlers, rapidly developing a community consciousness and desiring to

2. "The true coppie of the Agreement of Cambridge, August 26, 1629," *Winthrop Papers*, II, 152.

3. Additionally, William Vassall was in the Bay briefly in 1630 and presumably acted as an assistant. Frances Rose-Troup, *The Massachusetts Bay Company and Its Predecessors* (N. Y., 1930), 156.

4. *Assistants' Records*, II, 4.

establish relationships with authority on the local level, accepted as natural leaders those assistants who moved with them. Thus the settlers on Shawmut looked first to Isaac Johnson, "the chefeste stud in the land . . . the cheiffeste man of estate in the land and on[e] that woold a don moste good,"[5] and after his death to Winthrop. Very quickly the Assistants as a group regularized their local leadership, on August 23 appointing Winthrop, Dudley, Saltonstall, Johnson, Endecott, and Ludlow as "Justices of the peace" with "like power that Justices of peace hath in England for reformacion of abuses and punishing of offenders," presumably for Charlestown, Watertown, Boston, Salem, and Roxbury.[6]

The office assumed so easily from their English experience (Winthrop, for example, had been a justice for some twenty years) was primarily but not entirely judicial, for in addition to adjudicating or binding over for a higher court petty criminals and felons and resolving minor civil actions, the justices in England had been agents of the central government in reporting on conditions in their counties and in overseeing a host of economic and social statutes—in brief, they had been the major instrument creating workable local government. In the new commonwealth, terminology would change; the title of "justice" would quickly fall into disuse to be replaced by "magistrate." But the powers would remain and ultimately be considered an inherent part of the office of assistant.[7]

In the months that followed the dispersal, the emerging towns were governed by the leaders of the commonwealth, clothed in the mantle of their generally accepted superiority in the communities and bulwarked by their offices of assistant in the company structure and the traditional justice of the peace. Together they empaneled juries grand and petty, tried felonies and misdemeanors, heard civil suits, conducted probate and coroners' hearings, licensed and supported improvements within the towns; they also

5. [John] Pond to William Pond, Mar. 15, 1630/31, *Winthrop Papers*, III, 18.

6. *Assistants' Records*, II, 3.

7. Notestein, *English People on the Eve of Colonization*, 227; George Lee Haskins, *Law and Authority in Early Massachusetts: A Study in Tradition and Design* (N. Y., 1960), 174.

regulated wages and prices, taverns, trade, apprenticeships, and defense, and even determined liability in cases where one man's cattle wandered into another man's corn. Individually (or sitting in pairs) they acted on the local level, dispensing punishment for petty offenses and presenting the gross offender to the full body of Assistants, determining minor conflicts among the settlers, and administering such orders of the Court as that "for preservacion of good timber for more necessary uses" which proscribed the indiscriminate cutting of wood for fences and required the settler seeking to cut on vacant land to obtain the permission of "the nexte Assistant, or some whome they shall depute."[8] In all of this, they had the aid of constables, in England the right arm of the county justices of the peace in presenting offenders to their judgment, serving their writs, and enforcing their sentences. The constables were selected by the Court for individual towns as early as September 1630.[9] Lastly, though not least important, the leaders assumed the direction of the impromptu distribution of land within the towns.

There was no formal system of land distribution as the settlers dispersed, system being a luxury of the settled community. Land had occupied the attention of the company in England, however, and from fragmentary records it is clear that the original investors, considering land a proper return for investment and contemplating a settlement consisting of a single town surrounded by outlying farms, had established a basic policy accordingly. On the one hand, the company offered large tracts of land to actual investors in the enterprise, two hundred acres per fifty pounds invested. The fact that an individual transported himself, his family, and his servants to the settlement was, in itself, considered an investment and also subject to return. Hence those actual purchasers of the company's stock who traveled to the New World were to receive fifty acres for themselves and every member of their family; non-stockholders who paid their way were to receive fifty acres if a "Master of the familie" and more in proportion to "their charge and qualitie." Those transporting serv-

8. *Assistants' Records*, II, 28.
9. *Ibid.*, 5. On the English constable see Eleanor Trotter, *Seventeenth Century Life in the Country Parish, With Special Reference to Local Government* (Cambridge, Eng., 1919), 84ff.

ants for their own use were to receive fifty acres for each head "to dispose of at [their] discression," while persons engaged by the company to perform specific services were to be recompensed in land or other valuables according to the terms of their individual agreements with it. On the other hand, the company set aside one-half acre per fifty pounds invested on which the adventurer (and presumably the master of the family paying its own way) was to build his house, ordering "that if the plott of ground whereon the towne is intended to bee built bee sett out ... that then noe man shall presume to build his howse aney where else."[10] Given this scheme, the colony would have taken the form of a single town or village surrounded by large and small holdings, some worked as family units, others by servants, some in the hands of residents of the colony, others subject to absentee ownership.

This land policy the emigrants brought with them from England, Winthrop himself subscribing to the use of land as a dividend for investment in an address to the company late in 1629 and sketching house and garden lots of various sizes (quarter, half, and full acre) in his commonplace book.[11] But in the situation which prevailed in 1630, the policy could not be effected in any orderly manner. Some among the investors who arrived hurried out to engross large tracts of land for themselves. On September 6, 1631, for example, Winthrop was granted six hundred acres of land on the Mystic River by the Court of Assistants, but by that time his farm was already a well-established concern operated by servants living on the premises; a house stood on the property and at least one stone building.[12] Other farms—that of Matthew Cradock, London merchant and governor of the company prior to its transfer to the New World for one—were being

10. Nathaniel B. Shurtleff, ed., *Records of the Governor and Company of the Massachusetts Bay in New England*, 5 vols. in 6 (Boston, 1853-54), I, 43, hereafter cited as *Colony Records*. At the time the company was contemplating a single settlement at Salem but the occupation of Massachusetts Bay being considered necessary, building in that area was to be allowed "according to such directions as shalbee thoughte meete for that plase."

11. "Address of John Winthrop to the Company of the Massachusetts Bay [Dec. 1, 1629]," *Winthrop Papers*, II, 176 and the plates following p. 276; *Colony Records*, I, 64, 240.

12. *Assistants' Records*, II, 19; *Winthrop's Journal*, I, 68, 69.

laid out in the area. At the same time, the settlers moving into the emerging towns began setting up their houses and laying out gardens, sometimes at will, sometimes under the general direction of the assistants acting as the natural leaders of the new communities.

No formal order of the Court of Assistants—which, acting as the company, possessed the land under the charter—deeded land to the first towns as they were founded during the dispersal of 1630; indeed, given the agitation that year for a regrouping of the settlers into a single community, such an act of the Court was inconceivable. The occupation of Shawmut, and of the other towns, was validated, therefore, not by a specific pronouncement in the records of the Court, but by the implication of the Court in ordering the dispersal, assigning a name to the settlement, assessing rates upon it, and determining its boundaries in relation to other towns. Only with time would the Court accept what was growing up spontaneously, the ownership of the lands of the town by its inhabitants.

Similarly, no formal act of the Court either deeded land within the town to a specific individual or established a system whereby it could be deeded. In choosing house lots, the settlers on Shawmut merely obtained the approbation of, first, Isaac Johnson, and subsequently Winthrop. Presumably under Winthrop's direction they began, in 1631, to open the various fields of the peninsula, dividing them into allotments for each of the town's families—Fort Field, Mill Field, Colborne's Field, and the New Field being under cultivation as the town records begin in 1634. That the distribution was only an expedient improvisation was indicated in August 1632 when Winthrop, charged with exceeding his authority in that he "had disposed of lands to divers," answered that in actuality "he had disposed of none ... he had only given his consent, but referred them to the court" for final disposition.[13]

The gentry of the Winthrop fleet had assumed leadership in the new-born towns by virtue of their pre-eminent status among

13. *Winthrop's Journal*, I, 86, 87. The reference to Dudley's assigning lands at Newtown indicates that the disposition of land referred to was within the towns and not between them.

the settlers and of the dual office of assistant and justice, taking up individually and collectively the many-faceted role of arbiter of the peace, the land, and the communal good. But their authority was not to remain unchallenged. The inhabitants of Boston—and of the various towns of the Bay—were to form a parallel locus of power, organized first as a religious congregation and ultimately as the corporate town itself.

The precise form of the church that they were to establish was not fixed in the minds of the leaders of the Winthrop fleet as they arrived in mid-1630. They had apparently given little thought to church polity while still in England; their letters to each other and their statements about the reasons for their departure and their intentions are silent on the point. They had, however, sought ministers to serve the spiritual needs of the settlers. Great care had been expended in the selection, for the leaders desired conscientious and learned men who could preach the word of God well and truly. They turned, quite naturally, to friends in the ministry, to those men whose preaching had awakened their own piety—that portion of the ministry most ardent in its criticism of the dissolute and degenerate conditions prevailing in the greater number of the churches of England and most vehement in their rejection of the forms and practices ordained by the hierarchy. From them, the leaders sought advice about "such of their brethren of the Ministry whom we shall desire to single out for this employ" in the New World. Such lights of English nonconformity as John Cotton, Thomas Hooker, Hugh Peter, and William Ames came to their attention and were unsuccessfully solicited.[14] In the end, George Phillips and John Wilson— good, but lesser men—were engaged, Phillips the vicar of Boxted, county Essex, Wilson a lecturer at Sudbury, Suffolk.

The agreements under which Phillips and Wilson sailed with the Winthrop fleet have not survived, but it appears that they proceeded under contracts similar to others negotiated at the time with men whose occupations were considered necessary for success. Two additional ministers arrived in the Bay with them, John Maverick and John Warham, serving the independently

14. John Winthrop and others to [?], Oct. 27, 1629, *Winthrop Papers*, II, 164. See also Isaac Johnson to Winthrop, Dec. 17, 1629, *ibid.*, 177-79.

organized Dorchester settlers; two others were already ministering in the area, having been dispatched to Salem under contract
earlier, Francis Higginson (who died August 6, 1630) and Samuel
Skelton.   But the Court of Assistants, meeting on August 23,
provided support only for Phillips and Wilson, ordering that
houses be built for them "att the publique charge" and that they
receive annual compensation.[15]   The order was of the same sort
as that of the same date establishing public support for William
Gager, a man of "godlinesse and abilityes in the Arte of Chirur-
gerye" employed by the company before leaving England and
awarded thirty pounds a year in the Bay, that employing James
Penn as marshal of the commonwealth, and that of a subsequent
date establishing public support for a number of men engaged
to supply military leadership to the settlement.[16]

On arriving in the Bay area Phillips and Wilson immediately
set to work ministering to the settlers.   The wide-spreading limbs
of a tree at Charlestown formed the vaulted ceiling of their first
church, the total body of settlers their parishioners.[17]   Later, as
the settlers dispersed, the ministers separated, Phillips settling
at Watertown with Sir Richard Saltonstall's band, Wilson remaining with those at Charlestown and Boston.

If the question of formal church organization had not con-

15. *Assistants' Records*, II, 1-2. The assessment for their maintenance of Nov.
30, 1630 (*ibid.*, 9), indicates that Boston, Charlestown, and Winnisimmet were
being ministered to by Wilson; Watertown, Roxbury, and Medford by Phillips;
Saugus, by virtue of its exclusion, from Salem; Salem and Dorchester, by their
exclusion, by their own ministers.   The contracts with Higginson and Skelton
(Apr. 8, 1629), together with an earlier contract with Francis Bright (Feb. 2,
1628/29), can be found in the Early Files of Courts and Miscellaneous Papers,
Office of the Clerk of the Supreme Judicial Court for the County of Suffolk,
Boston.   Skelton's three-year contract was assumed by the undertakers—the ten
investors who, in return for commercial concessions, took on the obligations of
the old company following the transfer of the charter to America.   An undated
but *ca.* 1633 "Coppie of an Accompte of monies [of] Mr. Skeleton" in the files
indicates that the contract with him was not fulfilled by the undertakers.

16. John Winthrop and others to William Gager, n.d. but 1630, *Winthrop
Papers*, II, 199; *Assistants' Records*, II, 2, 4, 11.   Just as Phillips and Wilson
were supported by the central government and Warham and Maverick at Dorchester were not, Captains John Underhill and Daniel Patrick, engaged by the
company while in England, were supported by the central government of the
commonwealth and Captain Richard Southcote, engaged by the Dorchester settlers,
was not.

17. Thomas Prince, *A Chronological History of New England, In the Form of
Annals* [1736], ed. E. M. Goldsmid, 5 vols. (Edinburgh, 1887), V, 6.

cerned the leaders in England, it became at once a major question in the New World. The settlers had ministers; the association of the ministers with definite localities following the dispersal was to create a situation akin to the geographically based parishes of England. But in the absence of bishops and advowsons, the gift of parish livings held by the Crown, colleges, manor lords, corporations, and the like, who would nominate and install the ministers in their places? Lacking long-established vestries, those self-perpetuating groups of gentlemen and leading citizens dominating the English parishes, who would elect the churchwardens and other officers? Who would care for the physical property of the church? Overlaying these specific questions was the general problem: How was an institutional church to fit into the ideal of a "Citty upon a Hill"?

As it did in regard to town government, the commonwealth might well have drifted toward a solution, possibly by the Assistants collectively assuming the advowsons and forming the nucleus of local vestries. But an alternative existed—congregationalism. Limit the church (or churches following the dispersal) to those explicitly covenanting themselves "wholly unto the Lord Jesus, to do him faithful service, observing and keeping all his statutes, commands, and ordinances" rather than open membership to the whole populace;[18] accept the fact that authority over the church rested in this select congregation and in no higher body or man. The congregation could then select and install those ministerial and lay officers whose titles and duties could be found in the Bible and the writings of the fathers of the primitive church—pastor, teacher, elders, deacons. Given the traditional domination of the English parish by the gentry and the tendency of the villager to take his religion "from his landlord," referring it "wholly to his discretion," the decision rested with the leaders.[19] In a series of conferences in mid-1630, they argued out the question of organization. Samuel Fuller, Edward Winslow, and Isaac Aller-

18. From the Watertown Covenant of 1630, Mather, *Magnalia Christi Americana*, I, 377.

19. John Earle, *Microcosmographie: or, a Piece of the World Discovered, in Essays and Characters* (London, 1628), quoted in Isobel Bowman, ed., *A Theatre of Natures: Some XVII Century Character Writings* (London, 1955), 20; Hill, *Economic Problems of the Church*, 55.

ton from Plymouth, John Endecott, the Reverend Mr. Skelton, and others from Salem—both communities already committed to this congregational polity—joined with arguments and advice.

We do not know who first raised congregationalism as an alternative. At one time it was commonplace to ascribe it to the men of Salem and Plymouth, but Perry Miller's groundbreaking *Orthodoxy in Massachusetts* challenged that interpretation and asserted that the newcomers had congregationalism in mind all along, that they had imbibed a peculiar non-separating congregationalism (as against the separatism of Salem and Plymouth) while still in England. The truth would seem to lie between the two. A vague and imprecise leaning toward congregationalism existed among the leaders of the newcomers, but the positive example of Salem and Plymouth was necessary as a catalyst.[20]

Winthrop and others among the leaders were nonplused by their first encounter with the congregationalism of Salem, but the fundamental tenets of that polity were not entirely strange. The Biblical covenant between God and His people which congregationalism stressed was generally familiar to English Protestantism, Winthrop having spoken of it in his "Modell of Christian Charity," and the notion that man's social organization rested upon covenants between men was in the air of the seventeenth century. Covenants were not "peculiar to the Paedagogy of the old Testament," John Cotton would write, "for it is evident by the light of nature, that all civill Relations are founded in Covenant .... There is no other way given whereby a people ... free from naturall and compulsory engagements, can be united or combined together into one visible body ... but only by mutual Covenant; as appeareth between husband and wife in the family, Magistrates and subjects in the Commonwealth, fellow Citizens in the same Citie." "It is of the nature and essence of every society to be knitt togither by some Covenant, either expressed or implyed," Winthrop himself was to write.[21] It was not difficult,

<hr/>

20. See Appendix II, "Were the Emigrants of 1630 'Non-Separating Congregationalists.'"

21. John Cotton, *The Way of the Churches of Christ in New-England* (London, 1645), 4; Winthrop to Henry Paynter, n.d. but 1640, *Winthrop Papers*, IV, 170.

therefore, to apply the idea of a covenant to the forming of churches. Again, the power of the congregation generally and specifically in the determination of its own affairs was familiar. Anglican theory accepted it with qualification, defining the English vestry, for instance, as representative of the total body of the parishioners in its election of officers and control of church property. The election of ministers by the parish was not an idea unknown, being put forward frequently as one means to reform the clergy. Indeed, the point would entail little argument. The Reverend Mr. Warham, who, during the conferences, held out for a more traditional English church than the congregationalism urged upon him by Fuller, had been elected to his office (together with the Reverend Mr. Maverick) in a solemn assembly of all the Dorchester settlers before leaving England.[22]

Moreover, the leaders had emerged from English nonconformity, and the differences between the practices of Salem and those with which they were individually familiar through their association with nonconforming ministers in England were frequently differences of degree, not kind. William Coddington had been a parishioner of John Cotton in England, Dudley and Johnson at least acquaintances, and Cotton, although he disagreed with the extreme practices found in Salem, had at one time sought to draw the ostensibly godly members of his English parish into a select group covenanted "to follow after the Lord in the purity of his Worship." Increase Nowell, early in 1629, had recommended a minister to the Massachusetts Bay Company who had openly barred ignorant and scandalous persons from communion in his church. Richard Brown, who was to serve as elder of the Watertown church, had been one of the founders of a covenanted church in London in 1616.[23] On a more general level, the very fact that their search for ministers to journey with them had led the leaders to Hooker, Peter, and Ames implies an asso-

22. *Memoirs of Capt. Roger Clap* ... (Boston, 1731), in Young, comp., *Chronicles of the First Planters*, 347-48; Trotter, *Seventeenth Century Life in the Country Parish*, 18; Hill, *Economic Problems of the Church*, 57ff.

23. Larzer Ziff, *The Career of John Cotton: Puritanism and the American Experience* (Princeton, 1962), 49; Perry Miller, *Orthodoxy in Massachusetts, 1630-1650* (Cambridge, Mass., 1933), 130; Champlin Burrage, *The Early English Dissenters in the Light of Recent Research*, 2 vols. (Cambridge, Mass., 1912), II, 294.

ciation with dissenting English ministers who, while eschewing separation, had nevertheless tended to accept the congregationalism which the separatists practiced.[24] Of the two ministers they did successfully solicit, Phillips was very much in the congregational mold upon his arrival, while Wilson, although not a thorough-going congregationalist if we are to ascribe the reservations about his call by the Charlestown church to him, had been a student of Paul Baynes in England, a minister who had thundered against the hierarchy and the mixture of godly and ungodly in the churches.[25]

The practical ramifications, too, must have appealed to some. Congregationalism obviously answered the problems posed by the physical separation from England. More important, the church would be an integral part of Winthrop's "Citty upon a Hill"; consequently it could not be allowed to degenerate into the condition of the churches of England. Such degeneration was certainly conceivable. Already the optimism which Winthrop had expressed aboard the *Arbella* was disappearing as the settlers indicated by their actions that they would not necessarily accept God's will as a guide to their conduct, that they would not voluntarily subordinate themselves to the general good. In the months ahead "carpenters joyners brickelayers, sawers and thatchers" would take advantage of the shortage of skills and plenitude of work to charge exorbitant rates, and the Assistants would answer by dipping into their English precedents and applying price and wage limitations. "Stronge water" would be sold "to severall mens servants" occasioning "much disorder drunckenes and misdemeaner" and the Assistants would seize the supply of the leading offender. Among the settlers there would be Sabbath-breaking, adultery, theft, gaming, while one Nicholas Knopp would appear before the magistrates charged with promising to cure scurvy with "a water of noe worth nor value, which he solde att a very deare rate."[26] Quite

24. The implication is not necessarily of a direct knowledge, as Miller, *Orthodoxy in Massachusetts*, 123ff, writes. The leaders had solicited a number of ministers (presumably those known to them personally) for the names of such who might be suitable; the fact that the names of Ames, Peter, and Hooker came up implies only that these personages were foremost in the minds of the ministers canvassed.

25. Miller, *Orthodoxy in Massachusetts*, 78, 134.

26. *Assistants' Records*, II, 3, 5, 11. See also John Winthrop's letters to England of July 1630, in *Winthrop Papers*, II.

obviously the free admission of the generality into the church would put it in danger. A covenant church, however, would involve an inherent control if "such godly persons that are amongst them and known each to other" were to form the initial body of the church, entering "into covenant with the Lord to walk in his ways." This group could then act deliberately and without haste, "not . . . intending rashly to proceed to the choice of officers, or the admitting of any other into their society than a few, to wit, such as are well knowne unto them." Eventually, all those "as shall appear to be fitly qualified for that [church] estate" would be admitted.[27]

The conferences about the church began sometime before June 28, when Fuller wrote home of his talks with the Reverend Mr. Warham at Dorchester and with Winthrop, Coddington, Endecott, and the Reverend Mr. Phillips, presumably at Salem. For such men as Nowell, Brown, Wilson, and Phillips, familiarity with congregational thought in England would make the congregationalism of Salem and Plymouth a viable proposition. It was not long, undoubtedly, before they joined their voices to those of Endecott, Skelton, and Fuller, if indeed they had not raised the issue in the first place. And such men as Winthrop, more pious than dogmatic, more intent on a natural spirituality than the fine points of institutions, wavered, Fuller describing him during the Salem conferences as "a godly, wise, and humble gentleman," anxious for advice and counsel. The conferences probably continued in the governor's house at Charlestown. On July 26, from Salem, Fuller and Winslow reported to Plymouth that they had heard from Winthrop in the Bay area through Isaac Johnson. "The hand of God" was upon the newcomers, "visiting them with sickness, and taking divers from amongst them."[28] The sickness seems to have precipitated a decision, and four days later, both at Charlestown and Watertown (the dispersal having already begun) church covenants were drawn up. The Charlestown covenant—which, with the transfer of the church to Shawmut, would

27. Fuller and Winslow to Bradford and others, July 26, 1630, Mass. Hist. Soc., *Collections*, 1st Ser., 3 (1794), 75-76.
28. Samuel Fuller to William Bradford, June 28, 1630, Fuller and Edward Winslow to Bradford and others, July 26, 1630, *ibid.*, 74-75.

become the covenant of Boston's church—was the simpler document:

> In the Name of our Lord Jesus Christ, and in Obedience to His holy will, and Divine Ordinaunce

> Wee whose names are hereunder written, being by His most wise, and good Providence brought together into this part of America in the Bay of Masachusetts, and desirous to unite our selves into one Congregation, or Church, under the Lord Jesus Christ our Head, in such sort as becometh all whom He hath Redeemed, and Sanctifyed to Himselfe, doe hereby solemnly, and religiously (as in His most holy Proesence) Promisse, and bind our selves, to walke in all our wayes according to the Rule of the Gospell, and in all sincere Conformity to His holy Ordinaunces, and in mutuall love, and respect each to other, so neere as God shall give us grace.[29]

It was signed that day by Winthrop, Johnson, Dudley, and Wilson. Within three days Increase Nowell, Thomas Sharpe, Simon Bradstreet, William Gager, and William Colborne were allowed to add their names. Others were admitted in quick succession and some weeks later, on August 27, the congregation chose Wilson as teacher of the church, Nowell as elder, and Gager and William Aspinwall deacons. Upon Gager's death, Colborne was elected to replace him and, on October 23, "was invested by imposition of hands of the minister and elder."[30]

The covenanted church so created would in time evolve into a peculiar New England Way. But at the moment it did little more than effect minor changes in the practices of the English parish. From the standpoint of various individuals and groups in the community, there was more that was familiar about the church than was unfamiliar. The leaders among the population had been the first to adhere to the covenant (which they had probably

29. First Church of Boston, Records and Baptisms, 1630-87, manuscript copies in the Massachusetts Historical Society Library, Boston, hereafter cited as First Church Records, erroneously dated Aug. 27, 1630. Fuller's letters to Bradford correct the date. In all the discussions there was no indication of the thought that the division of the ministers and congregationalism would contribute to the demise of the single community idea and perpetuate the dispersal. That this was not considered, however, is evidence of nothing more than the confusion of the times.

30. *Winthrop's Journal*, I, 51-52, 53.

drafted in cooperation with the ministers), and quite clearly they intended having the final say in the admission of new members, the election of officers, and, generally, the affairs of the church. John Winthrop, formerly patron of St. Bartholomew's Church, Groton, would be comfortable in this situation. For his part, the Reverend Mr. Wilson need not break stride in his preaching. The changes effected had concerned polity, not doctrine, hence Wilson could continue the contradictions of the English pulpit, preaching a Calvinistic salvation by God's free grace while calling for a personal reformation, a coming closer to God through godly conduct.[31] Now, however, he need not merely exhort; he could hold out communion and baptism of children as rewards for those who would be struck by his words and, adhering to the covenant, bind themselves to reformation.

Finally, the church was familiar to the general populace. Its organization—the tendency toward one community, one church—was in essence a re-creation of the parish around which had revolved so much of the individual's life in England. As in England, the whole community attended and listened to the word of God, for while the congregation was technically limited to those communicants who had espoused the covenant, it was in practice the entire body of settlers. Not for five years would absences from church services be such as to require a law commanding attendance.[32] That the leaders dominated in the formation of the church was not unusual to the generality, nor was the fact that the communicants alone elected the first officers, or that the officers had unusual titles. The first communicants in a sense assumed the function of the vestry, from which the generality had been excluded in England, and officers were, nonetheless, officers.

Moreover, the intention would seem to have been that eventually all but the most incorrigible would be assimilated into church membership, that the congregation in terms of communicants would be nearly identical to the congregation in terms of the adult population.

31. The gist of the subsequent difference between Cotton's preaching and Wilson's was the former's emphasis on grace, the latter's on works.
32. Law of Mar. 1635, *Colony Records*, I, 140.

The ideal of unity within the community inherent in the early seventeenth century and reflected in Winthrop's "Citty upon a Hill"—the same ideal which made separatists and schismatics so alien to the socially orthodox—demanded a correspondence of church and community, while the nature of the church formed in 1630 made possible such a correspondence. The leaders had established a church encompassing only a few who were well known to each other. But they were not seeking to approximate the invisible church of saints, an approximation which would by definition exclude the great majority of the population. Certainly the covenant did not imply the creation of such a group of saints removed from the total populace. Indeed, there is a sense of unsurety in the covenant which belies the thought that here were professed saints gathering together. The covenanters wrote that they were "desirous" of forming a church "in such sort as becometh all whom He hath Redeemed," not of their certainty that they had probed the Bible and the literature of the primitive church and found the true polity of the church of Christ's elect. They "Promisse, and bind" themselves to walk in godly ways, to conform "to His holy Ordinaunces," but they do not promise as saints. Saints would have been hallowed by God's enduring grace, yet these covenanters recognized that they could abide by their promise only "as God shall give us grace." On the other hand, in the formation of the church, the few promised the many that they would admit all others "as shall appear to be fitly qualified."[33] And "qualified" did not imply "saint." The prospective member was to be evaluated on the basis of conduct and Christian faith, not—as would develop subsequently—on the basis of his profession of the evidence of grace within him.[34] Faith being the product of instruction,[35] and conduct subject to reformation, the Reverend Mr. Wilson's preaching, although illogical in the light of strict Calvinism, had a purpose—the bringing of all into the church and the fulfillment of Winthrop's op-

33. Quoting the covenant in First Church Records, and Fuller and Winslow to Bradford and others, Mass. Hist. Soc., *Collections*, 1st Ser., 3 (1794), 75.

34. A major thesis of Edmund S. Morgan's very excellent *Visible Saints* is that evidence of justification as a prerequisite to membership developed in Massachusetts Bay subsequent to 1630.

35. *Ibid.*, 43.

timistic hope for a community living as a single body, each individual part nurturing every other.

While the desire for unity required, and the nature of the church formed in 1630 allowed a correspondence between church and community,[36] acceptance of this ultimate goal was indicated within a few years when the town of Boston moved to insure that its free male inhabitants would all be property holders, participating citizens, and church members.[37] The intention was never fully realized, but the correspondence achieved during the first years was remarkable.

The town itself grew steadily. Approximately 175 men, women, and children arrived from the Winthrop fleet in 1630. Some left, others died; but more came and the community grew to slightly over 200 by the end of 1631, approximately 290 by the end of 1632, 400 by the end of 1633, and roughly 575 by January 1635.[38] All the while membership in the First Church grew, 132 adding their names by September 1633 to the original four subscribing to the covenant, 136 more by January 1635.[39] And the early records of the church from which these figures are drawn are not complete, as is evidenced by the demission from Boston of six persons—wives of church members—who were otherwise unrecorded as members, and by the omission from the extant list of members, for example, of Richard Gridley, acknowledged as a member in the baptismal records and admitted to freemanship in April 1634.[40] The exact proportion of church members to the total populace, excluding children who would not normally subscribe to the covenant, is difficult to determine in view of the known omissions from the church list and the necessity of approximating the total populace. But out of 131 adult men and women identifiable as having come to the town in 1630 and remaining

36. *Ibid.*, 105.

37. Below, chap. 6, pp. 141-42.

38. On population, see the chart of "Estimated Population of the Commonwealth and Town, 1630-50," below, chap. 7.

39. First Church Records. The Charlestown inhabitants, who withdrew to establish their own church in 1632, have been deleted from the count.

40. Dismissed to Charlestown in First Church Records but unrecorded as members: Arrald Cole, Margaret Hutchinson, Mary Sprague, Joan Hale, Bethiah Hall, and Amy Stowers. Richard Gridley, not recorded as a member, is referred to as "brother" in the baptismal entries, as is Richard Foxwell. Both became freemen. *Colony Records*, I, 366,368.

for any length of time, seventy-one were listed as members of
the church before September 1633, most presumably joining
shortly after its formation; eighteen more by 1636. The 131 is
an unrefined figure, however, including servant and free, single
man and head-of-family.   More significant than the ratio of
church members to this figure in view of the family orientation of
Boston's early society is the fact that of forty-five families arriving in 1630 and remaining in the town, forty-two are known to
have been represented in the church by at least one adult member, both husband and wife being members in at least twenty-two
instances, the husband only in eighteen, the wife only in two.[41]

In the years immediately following, the proportion of church
members to the total adult populace and the family/church percentage appears to have remained the same, the latter being indicated by a comparison of the birth and baptismal records for the
town and church through 1634.   All births were recorded, but
only the children of church members were baptized.   Yet among
sixty-three births recorded by the town, there are only three clear
cases in which the children were not baptized.   In two of these
cases one or both parents were to join the church within a year
or so of the birth; only one family with newborn children—that
of Nathaniel and Alice Bishop—remained apart from the church
for any length of time.[42]

The appearance of congregationalism in Massachusetts Bay
and (at least in Boston) the fact that the body of communicants
embraced with few exceptions the heads-of-families and a majority of the whole adult population must have had a profound
effect on the evolution of town government.   At the lowest level,
English local government in the countryside had been lodged in
the parish and in a variety of petty courts associated, for the most
part, with the manors and boroughs.   Under the general supervision of the justices of the peace of the counties, parish officers

41. Darrett B. Rutman, "God's Bridge Falling Down: 'Another Approach' to
New England Puritanism Assayed," *William and Mary Quarterly*, 3d Ser., 19
(1962), 410 and *n*.   The figures given here are a refinement of those in the
article.

42. First Church Records; "Boston Births, Baptisms, Marriages, and Deaths,
1630-1699," City of Boston, *Report of the Record Commissioners*, IX (Boston,
1883), 1-3.

had been responsible for the repair of highways and the direct administration of poor relief; parish churchwardens had constituted the lowest rung in the ladder of ecclesiastical courts enforcing church duties and moral conduct. Individual parishioners, sometimes under the auspices of the parish, at other times serving under one of the manorial or borough courts, had formed a local officialdom—constables, well-masters, ale-tasters, clerks of the market, produce inspectors, hog-ringers, swineherds, neatherds, scavengers, and the like. The first settlers of Massachusetts Bay, drawn largely from the country villages,[43] were familiar with this local government, far more than with the great world of the county and beyond. It had, to all appearances, regulated their economic affairs, taxed them, established whatever sanitary standards existed, governed their morals, afforded them justice at the lowest and most common level, recorded their land transactions, administered land usage in fields cultivated in common, and generally governed their relations with their neighbors.[44] Some among them had participated in this local government, serving on the vestries which controlled parish activity, as local officers, or in attendance at the local courts. But the number of those participating had been limited; local government in England was basically oligarchic.

In Massachusetts, however, congregationalism was initially the reverse of oligarchy. As a matter of church polity, the Massachusetts communicants were in essence presented with the rights and duties involved in the election of church officers which the English parish had largely reserved to the select vestry, and those rights were even expanded to give to the communicants the elec-

43. Note the origins of those settlers listed in Charles Edward Banks, *The Planters of the Commonwealth, 1620-1640* (Boston, 1930), 65ff. This is confirmed by samplings among those Boston inhabitants not listed in Banks who have been traced to their point of origin. From 1633 and 1634 on there was a larger percentage coming from incorporated boroughs, but the influence of the boroughs can be discounted to a large extent for by that time town government had emerged.

44. William E. Tate, *The Parish Chest: A Study of the Records of Parochial Administration in England* (Cambridge, Eng., 1946), Pt. II and *passim;* Trotter, *Seventeenth Century Life in the Country Parish, passim;* Sidney and Beatrice Webb, *English Local Government from the Revolution to the Municipal Corporations Act: The Parish and the County* (London, 1906), 224ff and *passim; idem, The Manor and the Borough,* 2 vols. (London, 1908), I, chap. 2 and *passim;* Mildred Campbell, *The English Yeoman Under Elizabeth and the Early Stuarts* (New Haven, 1942), chap. 9.

tion of the minister and the admission of new members. To en-
large the power of the communicants in church affairs in this manner and at the same time equate the communicants with the greater
number of the adult townspeople was to open wide the doors to
enlarging the political action of the populace. It was but an easy
step from the assumption of the power of the vestry within the
church to the assumption not only of the vestry's traditional rights
and duties to act in affairs outside the church but of the additional
powers which would naturally have devolved on the vestry in the
absence of manorial and borough courts.

In Boston, the affairs of the community came within the purview of the town's populace gradually, though as the records of
the town begin in September 1634 the process had already been
completed, the initial monopolization of authority by the Court of
Assistants generally and Winthrop specifically having become a
thing of the past. The paucity of records makes it impossible to
trace the course with exactitude. But the process seems to have
originated in the congregation's involvement in church affairs, the
congregation gathering at the call of the officers for special meetings or turning to business following the meetings for worship.
Those of the Charlestown side of the river, finding it difficult to
attend services on Shawmut, desire to form their own church and
ask "the rest of the Church for direction";[45] new members are to
be admitted—Mary Coddington, the wife of William, Anne Newgate, wife of John, Thomas Grubb and his wife Anne;[46] officers
to succeed those dead or gone must be elected; someone to share
the ministry with John Wilson is desired and the congregation
considers and solicits a number of candidates.[47] These were the
great issues, but undoubtedly lesser questions were considered and

45. First Church Records under date of Oct. 14, 1632. The decision appears
to have been made at a Thursday meeting of the congregation, the demissions on
the following Sabbath.

46. Admissions clearly followed the Sabbath services by the fall of 1633. See
Winthrop's Journal, I, 107, and note the dates of admissions as they are included in First Church Records from Dec. 1, 1633.

47. In soliciting John Stoughton in 1632, Winthrop and Wilson assured him
"of our stronge desires towards you" and carefully pointed out that "we meane
not of our selves onely but of the Church of Boston whereof we are"; letter of
Oct. 1632, *Winthrop Papers*, III, 88. See also *Winthrop's Journal*, I, 94, a reference to "one whom *the congregation* intended presently to call to the
office of teacher" (italics mine).

resolved: The thatch on the meetinghouse roof, dry, must be replaced. The common problems of the small community would naturally enter into the discussion; there was no other forum at which they could be considered but at the meetings of the church. The individual plots in the fields on the peninsula were initially laid out in common, and the times for breaking ground, sowing, and harvesting had to be agreed upon. Refuse cluttered the streets and not only must someone be appointed to clear it away, but preventive rules had to be drawn up. Someone had to be designated cowherder; a town watch had to be set.[48] At first such discussions probably involved little more than the leaders outlining the problem and its solution. But the men gathered in the congregation, certainly the men with families and responsibilities, who had a major stake in the affairs of the community—including both communicants and the few non-communicants, for we cannot assume that the latter were completely excluded from meetings of the congregation during these years[49]—would gradually take on a more active role when their individual interests were directly involved.[50]

Above all there was the question of the further allocation of the land. Here was an issue in which all were concerned, in which all would demand their say, particularly in Boston where the land immediately available for houses and tillage was limited. The discussions must have been prolonged, but only a scant hint of them has survived. In 1633 the Reverend John Cotton arrived in the town and those who had followed him from England desired land. Cotton, at the very meeting of the church at which he was installed as teacher, asked that they be "comfortably provided for." Subsequently, in November, the congregation met to consider the maintenance to be allowed Wilson and Cotton. Church business merged with town business as William Coddington rose to air his grievances against the continued predominance

48. That such questions were taken up in conjunction with church questions is a presumption based on (1) the fact that such problems existed; (2) they were solved; (3) there is no evidence that they were solved in any other way; (4) there is evidence (below) that problems involving the allocation of land in 1633 were intermixed with church business.

49. See below, chap. 6, pp. 160-61.

50. As they would at town meetings in 1634. See *Winthrop's Journal*, I, 143-44; "Boston Town Records [1634-1660/61]," City of Boston, *Report of the Record Commissioners*, II (Boston, 1877), 3, hereafter cited as "Boston Records."

of Winthrop in local affairs, notably in the distribution of land.
Sometime before this, Winthrop, presumably in just such a meeting, had been requested to appoint a committee to undertake the
allocations and had complied.   Now Coddington challenged Winthrop's appointments, holding that the Governor "took away the
liberty of the rest, because . . . he had named some men to set out
men's lands."   Tempers flared; harsh words were exchanged.
Winthrop most likely pointed out that he had acted "at the request of the rest"; probably, too, he vented his bitterness toward
those who had retreated from the difficulties of the first year
only to return to enjoy the fruits of their fellows' work. (Coddington, in Boston during the winter of 1630, had gone back to
England in the spring of 1631 and had only recently returned to
the commonwealth.)   In the end, the harsh words were passed
over, and at the meeting on the following Sabbath "they both
acknowledged openly their failing, and declared that they had
been reconciled."[51]

In general, it would seem that the tendency of the town to
assume authority over itself, even though town and congregation
as formal entities were as yet indistinguishable, was not opposed
by the assistants who had, in the first year, assumed a finite control over local affairs.   Winthrop, overburdened by his commonwealth duties, which steadily increased as the population and area
of the settlements expanded, was not at all reluctant to allow the
townspeople a role in local government.   His compliance with the
request to delegate the further allocation of land to a committee
and his acceptance of a debate on public issues with a fellow assistant (Coddington) before the congregation would indicate this.
Collectively, moreover, the Court of Assistants speeded the process by delegating more and more tasks to the towns, reserving to
itself only that general supervision which, in England, the justices
of the peace had exerted over the local community and its officers.

The slow accrual of power in the towns through delegation of
power by the Court can be followed in the records.   In March
1631 the Court found it convenient to give to "every Towne
within this Pattent" the responsibility of seeing that all persons
"except magistrates and ministers" were "furnished with good and

51. *Winthrop's Journal*, I, 111, 114.

sufficient armes." A few months later it was convenient to place upon the towns the responsibility of providing themselves with "common measures and waights" calibrated to sealed instruments kept by the governor. In 1631 various towns, including Boston, were ordered to maintain militia watches (although notably Boston's watch antedated the order of the Court). The following year, the two militia captains of the commonwealth were ordered to be supported by their town-based companies, Roxbury and Boston together to maintain Captain John Underhill. Town support does not seem to have been successful, however, for shortly thereafter the Assistants were levying a general tax for the maintenance of the militia captains. For a brief time after 1633 the responsibility of establishing just wages for laborers was shared with selected townsmen. In July of that year the Court ordered "the inhabitants of the Towne" to inspect the fencing surrounding cultivated land and give warning to the owners if their fences were insufficient; should the warning be ignored, "the Inhabitants shall mend the said fence, and the corne of the owner ... shalbe liable to pay the charges of the mending." In November "every plantacion" was instructed to "agree howe many swine every person may keepe winter and summer aboute the plantacion." At the same time—in consideration of a temporary shortage of foodstuffs—the Court forbade the feeding of edible corn to swine and delegated "2 or 3 neighbors" to determine whether particular corn was fit "for mans meate." Soon after, the Assistants surrendered, by default, the right to appoint the town constables, merely swearing into that office the free choices of the town.[52]

Parallel to this delegation of power to the town by the Court was the emergence of the town as the primary electoral unit of the commonwealth. The process began in May 1632, when the General Court—the total body of freemen meeting together— appointed "two of every plantacion" to confer with it about assessing a public levy (William Colborne and William Cheesbrough being appointed from Boston), and ended in the spring of 1634, when the General Court was reorganized on a representative

52. *Assistants' Records*, II, 12, 17, 26, 31, 33, 36, 38; *Colony Records*, I, 87; "Boston Records," 5.

basis, "two or three" men being elected "of each towne." By then, too, juries were being elected by the townsmen.[53]

All the while there was a general tendency to regard the land of the towns as belonging to the inhabitants, a fact indicated indirectly by the Assistants' and the General Court's determination of town boundaries, and directly by specific awards. In 1632, for example, the Assistants stipulated "that the necke of land betwixte powder horne hill and pullen poynte shall belonge to Boston to be enjoyed by the Inhabitants thereof for ever"; in 1633, land in dispute was adjudged to belong "to the inhabitants of Charlton." In April of the next year, when the informality of the earliest town allotments had created a situation in which individual ownership was at best shaky, the Assistants ordered "that the Constable and [four] more of the cheife inhabitants of every Towne (to be chosen by all the free men there, att some meeteing there)" should survey and record all existing holdings and that "the same soe entered and recorded shalbe sufficient assurance to every such free inhabitant" of his legal title.[54]

First within the congregation, it would seem, and subsequently in their town meeting, the people of the towns dealt with the responsibilities being assigned them. Exactly when the formal division of functions took place, when public affairs were formally recognized as separate from church affairs, is unknown. Dorchester's town government was fully separate from its church by October 1633,[55] but the call of the Assistants for the election of property surveyors "at some meeteing" in each town in April 1634 indicates that at that time there was a lack of uniformity. In Boston, it is evident that the division took place between November 1633, when public affairs were demonstrably dealt with in conjunction with church affairs, and September 1, 1634. By the latter date, the town records indicate that a standing committee, "the 10 to manage the affaires of the towne," was operating as an executive body for the community, while the assembling of the

53. Colony Records, I, 95, 118; John Winthrop to Sir Nathaniel Rich, May 22, 1634, Winthrop Papers, III, 167.

54. Assistants' Records, II, 29, 33, 45.

55. Dorchester Antiquarian and Historical Society, The History of the Town of Dorchester, Massachusetts (Boston, 1859), 32.

town for business in "a general meetinge upon public notice" was a regular procedure.[56]

In a sense the distinction between meetings of the town and church in Boston was merely semantic, for the correspondence between the adult population and the congregation was still very great. The town was not as yet distinguishing between freemen (newly defined as members of the church admitted to participation in commonwealth affairs) and the mere inhabitants; all free, male residents participated in the town meetings, and most were members of the church. Women and servants, although members of the church, were excluded from town affairs, but even in the church they would have been but mute observers. Similarly, if the town business no longer took up time during meetings of the congregation, the town assemblies were still, at least on occasion, held in conjunction with religious assemblies, Winthrop on December 11, 1634, recording that "the inhabitants of Boston" met for public business "this day, after the lecture."[57]

The formal separation of church and town by function seems a natural evolution, not a conscious development dictated by a peculiar thought. There was a general notion that the separation of civil and religious affairs was in order, for the First Church in July 1632 asked its sister churches whether a person might be a civil magistrate and a ruling elder of the church at the same time and received a unanimous reply in the negative. But this consensus did not prevent the ruling elders of the First Church from holding major offices in the town. Indeed, both elders in 1634— Thomas Oliver and Thomas Leverett—were included among "the 10" while Leverett was keeping both church and town records.[58] A more reasonable presumption would be that the division took place as a result of the extensiveness and secular nature of the duties devolving upon the town, the increasing amount of town business making it unfeasible to deal with it in the limited time available at Sabbath or other meetings of the congregation, while the secular nature of the business was making it inappropriate as

56. "Boston Records," 1 ff.

57. *Winthrop's Journal*, I, 143.

58. *Ibid.*, I, 83; Charles E. Park, "Two Ruling Elders of the First Church in Boston: Thomas Leverett and Thomas Oliver," Col. Soc. Mass., *Publications*, 13 (1912), 95.

religious ardor began to grow following the arrival of John Cotton.

Whatever the reason, the division was effected. By the beginning of 1635 town government, in the form of the town meeting and the embryonic selectmen (in Boston "the 10") was an accomplished fact. It was at one and the same time similar to that of old England and dissimilar. The similarity rested in the balanced relationship of the locality to the central government. In England, the law assigned tasks to local officials under the supervision of the justices; where the former ignored their duty, the justices commanded their compliance and, *in extremis,* moved against them judicially. So it was in Massachusetts as the towns developed, the commonwealth law as established by the General Court and the Court of Assistants delegating responsibilities to the localities, and the Assistants, operating together as the Court or independently as magistrates, enforcing compliance. The dissimilarity was in the town meeting, the product of a peculiar evolution. Only occasionally in England would one meet with a locality in which the inhabitants controlled their own activity apart from church, manor, or an all-powerful and institutionalized local oligarchy such as the English closed vestry represented.[59]

Statute caught up with the existence of town government only after the accomplished fact, for notably no single act of the general government recognized the town meeting until long after its appearance. Power continued to accumulate in the towns. In September 1635, the General Court cited the freedom of the towns in "receaving inhabitants and layeing out lots"; subsequently it was decreed that where persons built in the communities "without leave from the townes" the "inhabitants of the said towne shall have power to demolishe the said howses and remove the persons."[60] But not until March 1636, following conversations among the lay leaders and ministers to the effect "that trivial things, etc., should be ended in towns," did the law formally define town government. Then the General Court, noting that "particular townes have many things which concerne only them-

59. S. and B. Webb, *The Manor and the Borough,* I, 128ff., gives examples of such.

60. *Colony Records,* I, 161, 168.

selves," gave to "the freemen of every towne, or the major parte of them" the power to

dispose of their owne lands, and woods, with all the privilidges and appurtenances of the said townes, to graunt lotts, and make such orders as may concerne the well ordering of their owne townes, not repugnant to the lawes and orders here established by the General Court; as also to lay mulks and penaltyes for the breach of thei[r] orders, and to levy and distreine the same, not exceedeing the somme of 20s; also to chuse their owne particular officers, as constables, surveyors for the high wayes, and the like.[61]

The list, for the most part, merely recognized the *ad hoc* arrangements of the past years.

61. *Winthrop's Journal,* I, 172; *Colony Records,* I, 172. The classic description of town formation in *Johnson's Wonder-Working Providence,* 212ff, has had no place in the above discussion. Johnson, writing in the early 1650's of a town founded in the early 1640's was describing an established pattern; Boston's town government emerged before that pattern had evolved.

IV

"PLACES FOR HUSBANDRY"

W ILLIAM CODDINGTON, in rising in the congregation to challenge Winthrop's appointment of a committee "to set out
men's lands," had been at best ill-informed of the course of events;
at worst he had been seeking to assert himself in Boston by attack-
ing Winthrop. In either event, he had touched on a crucial issue,
one which both preceded and followed the appearance of town
government.

The problem of the land was initially two-fold: the limited
area available to the settlers on Shawmut with the consequent
necessity of expanding the limits of the town beyond the peninsula, and the establishment of a formal system for the distribution
of the land.[1] The first could be met in large part by soliciting
the commonwealth government, which retained authority over the
bounds of the towns. The second was more difficult to resolve
and precipitated sharp conflict between the generality and gentry
of Boston. By engendering conflict and, ultimately, a tendency
toward dispersal within the town (as in 1630 there had been dispersal into the towns), the land would prove disruptive of the
Winthropian ideal of a cohesive community.

The impromptu division of land on Shawmut in 1631 and
1632, when the settlers took up land under Winthrop's approving
eye, had afforded each family but a bare minimum, a house-and-
yard lot which normally did not exceed a half-acre, and an allot-

---

1. The satisfaction of Indian claims to the land constituted a third but minor
problem, the local Indians, depleted by recurrent plagues and threatened by
stronger tribes farther off, immediately putting themselves under the protection
of the new arrivals. See, for example, *Winthrop's Journal*, I, 59-60 and *passim;
Assistants' Records*, II, 40; *New Englands First Fruits* ... (London, 1643), reprinted in Samuel Eliot Morison, *The Founding of Harvard College* (Cambridge,
Mass., 1935), 428; Mass. Hist. Soc., *Proceedings*, 1st Ser., 17 (1880), 52-55;
"Boston Records," 6, 11-12; *Colony Records*, III, 252.

ment in the town's fields as they were opened for cultivation. Additionally, the inhabitants had established their right to harvest fodder and thatch from the marshes rimming the peninsula, to cut wood on town lands and in those areas on the mainland and harbor islands assigned them by the commonwealth for the purpose, and finally, to run livestock on the uncultivated lands of the peninsula. And yet the settlers at Boston, who had largely paid their own way to the New World, some of them going deeply into debt to make the journey,[2] assumed that by virtue of the company's policy, as enunciated in England and carried to the Bay, they had a right to broader acreage, an assumption in accord with their own inclinations as well. Many of the newcomers arriving in 1632 and 1633 paid their own way, too, and expected house and garden land in the village and larger allotments beyond. The opening of additional land on the peninsula—New Field, the largest of the four on Shawmut—could not answer the demand; hence an appeal was made to the Court of Assistants.

The augmenting of the town's lands by the commonwealth government was a steady process in the early 1630's. On November 7, 1632, the Court of Assistants gave the town possession of a peninsula thrusting down from the North Shore into the harbor to Pullen Point at the harbor mouth. By then, too, the Court had recognized Boston's interest on the mainland to the south, pushing the town boundary outward to include the base of the Neck. Much of this ground was marshland, but there was enough above water to afford a respectable pasturage beyond the town gate, soon to be built at the narrowest point of the Neck. By March 1633 the Bostonians had obtained still more acreage on the mainland, an alternating pattern of hill land and tidal swamp beyond Roxbury, along the banks of Muddy River.[3] A few months later, however, the influx of newcomers accompanying the Reverend John Cotton brought about a crisis. It was generally agreed that Boston was "the fittest place" for Cotton, and he and the First Church quickly came to an amicable relationship. But "those who came with him desired he might sit down where

2. See, for example, John Winthrop to John Winthrop, Jr., July 23, 1630, *Winthrop Papers*, II, 305-7.
3. *Assistants' Records*, II, 29, 31, 34; *Colony Records*, I, 129-30.

they might keep store of cattle," and since Boston could not meet this requirement the Assistants determined that "those of Boston might take farms in any part of the bay not belonging to other towns." This permissive grant was formalized by the General Court in September 1634, when it gave the town "inlargement" at Mount Wollaston on the south shore and Rumney Marsh on the North Shore.[4] At the same time the tiny village of Winnisimmet which had grown up at the mouth of the Mystic opposite Charlestown, previously given the choice of joining itself to Charlestown or Boston, chose the larger town. Earlier—in April 1634—three islands in the harbor (Long Island, Deer Island, and Hog Island) had been leased to the town for a twenty-one year period. The next year the three pounds paid in rent were remitted by the General Court, the old lease canceled, and the three islands—plus a fourth (Spectacle Island)—were "graunted to the inhabitants of Boston, to enjoy...for ever," subject only to a token annual rent of four shillings.[5]

In still another way, Boston sought and obtained enlargement. On Shawmut, on Noddles Island, and on the mainland around Winnisimmet, earlier settlers had engrossed large areas—the Reverend Mr. Blackston on the peninsula and Samuel Maverick on the island and the mainland. In April 1633 the Court of Assistants recognized Maverick's possession of Noddles Island upon payment of a quitrent of "either a fatt weather a fatt hogg" or eleven shillings, and of Blackston's ownership of fifty acres on Shawmut in fee simple. Both men soon received delegations from Boston seeking to buy them out. In 1634 an agreement was reached with Blackston for the purchase of all but a six-acre house lot for thirty pounds, the town soliciting six shillings from each householder to raise the purchase price. Maverick's Winnisimmet lands passed to Boston's Richard Bellingham by private sale in 1634, but he held on to the island's 663 acres, only granting an undetermined part of it to the temporary use of the town in late 1634 or early 1635. Subsequently Boston obtained jurisdiction over the whole island, but the land remained in the pos-

4. *Winthrop's Journal*, I, 108-9; *Colony Records*, I, 119, 130.
5. *Colony Records*, I, 119-20, 125, 139; *Assistants' Records*, II, 44. The rent for the islands seems to have fallen into abeyance immediately.

session of the Maverick family until sold at the end of the second decade to a West Indian merchant.[6]

In the face of a steadily increasing population, the enlarged boundaries of the town, and the political maturation of the towns-men, the rough, impromptu allocations under Winthrop's auspices of the first years had, of necessity, to give way, in 1633, to grants by a committee appointed by Winthrop "at the request" of the town, and in 1634, to those of the town itself. But the assumption of control of the land by the town, a corollary to the emergence of town government, did not mean the exclusion of the

6. *Assistants' Records,* II, 31; "Boston Records," 2, 3; "Deposition of John Odlin and other Inhabitants of Boston, respecting Blackstone's Sale," Mass. Hist. Soc., *Collections,* 2d Ser., 4 (1816), 202-3; *Colony Records,* I, 189; Suffolk County, Mass., Registry of Deeds, *Suffolk Deeds,* 14 vols. (Boston, 1880-1906), I, 15, 122-23, hereafter cited as *Suffolk Deeds;* Deed of Sale, Oct. 28, 1650, Greenough Collection, Office of the Clerk of the Supreme Judicial Court, Suffolk Co., Boston.

commonwealth leaders from a voice in the disposing of the land or from power generally in the affairs of the community. On the contrary, men of Winthrop's ilk, while acquiescing in and even furthering the political growth of the town, nevertheless maintained a strong position in local affairs. Inevitably, their positions in commonwealth government, their conviction that led Winthrop in his "Modell of Christian Charity" to speak of men "highe and eminent in power and dignitie; others meane and in subjeccion," and their acceptance by the generality as natural leaders, all demanded their continuing activity within, though not the domination of, the town.

Moreover, the emergence of the town and town meeting did not imply egalitarianism. There was a stratification within the town, a rough division of the free populace into what can be termed gentry, both greater and lesser, and generality. Some men were possessed of more worldly goods than others, having been men of substance and status in England. In New England they expected—and given the traditions of English society they received—deference in social and political matters. Others, of little status in English society, nevertheless arrived with property and connections with more eminent worthies which placed them a cut above the general populace. The division had, of course, always existed. The deference paid to Isaac Johnson and John Winthrop by the first settlers on Shawmut was largely due to the wealth and status which they brought with them from England. But in Boston the distinction was exaggerated after 1633 by the arrival of John Cotton's well-to-do friends and parishioners from Boston and the nearby countryside in England, families which had the desire and wherewithal to follow their beloved minister to the New World—the Haughs, Leveretts, and Hutchinsons, for example.

Boston's gentry as it existed in 1636 was revealed in two instances when the townsmen volunteered funds for community purposes, in February for the building of a new fortification on Fort Hill, and in August when a "general meeting of the richer inhabitants" contributed over 40*li* toward the maintenance of a free school in the town. The twenty-seven Bostonians listed as contributing more than 6*s* formed the core of the early commu-

Contributors to Fort and School*	Arrived	li	s	d	Servants**	Common-wealth	Dep.	Town	Comm. Posts***	Church Offices****	Acres	Location	Comment
Group I													
John Winthrop	1630	15	0	0	12	7	—	—	2	—	200+	North Shore	English gentry family
Henry Vane	1635	15	0	0	2	1	—	—	2	—	200	"	Prominent English family. Departed 1637.
Richard Bellingham	1634	7	10	0	5	2	—	1	3	—	?		Purch. extensive farm; Recorder, MP, Bost., Eng.
William Coddington	1630	6	10	0	6	8	1	1	4	—	530	Mt. Wollaston	Prom. citizen, Boston, Eng.
(Atherton Haugh)	1633	—	—	—	4	1	—	1	—	—	700	"	Mayor, Alderman, Boston, Eng.
Sub-total		43	10	0	29	19	1	3	11				
Group II													
John Coggan	1633	6	0	0	1	—	—	2	1	—	210	North Shore	Not ch. mem. but frman. 1633 & wf. Ann mem. '34
John Winthrop, Jr.	1631	6	0	0	—	—	—	1	1	—	—	Mt. Wollaston	Connection to Boston tenuous
William Hutchinson	1634	6	0	0	4	—	3	1	5	Deac.	600	North Shore	Prom. Old Boston & London family
Robert Harding	1630	3	3	4	1	—	—	2	—	—	100	North Shore	Shipcaptain; infrequently in town
John Coggshall	1634	3	3	4	8	—	2	2	3	—	200	Muddy River	Ard. Roxbury '32; to Boston '34
Thomas Oliver	1632	3	0	0	1	—	—	3	4	Elder	115		
Thomas Leverett	1633	3	0	0	4	—	2	2	3	Elder	115	North Shore	Alderman, Boston, Eng.
(William Brenton)	1633	—	—	—	7	—	—	2	7	—	228		Ard. Watertown '30; to Bost. '32; '34
(Giles Firmin)	1632	—	—	—	7	—	—	—	—	Deac.	—		d. ca. 1636-37
(Edmund Quincy)	1633	—	—	—	6	—	—	—	3	—	?	Mt. Wollaston	
Sub-total		30	6	8	32	—	7	15	27				
Group III													
John Wilson	1630	1	0	0	6	—	—	—	1	Pastor	200	Mt. Wollaston	
(John Cotton)	1633	—	—	—	8	—	—	—	—	Teacher	250	Muddy River	
William Peirce	1632	1	0	0	—	—	—	—	—	—	100	North Shore	Shipcaptain; infrequently in town
Robert Keayne	1635	1	0	0	4	—	—	1	—	—	314	"	Eventually obtained recognition of 530 acr.
John Newgate	1632	0	10	0	3	—	—	—	—	—	112	"	
Samuel Cole	1630	0	10	0	—	—	—	1	—	—	105	"	
Richard Tuttle	1635	0	10	0	—	—	—	—	—	—	161	"	
Ralph Hudson	1635	0	10	0	1	—	—	—	—	—	50	"	
Samuel Wilkes by	1634	0	10	0	1	—	1	—	—	—	—	—	No rec. as ch. member; left Bost. ca. '36
William Colborne	1630	0	8	0	6	—	5	1	10	Deac.	160	Muddy River	
William Aspinwall	1630	0	8	0	1	—	—	1	5	Deac.	186	North Shore	
John Sanford	1631	0	8	8	1	—	—	1	7	—	106	—	
William Baulston	1630	0	6	8	—	—	—	1	6	—	(90+)	Mt. Wollaston	
James Penn	1630	0	6	8	1	—	—	1	2	—	50	North Shore	"Cannoneere" of Fort, '32
Jacob Eliot	1631	0	6	8	—	—	—	—	2	Deac.	?	Mt. W. & Muddy R.	No allot. rec., but sold 90 acr. '38
Richard Wright	1631	0	6	8	3	—	—	—	—	—	(130)	Mt. Wollaston	"Beadle" (marshal) of colony '30
Thomas Marshall	1633	0	6	8	—	—	—	—	3	—	70	North Shore	Elder bro. of Rev. John Eliot
(Edward Gibbons)	1623	—	—	—	1	—	1	1	—	—	110	"	No allot. rec. but sold 130 acr. '38/9
(William Chees-brough)	1630	—	—	—	—	—	—	—	—	—	(200)	Mt. Wollaston	No allot. rec. but sold 200 acr. '39
Sub-total		8	7	4	36	—	7	8	45				
Total		82	4	0	97	19	15	26	83				
Contributors of less than 6s and non-contributors		3	2	0	12	—	—	4	11	—			

*The names of those added to the list of known contributors are in parentheses.

**"Servant" includes men, women, children indicated in the extant documents as "servant" or "apprentice" through 1638.

***Offices and committee posts are through the spring elections of 1636. Commonwealth offices include governor, deputy-governor, assistant, treasurer.

****Through 1640.

nity, with a few obvious additions—William Brenton and John
Cotton, who undoubtedly subscribed at least this amount, although
there are blanks following their names on the extant list; Atherton Haugh, a former alderman and mayor of old Boston; Edmund Quincy, near death as the meetings in 1636 took place;
William Cheesbrough.[7] Their ranks were regularly augmented
as newcomers of stature arrived. William Tyng, for example,
made his appearance in the midst of a religious dispute and with
the advantage of ready cash and relative neutrality easily inserted
himself into a prominent position in the town. They led in the
First Church, in which all but two were recorded as members;[8]
for while Wilson and Cotton were in part counted among the
gentry by virtue of their ministries, elders Thomas Oliver and
Thomas Leverett and deacons William Hutchinson, William Colborne, William Aspinwall, and Jacob Eliot received church offices
by virtue of their lay prominence. They dominated political
activity in the town, as can be readily seen in the accompanying
chart of "Boston's Gentry: ca. 1634-36," a compilation of data
from commonwealth, town, and church records. Nine of them
appeared for Boston as deputies to the General Court during the
period; among "the 10 to manage the affaires of the towne" as
the records open in 1634 were Winthrop, Coddington, elders
Oliver and Leverett, John Coggshall, William Peirce, Robert
Harding, and William Brenton. Giles Firmin of "the 10" had
died before the 1636 subscription lists were drawn up, but would
undoubtedly have contributed handsomely to both causes. Indeed, of the ten, only John Underhill was not in the rank of the
contributors, and his place in high councils was insured by his
position as the town's outstanding soldier and military leader.
Moreover in October 1634, when Firmin (deceased) and Hard-

7. See the accompanying chart of "Boston's Gentry: ca. 1634-36" based on
"Boston Records," 8, 160n. There was still a fourth group, consisting of persons
contributing less than 6s to the school: John Odlin, Edward Bendall, Isaac Grosse,
Zaccheus Bosworth, William Salter, James Penniman, John Pemberton, John
Biggs, William Talmage, Richard Gridley, Thomas Savage, Edward Rainsford,
Edward Hutchinson. With the exception of the last—the son of William Hutchin-
son—this group was peripheral to "the richer inhabitants."

8. The exceptions are John Coggan, whose wife Ann became a member in
1634 and who was himself listed as a freeman in *Colony Records*, I, 368, under
date of Nov. 5, 1633, and Samuel Wilkes, who was in the town in 1634, presumably had no family, and left in or shortly after 1636.

ing (trading in Virginia) were replaced on the ten, Richard Bellingham and John Coggan, two other contributors of note, were elected. Again, of 124 town offices and committee posts filled to March 1636—committees for surveying land, viewing fences, assessing town and commonwealth levies, investigating the overcutting of wood on the Neck, setting prices upon "cattell comodities, victualls and labourers and Workmen's Wages,"[9]—109 were filled from among "the richer inhabitants" charted.

That the gentry were not undifferentiated is indicated by their contributions to the 1636 funds. The more prominent men in terms of public office, who generally held commonwealth positions, were the more prominent in terms of contributions (Group I on the chart). The lesser members of the gentry in terms of contributions (Groups II and III) were content with the smaller stage of the town. These lesser members were similarly differentiated, the larger contributors among them (Group II) tending to hold town offices to a greater extent than the smaller (Group III), the latter tending to confine their activities to town committees. Some among the gentry were politically more active than others, the fourteen most active—a group including nine of the largest contributors from Groups I and II and five lesser contributors who had been in the town since 1630—holding 85 of the 124 town offices and committee posts and being selected deputy on fourteen of fifteen occasions. Of the rest, some were only tenuously connected to the town—John Winthrop, Jr., for example, whose travels took him to England and Ipswich during the period, ship captains William Peirce and Robert Harding. Others, like Robert Keayne, had arrived in the town late in the period and were not yet fully accepted within the community. Still others were like Atherton Haugh, who took up residence at Mount Wollaston, far from Boston's center and political life, soon after his arrival. A few, merchant John Newgate and tavernkeeper Samuel Cole, for example, simply refrained from (or were not awarded) public office.

In 1634 gentry and generality formed two distinct interests with regard to the land. The latter advocated a quick division of all available acreage on an equal basis, and at times achieved

9. "Boston Records," 5.

limited success. When, for example, Hog Island's 450 acres passed into possession of the town, a general meeting was called to determine its use, and it was ordered that the land there should be "lette out unto the inhabitants and freemen of this towne according to the number of names in every family.[10] The gentry, on the other hand, while not disregarding the needs of the generality, resisted their demand for precipitous action and argued for a policy which, in the words of the General Court, would take into account the ability of the individual "to improve lands." For some a selfish motive undoubtedly prevailed; having money, servants, equipment, they would be better fitted to improve more land than others and hence would receive it. Winthrop, who stood with the gentry and "oft persuaded" the town to move slowly in its divisions, leaving "a great part at liberty for new comers and for common," would similarly profit by a division made on the basis of the ability of the individual to use the land. But his stand seems to have been based on his concern for the welfare of the community. "The reason why some were not willing that the people should have more land in the bay than they might be likely to use in some reasonable time," he wrote, "was partly to prevent the neglect of trades, and other more necessary employments, and partly that there might be place to receive such as should come after." To him, it would be "very prejudicial" if newcomers "should be forced to go far off for land, while others had much, and could make no use of it, more than to please their eye with it."[11]

In December 1634, the issue reached a crisis. "The inhabitants" of the town met following a lecture in the meetinghouse to elect, by secret ballot, a committee of seven men to divide the town lands. Winthrop, Coddington, "and other of the chief men" failed of election as the townsmen, "fearing that the richer men would give the poorer sort no great proportions of land," chose "one of the elders and a deacon, and the rest of the inferior sort." Apparently the election was challenged, Winthrop claiming that he "had the greater number before one" of the success-

10. *Ibid.*, 2. Though "lette" implies rent—and this might have been the original intention—the land was subsequently held in fee simple.
11. *Colony Records*, I, 240; *Winthrop's Journal*, I, 143-44.

ful candidates "by a voice or two." But he would not press the point; on the contrary, he would refuse to serve by virtue of "such an election as was carried" by so few votes. He did evince his displeasure, however; while "he did not apprehend any personal injury, nor . . . doubt of their good affection towards him, yet he was much grieved that Boston should be the first who should shake off their magistrates, especially Mr. Coddington, who had been always so forward for their enlargement." Others added their voices to his. The Reverend Mr. Cotton spoke of "the Lord's order among the Israelites" by which "all such businesses" were committed "to the elders," arguing that "it had been nearer the rule to have chosen some of each sort."

Faced by this phalanx, the generality, unused to power, gave way and agreed to a new election to be held the next lecture day. The extent of their surrender then became clear. Winthrop, Coddington, Bellingham, Cotton, Oliver, Colborne, and William Baulston were elected and empowered "to devide and dispose" of all land "not yet in the lawfull possession of any particular person" (and this included the islands), "leaving such portions in Common for the use of newe Commers, and the further benefitt of the towne, as in theire best discretions they shall thinke fitt."[12]

The result of the dispute determined the question of policy. Land would be held in reserve for newcomers, but the generality would have expansion beyond their home lots and gardens on the Neck, receiving "places for husbandry" abroad on the basis of family size. The better sort, too, would have their house lots and gardens, but beyond the Neck they would have broad acres allotted to them in proportion to their ability to use them, or by virtue of their position and status in the community.

For the moment, however, there was a moratorium on land grants. The "Allotters"—the committee elected in December 1634—set to work surveying the town's populace and determining the amount of land each family should have; but other than the assignment to newcomers of house and garden lots in the town, no permanent allotments were made. As the planting season approached that spring, temporary allocations were made, the inhabitants being allowed to plant "eyther upon such ground as

12. *Winthrop's Journal*, I, 143-44; "Boston Records," 3.

is alreadie broken up or inclosed in the neck" or upon Maverick's
Noddles Island grant, "every able man fitt to plant" to have two
acres, every youth one.   Hutchinson, Coggan, John Sanford,
Brenton, and William Cheesbrough were designated to make the
assignments.[13]   In March 1635, steps were taken to protect future
allocations by an order of the town providing that "noe Wood
shalbe felled at any of the Islands, nor elsewhere, untill they bee
lotted out"; two months later an interloper building at Muddy
River, one Griffin Montague, was dispossessed by order of the
Court of Assistants, presumably at Boston's request.[14]   In November, a town meeting considered the question of who among
the newcomers flooding into the town should share in the land,
determining that no land should be "graunted unto any ... but
such as may be likely to be received members of the Congregation."   To preserve the intention of the order no one was to sell
property "to any new comers, but with the consent and allowance
of those that are appointed Allotters."   And since the earlier
impromptu divisions of the peninsula had been marked by an
"unequall disposing of the planting ground," the town attempted
to clear the way for a new division of land within the fields by
voting in December 1635 that "none of the inhabitants shall be
accounted to have any estate of inheritance ... upon the necke,
save onely in theire house plotte, gardens and yards, untill the
towne shall take order for a more equal disposing."[15]   The
records of the town give no hint of a redivision of the fields, however, and the order lay ignored for seven years.

    That same month, December 1635, the formal process of
setting out permanent allotments beyond the Neck began.   The
allotters had completed their survey of the town's residents.
Now they reported their decision as to how much land each family should have, and committees were appointed to lay out the
actual ground.   Hutchinson, Quincy, Samuel Wilbore, Cheesbrough, and John Oliver were appointed to lay out "allottments
for farmes att Rumley [sic] Marsh" according to "the assign-

    13. "Boston Records," 3.
    14. Ibid., 4.   Muddy River and Noddles Island were temporarily excepted,
as was an area on Dorchester Neck temporarily allotted to Boston for wood
gathering.
    15. Assistants' Records, II, 53; "Boston Records," 5-6.

ments of the Allotters." Coddington, Colborne, Aspinwall, Quincy, and Richard Wright were to lay out allotments at Mount Wollaston, adding to each "a convenient proportion of meaddowe...according to their number of cattell." Still another committee—Colborne, Aspinwall, Sanford, Baulston, and Wright—was to lay out at Muddy River the lands of "the poorer sort of the Inhabitants, such as are members [of the church] or likely so to be, and have noe Cattell," allocating four acres for every member of a family where the land lay close to Boston, five acres per head "farther off." Committees were appointed, too, to "take viewe" of certain localities and "bound out...what may be sufficient" for persons apparently not considered by the allotters for one reason or another. Coddington, Quincy, and Hutchinson were to receive "their particular farmes" at Mount Wollaston; Colborne, Leverett, Thomas Oliver, and John Cotton, at Muddy River. In at least one case, that of Colborne's land, the committee was to take into account a prior interest in the area, being instructed to lay out his farm "neare unto and about his house which he hath there built."[16]

The work of the surveyors proceeded erratically. The larger allotments were apparently laid out quickly, facilitated perhaps because many of the more substantial inhabitants had anticipated the results and begun improving their lands prior to their actual setting out, as Colborne had done. But the surveying of the lands of the lesser inhabitants dragged, and in 1636 a provision was made that those whose allotments were not yet laid out could plant their crops temporarily upon "such part" of the land already surveyed at Muddy River as the owners were not able to cultivate at the moment.[17]

When, finally, the surveyors' work was completed, probably in 1637, the record of allocations to the townspeople of 1635 gave tangible evidence of the decision of December 1634.[18] Allotments to the gentry (indicated on the chart of "Boston's Gentry:

16. "Boston Records," 6-7.
17. Ibid., 8.
18. The allotments were recorded in "Boston Records," under date of Jan. 8, 1637/38, but this was merely the final act of a long process. The division of land to the inhabitants of 1635 had obviously been completed earlier; the division to those arriving since 1635 was even then in progress.

ca. 1634-36") averaged just under 200 acres and exceeded 5,000 acres in all. Almost the whole of the harbor shore at Mount Wollaston had been awarded to four men: Atherton Haugh, who received 700 acres, William Coddington with 530 acres, Edmund Quincy, and the Reverend Mr. Wilson, who manipulated several grants from commonwealth and town and eventually obtained recognition of a 565-acre farm. Back from the shoreline were other large holdings, including 600 acres awarded to William Hutchinson. Along the North Shore, less extensive but nevertheless large holdings predominated. Winthrop himself received grants of 150 and 50 acres, plus an undetermined grant embracing the whole lower part of Pullen Point; Robert Keayne was allotted 314 acres; William Brenton, 228. At Muddy River five large farms had been laid out, for William Colborne, John Cotton, Thomas Leverett, Thomas Oliver, and soldier John Underhill.

Allotments to the generality totaled less than 1,500 acres and averaged below 30 acres. Some were laid out at Mount Wollaston, although it was the obvious intention of the allotters to hold the greater part of the land there in reserve. On the North Shore a few small plots were tucked in between the large allotments of the gentry. However, the great majority of small holdings were laid out at Muddy River, 55 grantees receiving an average of 15⅔ acres, the smallest being eight acres, the largest 25 and 35 acres.

All the while, as the allotments were being assigned and laid out to the population of 1635, the town had been growing— doubling in size between 1635 and 1638, exceeding two thousand by the turn of the decade.[19] The allocations of 1635 were outdated long before the surveys were completed. Newcomers asked for lands on and off the Neck, the established system of allotments justifying their request; sons of the older settlers grown to manhood sought land of their own, as did servants freed of their service.

At first these requests for land were considered in the town meeting itself. But this quickly proved to be a cumbersome and disorderly assembly, constantly growing more so as newcomers

19. See below, chap. 7, the chart of "Estimated Population of the Commonwealth and Town, 1630-50."

swelled attendance. The Boston records do not indicate the disturbances found later in Dorchester: "intemperate Clashings," "divers things . . . spoken of and few matters . . . issued by reason that new matters have been upstarted while a former hath been in hearing," "so much time spent and little work done," "unorderly departings of sundry before other brethren and Neighbors."[20] Yet in March 1635, the town had found it necessary to levy a fine of twelve pence on those who "fall into pryvate conference, to the hindering of the publique businesses." To some extent, the allotters served as a screening committee for the meetings in presenting business for the town's action, perhaps in conjunction with the ten, though that group seems never to have had much power and certainly lost its identity after the allotters made their appearance. Such screening, however, could only be informal.[21]

The town itself, certainly the gentry, recognized the difficulties of conducting more, and more complicated, business in such a body. The solution lay ready to hand: re-establish the ten as a select committee along the familiar lines of the governing councils of the English borough and of the select vestries of England, to which major community responsibilities in the villages had been delegated. And in March 1636 such a committee made its appearance in Boston, the town electing Elders Oliver and Leverett, Hutchinson, Coggshall, Colborne, Sanford, Richard Tuttle, Aspinwall, Brenton, Baulston, Eliot, and Penn. Whatever authority the ten had, together with that of the allotters, was delegated to this group, the town empowering it to "oversee, looke unto and sett order for all the Allottments within us, and for all Comers in unto us, as also for all other the occasions and businesses of this Towne."[22] For the remainder of the decade the town as a whole was to meet only sporadically: to elect the committee, initially every six months then every year; to elect deputies to the

20. Quoted in Charles Francis Adams, "The Genesis of the Massachusetts Town and the Development of Town-Meeting Government," Mass. Hist. Soc., *Proceedings*, 2d Ser., 7 (1892), 181, 184.

21. "Boston Records," 4. The town records contain no indication of a meeting of the ten or any other body which can be described as a steering committee from Sept. 1634 through Feb. 1636.

22. "Boston Records," 9.

General Court; and occasionally to ratify important actions. In all other business, the selectmen (though the name was not then in general use) acted for the town.

It was to the selectmen, therefore, that those seeking land within the town after the allocations of 1635 appealed. And the selectmen—chosen during the decade almost exclusively from the same group of "richer inhabitants"[23]—sought to accommodate them within the policy previously adopted. House lots and gardens on the peninsula were granted to them or bought by them from older settlers with the approval of the selectmen; the allotment of great lots beyond the Neck followed. In this regard, the dichotomy between generality and gentry was maintained. On the one hand, Stephen Kinsley, a laborer who had been allotted a house plot in 1637, was granted a great lot of thirty-six acres at Mount Wollaston, the proportion due to a family of nine; Edward Belchar, William Talmage, Thomas Snow, William Dening, and John Arratt, former servants of William Brenton, received house lots and great allotments at Muddy River of ten and fifteen acres in 1636. On the other hand, Benjamin Keayne, the son of Robert Keayne, was awarded two hundred acres at Mount Wollaston on the basis of status and worth; William Tyng, after obtaining house and garden lots, was in 1638 granted "his great Lott" of five hundred acres at Muddy River "for Eight persons, and Fortie and twoe heads of Cattell in present possession, and thirtie heads to come." Subsequently, his previous grant "not yet layd out" and "the number of his Persons and Cattell . . . increased," an additional one hundred acres was granted him.[24]

Land was awarded by the selectmen for public service, usually as grants to an office or an individual: the "Canoneere of Boston wheresoever he is, or shall be, in the service thereof from time to time" receiving five hundred acres at the Mount in 1640; Richard

23. Serving terms from 1636 through 1639 were: Oliver, 7 terms; Leverett, 7; Colborne, 7; Eliot, 6; Penn, 5; Coggshall, 4; Harding, 4; Sanford, 4; Keayne, 4; Baulston, 4; Hutchinson, 4; Brenton, 3; Aspinwall, 2; Newgate, 2; Tuttle, 1; Coggan, 1; Edward Gibbons and William Tyng, 1 each in 1639. The last two represent the new faces among the gentry, Tyng a newcomer, Gibbons having risen in wealth and stature within the commonwealth.

24. "Boston Records," 14, 17, 26, 32, 35, 47, 48.

Wright at Mount Wollaston granted "a narrow piece 60 rods in length for furtherance of a mill" there. But sometimes they were made to a group. Thus, in 1638, the associates who built a "Wharfe and Crayne" at Boston received one hundred acres at the Mount to support its repair and maintenance on the basis that it served the community's interest; in the early 1640's, a group of English and commonwealth associates were granted three thousand acres of Boston land at Mount Wollaston (in addition to land obtained from the commonwealth government) to forward iron mining.[25]

The record of allotments large and small is a continuous one from 1636 to the end of the decade and on into 1641. For the most part, the newcomers were awarded their lots at Mount Wollaston, over one hundred allotments being made there, the land, together with a fifteen hundred acre common, being laid out inland along Town Brook and behind the earlier Coddington and Haugh grants. A quarter that number were made at Muddy River, while virtually none were made on the North Shore where the earlier division had resulted in the distribution of almost all the ground. The allotments were made only to actual settlers, for while non-residents of the commonwealth were allowed houses and lots in the town in anticipation of the day they removed to New England, larger grants from the town were denied them. For example, Owen Roe, a London tradesman, dispatched cattle and two servants to Boston in 1635 to prepare the way for his own coming. By purchase or grant he obtained a house lot which was subsequently rented out for him; after he appealed to Winthrop to "help forward" his servants in obtaining land on which to graze his stock the town gave him the use of two hundred acres at the Mount "for the present releife of his cattell." But he was to receive a permanent allotment "whenas he shalbecome an Inhabitant amongst us, and not otherwise." The town's decision was a wise one. Roe procrastinated and when the English Civil War broke out chose finally not to come. His house on the peninsula remained in his possession, however, and he was still collecting rent for it in 1645.[26]

25. *Ibid.*, 37, 48, 77.
26. Owen Roe to Winthrop, Feb. 18, 1635/36, *Winthrop Papers*, III, 226;

At the end of the decade the town turned to selling land, the purchasers being those settlers who had received grants and who were willing and able to pay for additional meadow or marsh. In 1640 it was necessary for the selectmen to choose a treasurer to receive and, on order, disburse "the towne stock, which shall arise of sale of Lands, or by any other waies then by ordinary rates."[27] Initially, the price of land was between 8 and 12s an acre for marsh (depending upon the accessibility of the tract) and between 12 and 15s for meadow. But land rose steadily in value, slumping momentarily during an economic setback in the early 1640's. In 1643 Christopher Stanley bought marshland on the peninsula for 2li an acre; Alexander Beck, two years later, paid 3li 10s an acre.[28]

Increasingly as the period advanced there were indications that land, both on the peninsula and abroad where the allotments were laid out, was becoming scarce. The rising price of land bought from the town was one such indication. Another was the fact that while in the early years of the decade the inhabitants had received both home lot and a garden in the fields, the selectmen began granting only house plots on the peninsula. There was a tendency, too, to qualify grants both on and off the peninsula with such phrases as "if any yet remain to be disposed of," "yf it bee there to be had," and in 1640 the selectmen ordered a complete stoppage of grants at Muddy River and the Mount "untill such lands as are already graunted are layd out, and the residue of the land knowne what the acrs are."[29]

Still another indication that the better lands were becoming unavailable was the resort to the use of the islands. Hog Island, close to Pullen Point, had been divided among the inhabitants following the 1634 vote of the town meeting, but it was little used during the 1630's except to gather wood and marsh-grass, some of the settlers trading their allotments there for additional

"Boston Records," 11; "The Book of Possessions," in City of Boston, *Report of the Record Commissioners*, II (Boston, 1877), 201, hereafter cited as "Boston Book of Possessions"; "A Volume Relating to the Early History of Boston Containing the Aspinwall Notarial Records from 1644 to 1651," in City of Boston, Registry Department, *Records Relating to the Early History of Boston*, XXXII (Boston, 1903), 35-36, hereafter cited as "Aspinwall Notarial Records."

27. "Boston Records," 53.
28. *Ibid.*, 53ff, 71, 83.
29. *Ibid.*, 56, 57.

land in their great allotments. But by the latter part of the decade a brisk market had developed, Hog Island land bringing eight shillings an acre.[30] Spectacle Island and Long Island, farther out in the harbor but within reach of the Mount Wollaston shore, had, again, been useful through the 1630's only for the wood they provided; by the end of the decade the town was allocating temporary planting lots on them, and requiring the clearing of underbrush. Ultimately permanent allotments would be made, fifteen on Spectacle Island, thirty-seven on Long Island; but unlike most of the lands disbursed by the town, these would be granted upon condition that the holder pay a yearly quitrent of six pence an acre.[31] Deer Island, extending south from Pullen Point at the harbor mouth, was little used in the 1630's. But in 1640 the selectmen considered the feasibility of the island "for Tilleg." Apparently they discounted the idea, for the next year it was being used as a place to keep stray hogs and goats picked up on the Neck, while in 1642 Edward Gibbons obtained the temporary use of the land as a grazing ground for cattle in return for buying off a squatter. At the end of the second decade it was still being used as grazing ground, Edward Bendall paying the town fourteen pounds a year for the privilege.[32]

The growing scarcity of land both on and beyond the peninsula created stress in the town. Newcomers continued to arrive, but as the decade turned it was increasingly difficult for the selectmen to find land to satisfy them; older settlers, too, found it difficult to obtain additional land for themselves or their grown children from the town. On Shawmut, the selectmen revived an earlier policy of requiring recipients of house lots to build within a set period or see the land forfeited to the town and regranted.[33] Pressure from the generality undoubtedly brought about a review by the selectmen of the larger grants beyond the peninsula, though to little purpose. John Oliver's work, presumably in surveying North Shore tracts, was validated *in toto*

30. *Ibid.*, 15, 53-58. Ultimately all allotments would be brought under one ownership and the island operated as a single farm. Shurtleff, *Topographical and Historical Description of Boston*, 448.

31. "Boston Records," 46, 51, 53, 94, 95.

32. *Ibid.*, 58, 60, 65-66, 92, 93.

33. *Ibid.*, 9, 52 ff.

despite the fact that he had made "allowance for Rockes or swampes" and laid out more than had been allotted. A review of the holdings of Elders Oliver and Leverett indicated that "their Lotts doe amount to a greater quantity of land than was intended at the graunting thereof," but the selectmen confirmed the boundaries as they existed; similarly, William Hibbens was discovered to have almost twice the marshland his grant stipulated, but again the "overplus" was confirmed by the selectmen. On the other hand, smaller holders frequently discovered that they had less land than they were entitled to—William Talmage, Brenton's old servant, having been granted fifteen acres, discovered that he had only ten and applied to the selectmen for a rectification.[34]

The results of the review of land distribution by the selectmen, and of a depression which descended upon the commonwealth in 1641, prepared the way for an upheaval in the town. But turbulence developed only when the selectmen, apparently to obtain more room on the peninsula for house lots, attempted early in 1642 to revitalize the long-ignored order of December 1635, which denied the inhabitants permanent possession in the Boston fields until they had been allotted on a more equitable basis. The reaction was swift. For the first time since the selectmen had begun their work, the town met for more than an election or a brief ratification of the selectmen's decisions. The discussion must have been clamorous, for at its close the meeting, "for peace sake, and for avoyding of confusion in the Towne," repealed the 1635 order. At the same time the allotment of land was removed from the jurisdiction of the selectmen; the town itself would assume control.[35]

Yet the factors which had led the town to delegate responsibility to the selectmen in the first place still existed; indeed, they were even exaggerated, given the fact that the town of 1642 was much larger than that of 1636. The authority to allocate lands was of necessity returned to the selectmen within six weeks. In the interval, however, a basic change of policy had been effected.

34. *Ibid.*, 56, 59, 60, 61.
35. *Ibid.*, 65. Subsequently (1645) the fact that grants had been made "to the partyes themselves without mention of their heyres" brought about a declaration that all "graunts were, and shall be Intended to be estates in Fee simple, with all due and usuall priviledges and appurtenances"; *ibid.*, 85.

The town's order re-empowering the selectmen provided that "the residue of the Townes Lands not yet disposed of"—the established common ground excepted—should be divided "amongst the present Inhabitants" and those admitted to the town within the following two months. The guiding principle of this last division was laid down, too: "a greater Proportion to them that have had lesse than their due, and the lesse to them that have had more, and proportionable to them that have had none."[36] The wheel had come full circle, and what the generality had desired in 1634 was finally embodied in a town ordinance. But it was a paper victory; there is no indication in the records that the selectmen carried out the mandate of the town, perhaps because the better land was to all intents and purposes gone. Less than thirty grants (other than on the islands) were to be made in the years through 1649.

In the end, Boston's gentry—some thirty families—had received almost one-half of the land granted by the town. Some had, additionally, obtained land from the commonwealth government which regularly granted land outside the towns in return for investments in the old company or for public service. The practice, based upon the land system envisioned by the company while still in England, was regularized in 1639 when the General Court, "for avoyding the trouble[ing] of this Court about granting of lands, and the more equall proceeding therein" established a committee "to take the names of all such as will demand alowance of lands" and consider the requests in the light of "their adventures in the common or joynt stock, and their abilities to improve lands, and also to such lands as have bene already granted them, either by the towne or by the Court."[37] And some among the Bostonians had engrossed land by purchase from their fellows.

John Winthrop's far-flung lands, although more extensive than most, exemplify the holdings of the gentry at the end of the first decade.[38] At that time he owned, in addition to a house and

36. *Ibid.*, 66-67.
37. *Colony Records*, I, 240. Unlike the town, the commonwealth frequently granted extensive land to non-resident investors.
38. The examples following are drawn from a survey of land holdings at the turn of the decade based upon "Boston Records"; "Boston Book of Possessions"; *Suffolk Deeds; Assistants' Records; Colony Records; Winthrop Papers;* and

garden in Boston (the former referred to as his "mansion" when sold in 1643), two farms on the North Shore of the harbor which he had received from the town, one of 150 acres at Rumney Marsh, the other of over 200 acres at Pullen Point; the Governor's Garden (Conant's Island) in the harbor, which he had received from the Court of Assistants on condition of paying a token yearly quitrent; a Mystic River farm of 600 acres and another 1,260 acres on Concord River farther in the interior. The Mystic River property had been given him by the commonwealth in 1631; the Concord River land he had hoped to obtain from the town of Concord, but that project failing, he had applied for and received it from the central government. Far off in Narragansett Bay, Winthrop had a half interest in Prudence Island, which he had purchased in conjunction with Roger Williams from a coastal trader who had, in turn, bought it from the Indians. Finally, another 3,000 acres in the Bay was granted to his wife Margaret by the General Court in 1640, although it was not to be laid out in either of their lifetimes.

Of his land, four parcels—Rumney Marsh, Pullen Point, "Ten Hills" on the Mystic, and the Governor's Garden—were in operation under the general direction of James Luxford, Winthrop's steward, whose dishonesty and falsification brought the Governor to bankruptcy in the early 1640's. "Ten Hills," worked by servants living on the property, was at least partly under cultivation, one section being laid out as an orchard. But it seems to have been primarily devoted to raising livestock, some of it sent over by English investors and grazed by Winthrop acting as their agent. Rumney Marsh and Pullen Point were, similarly, worked by resident servants, though in the early 1640's Winthrop's son Deane lived at Pullen Point and in 1647 the property passed to him. Corn and wheat were cultivated on the properties and cattle pastured there, while the ever-present marshes and woodlands supplied the Governor with building materials, fodder, and firewood. The seventy acres of the Governor's Garden were

---

Edward E. Hale *et al.*, eds., *Note-book Kept by Thomas Lechford, Esq., Lawyer, In Boston, Massachusetts Bay, from June 27, 1638 to July 29, 1641* (Cambridge, Mass., 1885), hereafter cited as *Lechford Notebook*. Specific citations refer to quotations.

worked by servants sent out from Boston by boat. Winthrop had apparently planned to cultivate grapes on the island and process his own wine, for in 1635 the original quitrent of twelve pence was commuted to "a hogshead of the best wyne that shall grow there." That this project did not work out is indicated by a further commutation in 1640 to two bushels of apples. Subsequently "apples, peares, grapes, plumes" were growing there. The same servants who worked Governor's Garden tended the land about the house in Boston, growing garden vegetables for Winthrop's table and tending the goats and milk cows there. The far-distant lands—on Concord River, at Narragansett—and Margaret's 3,000 acres were for future development.[39]

Typical also were the holdings of the Reverend Mr. Wilson. In Boston he had consolidated two gardens and a yard into a single plot on which stood a house and barn; at the Mount he owned one farm of 565 acres which he had obtained from the town; on the Mystic was another of 200 acres which had been awarded him by the General Court. William Tyng, having obtained 600 acres from the town at Muddy River in 1638, proceeded to augment his holdings by purchase. In 1639 he bought out William Coddington for 1,300*li*, purchasing a house and property on Shawmut, an interest in Spectacle Island, and 530 acres at the Mount, a portion of which Coddington, using resident servants, had planted in grain. Soon after, Tyng acquired additional acreage at the Mount: 112 acres from Thomas Cornell (who had bought them earlier from William Baulston), 160 acres from Edward Hutchinson at 13*s* 4*d* an acre, possibly an additional 200 acres from Coddington. Robert Keayne owned two plots on the peninsula, a house and yard and a "great garding," in addition to his 314-acre farm at Rumney Marsh, where in 1640 Boston carpenter Thomas Joy built him a barn 72 feet long by 26 feet wide for 98*li* 1*s*. Later, Keayne would receive from the General Court 1,074 acres in the northern interior.[40] John Coggan had a house and garden in town and 210 acres on the North Shore, including a farm "at the Rocks goeing to Lin."

39. *Suffolk Deeds*, I, 25, 45; *Colony Records*, I, 139.
40. "Boston Records," 17. See also the order of the General Court, May 24, 1650, Manuscript Photostats, Box 4, Mass. Hist. Soc. Lib.

There, a few years later, he would have a dwelling house, barn, four oxen, and four cows "in the Custody of the tenant." But even in 1641 he was having trouble with Nicholas Bacon, presumably the tenant, and sought an attachment against his cattle "for the payment of his rent."[41]

Among those Boston men engrossing large tracts, some took up residence on the land, directing the activities of their many servants themselves. Deane Winthrop, in the 1640's, was one; Samuel Maverick was another, remaining through the 1630's on the Noddles Island farm which boasted "Mansion house millhouse and mill, bakehouse . . . outhouses barnes stables." Richard Tuttle, described as a "husbandman" on admission to the church, was still another.[42] Arriving from Northamptonshire in 1635 with his mother, wife, and three children, he obtained a house lot from the town and 161 acres at Rumney Marsh. The house lot was ignored, and in 1636 the town revoked the allotment on the ground that it had not been built upon. But prior to his death in 1640, Tuttle had erected his home and farm buildings on the North Shore—including a windmill which his widow moved to Boston's Fort Hill in 1642—and had doubled his acreage, buying 50 acres from Robert Harding, 84 acres from John Odlin, and 49 acres from Nicholas Willis at a total cost of 93*li* 6s 2d.

The tenantry and the use of stewards noted in regard to Winthrop's and Coggan's property and familiar from the English manorial tradition were common features of the Massachusetts landscape. Such men as Coggan, Keayne, Tyng, Wilson—and one can include Cotton, Colborne, Leverett, the Hutchinsons, indeed, the greater number of Boston's gentry—were too occupied in town to give their direct attention to the land. Only a few of the agreements involved in the system have survived from these early years, however.[43] Among them is that of April 1639 between William Tyng and John Read for the rent of "Salter's

41. *Suffolk Deeds*, I, 68; *Assistants' Records*, II, 104.

42. *Suffolk Deeds*, I, 122; First Church Records under date of Dec. 29, 1635.

43. More common are leases of a later date: for example, in the farm accounts between Samuel Townsend and Richard Bellingham, Massachusetts Archives, Boston, C, 169-71; John Pemberton's lease to the Cotton Farm at Muddy River, *ca.* 1670, Mather Papers, Prince Collection, Boston Public Library; various North Shore leases in Miscellaneous Farm Papers, Winthrop Public Library, Winthrop, Mass.

farme," a part of the land purchased from Coddington. By its terms Tyng was to let the farm to Read for a period of ten years, stocking it with ten milk cows, twenty heifers, ten "cowe calves," a bull and a bull calf, ten oxen, four mares, twenty goats and a ram, three sows and a boar, ten hens and a cock, two turkeys and a turkey cock, four geese and a gander, four ducks and a drake. Read, for his part, was required to pay all town rates levied on the farm and his person, supply all seed corn and tools necessary, and engage at his own expense nine servants (seven men and two maids). Should additional help be necessary in "planting, reaping mowing, and making of hay," Tyng was to pay half the cost. Employing "his owne labour and industry" as well as that of the servants, Read was to keep and improve all livestock on the premises, giving an account of any increase upon a month's notice from Tyng; build a barn seventy-four feet long by forty feet wide within fifteen months; maintain and repair all other buildings, fences, gardens, and trees; plant eight acres of arable land "that hath not ben formerly broken up or ploughed" each year; and lay compost "in husbandly manner where most need shall be from time to time." He was, finally, to provide Tyng with "lodging and Dyet for himself and horsemeat and stableroome for his horse when he shall come to the sayd farme to survey the same . . . which he shall have liberty to doe at one or more times in the yeare, for the space of one moneth in the yeare." The proceeds of the farm—both crops and the increase of stock—were to be divided equally between the two.[44]

Another surviving lease, an agreement between a Mount Wollaston "husbandman" and the Reverend Mr. Warham of May 1639, exemplifies a slightly different arrangement. The husbandman was to take possession of the "Newberry Farm" just over the Dorchester line from John Wilson's Mount Wollaston property, together with its livestock, for a period of four years, assuming all the expenses of labor, equipment, and seed. Rather than sharing the proceeds, however, the tenant in this case agreed to

44. *Lechford Notebook*, 94-100. A lease of May 1640 between Richard Parker of Boston and John Parker of Dedham by which John agreed to work Richard's Dedham farm is similar; *ibid.*, 244-47.

pay a flat rate of 60*li* a year, taking the crops and the increase of the stock for himself.[45]

Side by side with these large tracts were the holdings of the generality. Some were but a step down in size from the establishments of the gentry. At the end of the 1630's, Zaccheus Bosworth owned a house lot, two plots in the New Field—one of two acres, the other of one-and-a-half acres—and fifty-one acres at the Mount; within a few years his house lot would be described in a mortgage as "his dwelling house in Boston together with all cow houses barnes stables yards orchards or gardens thereto belonging."[46] William Dyar, before leaving the town in the late 1630's, had obtained a house and lot on Shawmut and forty-two acres on the North Shore. William Dinely, the town's "Barber-Chirurgion,"[47] owned a house and yard, a two-acre garden in Colborne's Field, and twenty-four acres at Muddy River prior to his death in a 1639 snowstorm. Thomas Savage, in 1636, had a house on the peninsula and was granted seven acres of marsh at Muddy River for the maintenance of his five head of cattle; subsequently, by grant and purchase, he obtained a garden plot and possibly another house, two farms at Muddy River, one of thirty-eight and a quarter acres, the other of twenty-six acres, ten and a half acres of wood, meadow, and marsh ground at Hog Island, and a small Mount Wollaston marsh.

Other holdings were quite small, mere supplements to the land on the peninsula. Edmund Jackson, a shoemaker on admission to the church in 1635, received a houseplot from the town, some three acres of planting ground in the New Field, a lot on Long Island, and eight acres at Muddy River. William Courser, described as a cobbler, had, at the turn of the decade, a house on the peninsula and ten acres at Muddy River. Abel Porter, a former servant of Thomas Grubb, leather-dresser, had, by the

---

45. *Ibid.*, 124-26. There is a similar lease *ca.* May 1640—with the rent payable in produce—*ibid.*, 249-50. Another form of tenantry, but not common, is represented by Matthew Cradock's agreement with Josiah Dawstin of Apr. 1641. By this Dawstin was to take possession of "Dixes howse" and "Rock meadowe" in Medford in return for his eight days' service on Cradock's property each year; *Suffolk Deeds*, I, 11. No such arrangement has been discovered in Boston.
46. *Suffolk Deeds*, I, 92.
47. *Johnson's Wonder-Working Providence*, 191.

early 1640's, a houseplot at Boston, a "great lot" for two heads (eight to ten acres) at Mount Wollaston, and a small parcel on Long Island. His former master had property on the peninsula and about twenty acres in several plots at Muddy River. Ultimately both servant and master would share in Spectacle Island.

Some of these lesser holders might well have resided in town and made use of tenants as their larger neighbors did, though there are no records of such arrangements. Others, such as the Mount Wollaston husbandman renting the Reverend Mr. Warham's farm, or John Coggan's tenant on his farm at "the Rocks," were freeholders as well as tenants, working their own land and that of others. Most of the lesser men seem to have commuted to their various properties from their homes on the peninsula. With their servants (if they had any) they trudged the miles to Muddy River or took a boat to the North Shore or the islands or the Mount. In the winter they went to cut wood, sometimes piling it up to be brought into town during the slack summer months, sometimes sledding it in over the snow or, in those winters when the river and occasionally the inner harbor itself froze over, across the ice. In the spring they went out to plow and plant; in the summer to make hay on the meadows and in the marshes; in the fall they went to harvest wheat and grain. Their time was, of necessity, divided between their planting lots and gardens on Shawmut and the allotments farther out, but sometimes in the busiest seasons the men left the care of the peninsula lands to their wives and families and camped out in temporary shelters for a week or two. At other times they built shacks and housed sons or servants on the land, particularly if they had cattle grazing.[48]

There was, however, a tendency on the part of some to divorce themselves completely from the town on the peninsula, notwithstanding the commonwealth law of 1636 prohibiting the building of houses above a half-mile from the meetinghouse ("myll howses and ferme howses of such as have their dwelling howses in some towne" excepted).[49] Just as Richard Tuttle of the gentry pre-

48. Edmund Browne to Sir Simonds D'Ewes, Sept. 7, [1639], Col. Soc. Mass., *Publications*, 7 (1905), 75.
49. *Colony Records*, I, 157, 181. Even the Court realized the futility of this

ferred to live on his broad acres on the North Shore, others chose
to live on their smaller acres. Thus one finds a number of small
peripheral villages growing up around Boston, a phenomenon
common elsewhere but exaggerated by the peculiar geography of
the town, spread out around the harbor as it was.[50] Winnisimmet
to the north of Noddles Island appeared early, collecting a few
people even before the Winthrop fleet arrived—Maverick's first
house being in the vicinity—and even more during the dispersal.[51]
At Muddy River a small permanent village of perhaps two dozen
families grew up, with a 300-acre common set aside by the town in
December 1639 for the use of "the Inhabitants there."[52] Some
lived on their own land, others as tenants, William Franklin, for
example, who farmed Tyng's Muddy River property. Similarly
Pullen Point and Rumney Marsh on the North Shore became
identifiable localities, though their inhabitants were dispersed on
their various properties. Both the people and the lands of these
communities were accounted as "belonging to Boston," but the
link was a tenuous one, for the town and its church were far away.
Those on the North Shore very early sought the establishment of
a local chapel and lay reader that they might have the comfort
of religion without the discomfort of a trip across the harbor.
Others sought religion in churches nearer than Boston's First
Church, Elias Maverick of Winnisimmet joining the Charlestown
church; tenant Franklin spending his Sabbath at Roxbury and
"after a season" soliciting membership there; William Thorne—
his wife a Boston member—taking his children Desiretruth and
Hannah to Roxbury for baptism; Richard Bulgar, a Boston church

order, for in a 1636/37 order regarding defense (*ibid.*, 190), it provided for
"all such as keepe families at their farmes, being remote from any towne"; in
1639, on the petition of five men, the Court (*ibid.*, 257), allowed them to
maintain their homes farther than the requisite distance; in 1640 (*ibid.*, 291) the
act was finally repealed.

50. For example, Manchester (formerly "Jeofferyes Creeke"), Andover, Tops-
field, Reading, Malden, Medfield, Hull, and Haverhill all began as villages.
Colony Records, I, 147, II, 5-6, 73, 266, III, 30, 39, 47, 73-74, 106, 156, 162,
181; *Winthrop's Journal*, II, 262-63; Mass. Hist. Soc., *Collections*, 2d Ser., 4
(1816), 169-70; Early Files of Courts and Misc. Papers, Office of the Clerk of
the Supreme Judicial Court, Suffolk Co., Boston, under date of May 10, 1643.

51. Charles Knowles Bolton, *The Real Founders of New England* (Boston,
1929), 94-95, 177. Note in the *Assistants' Records*, II, that Winnisimmet is
assessed separately until joined to Boston.

52. "Boston Records," 44.

member, yet accounted of Roxbury when proceeded against as a Hutchinsonian in 1637.[53]

Mount Wollaston is the most notable example of such a peripheral village. The original grants at the Mount were intended, as those elsewhere, to be complementary to land on the peninsula; hence one finds the early allotments there being granted in conjunction with house lots in the town. But very quickly this proved infeasible. As early as the fall of 1636, Winthrop recorded that "the inhabitants of Boston, who had taken their farms and lots at Mount Woollaston" were "finding it very burdensome to have their business, etc. so far off." A movement to set up a congregation—apart from Boston's church, as Charlestown had done earlier—and a town were well under way. There was resistance, the problem being that the land had been "given to Boston for upholding the town and church there [on Shawmut], which end would be frustrated" by secession.[54] Nevertheless, the First Church and the town gave way in October 1636. The former agreed that a separate congregation should ultimately be formed and allowed the Reverend John Wheelwright to move to the Mount and begin preaching immediately; the latter agreed to a new town provided that the inhabitants made suitable payment to Boston to cover the loss. The formation of the new church and town was not completed for several years, however. The founding of the church was delayed by the Hutchinsonian schism, which resulted in the expulsion from the commonwealth of Wheelwright and others, and it was not completed until November 1639. Until then the Mount Wollaston people remained in the Boston church or without formal church affiliation.

Arrangements for the new town were delayed in part by the religious question, but even more by the failure of Boston and the Mount Wollaston settlers to agree on financial terms. The eventual agreement, recorded January 27, 1640, and ratified by the General Court in May, established the town of Braintree. But large tracts of the new community's land remained in Boston's

53. Thomas Lechford, *Plain Dealing; or, News from New England* [London, 1642], ed. J. Hammond Trumbull (Boston, 1867), 40; "Roxbury Church Records," City of Boston, *Report of the Record Commissioners,* VI (Boston, 1881), 187.

54. *Winthrop's Journal,* I, 190.

possession to be granted by it to additional newcomers, perhaps as much as a quarter of the new town's area. Moreover, such holders of Braintree land as John Wilson were to continue being accounted Boston inhabitants and pay Boston rather than Braintree rates if they so desired, a situation which existed until 1649, when, for fifty pounds payable over five years, Braintree purchased the right to levy taxes on all holders of its land, Pastor Wilson and his farm excepted. Finally, the Braintree inhabitants were to pay 8*s* for every seven acres granted by Boston before the secession and 3*s* for every acre "that hath beene, or shalbe, granted to any others whoe are not [accounted] Inhabitants of Boston." The payment due from the initial Braintree inhabitants was apparently made in two installments in 1640 and 1641.[55]

The appearance of peripheral villages—indeed, the whole of the allotment system which gave rise to them—posed a fundamental problem to the community quite apart from the financial one which so concerned the Bostonians with regard to Braintree. Winthrop, speaking aboard the *Arbella* of his godly "Citty upon a Hill," had admonished the settlers to be "knitt together in this work as one man." John Cotton had commanded that they "goe forth, every man that goeth . . . looking not on your owne things onely." But the land with its material opportunities was proving disruptive of the communal spirit which both had advocated. Men were seeking their own aggrandizement, not God's; generality was at times arrayed against gentry, defying the notions of proper society. Moreover, the land was tending to frustrate all efforts of the community to enforce godliness and morality by law or in the church and family. The men of Plymouth in 1639 pinpointed the problem in a letter to the Boston congregation beseeching advice "concerning the holding of Farmes of which there is noe lesse frequent use with your selves then with us." Where men chose to live abroad from the church and community, they obviously cut themselves off from the discipline of their

55. *Ibid.*, 197, 310; "Boston Records," 47, 55, 96-97; First Church Records, [xiii], under date of Oct. 30, 1636; *Colony Records*, I, 291. Boston delayed completion of many of the Mount Wollaston grants until after the agreement, thus collecting 3*s* per acre from perhaps half of the inhabitants of the new town.

fellows. But even when they lived in the town, the fact that "places for husbandry" were "distant from the place of a mans habitacion and of the churches assembling" by "three or foure miles or there aboute" presented difficulties, "seing by meanes of such farmes a mans famylie is Divided so that in busie tymes they cannot (except upon the Lords day) all of them joyne with him in famylie duties." And what of servants and tenants "employed abroad at farmes"? Not all could "report Duly before the Lords day to the famylies they belong too and continue there till the Second Day" for someone "is necessaryly Detayned" abroad to look after the property and cattle; and all would be away from the guidance and control of the family and community during the week. To the Plymouth men these were "darke and doubtfull" things to be seriously considered; apparently Boston men viewed them in the same light, for the letter was read to the church the day following its receipt.[56] There was, however, no adequate answer.

56. John Reyner and William Brewster "in the name and with the consent of the rest" of the Plymouth Church to the "reverende brethren the church of Christ in Boston to the Elders there," Aug. 5, 1639, Cotton Papers, Prince Collection, Boston Public Lib., hereafter cited as Cotton Papers.

V

TOWARD A NEW JERUSALEM

THE CHURCH organized in Boston in the summer and fall of 1630 was not the mature and elaborate church found there a decade later. Maturity and elaboration would come only with time and in response to events and changing circumstances. Neither was it an orthodox establishment in a milieu of Massachusetts orthodoxy. Indeed, there was initially no orthodoxy in Massachusetts Bay.

At the moment the church satisfied the general assumption that religious and moral teaching was an indispensable part of life and a necessary preparation for death. But to the early Bostonians it served as a unifying social and political organization as well as a haven for their souls, the focal point of their new environment, a bond with their neighbors, and a familiar reminder of the English parish. Similar in background,[1] the Bostonians were still very largely strangers to each other until, within the first, small, windowless "Mud-Wall Meeting house,"[2] strangeness died. The weight of evidence indicates that the church was meant to embrace eventually all but the most reprobate; and to the extent that this goal was achieved among the original inhabitants and those coming to Boston in the years immediately following, it impressed a unity upon the population by demanding that all communicants undergo the common experience of formal admission: the confession of faith publicly given, the ceremonial offer and acceptance of the "right hand of friendship," and the acceptance of the burden of the covenant to walk in godly ways and give love and respect

1. See below, chap. 6, p. 138.
2. [Joshua Scotto], *A Narrative of the Planting of the Massachusetts Colony* ... (Boston, 1694), reprinted in Mass. Hist. Soc., *Collections*, 4th Ser., 4 (1858), 292.

to all of the church. The ideal was never fact, although, as has been suggested, it approached actuality in the first years. However, even the non-communicant attended the church, partaking of its brotherhood and guidance while excluded from its sacraments.

To the leaders, during the first years, the social aspect of the church was all important. Necessity, an inclination toward congregationalism among some of them, and the example of Salem and Plymouth had led them to a congregational polity, while a more general opinion that "the observation of indifferent ceremonies which Christ had not commanded" was "unlawful" had led them to abandon the Book of Common Prayer and adopt a simplified version of the English church service.[3] The Scriptures and the ministers guided the leaders in such matters, but when disparate views appeared the unity of the community rather than dogma was their primary concern. In the spring of 1631, for example, Winthrop and the newly arrived Roger Williams debated separatism, and the Governor adamantly resisted the notion, which he felt would eventuate in the harmful division of the populace between godly and ungodly. Bitterly he lashed out against what today's historian might term the "tribalism" of the separatists: The ungodly, whom the separatists would leave for the Devil's spoil, were merely "weake Christians," Winthrop wrote, "the weaker for want of that tender Care, that should be had of them ... and next for that spirituall pride, that Sathan rooted into the hearts of their brethren, who when they are Converted, doe not, nor will not strengthen them, but do Censure them, to be none of Gods people."[4] Midway in 1631, Winthrop and others of the Boston church rode out to debate with Watertown's pastor and elder on their view "that the churches of Rome were true churches." The Bostonians won the day, all but three of the Watertown church concluding the proposition to be an error. But the three—one of them Elder Richard Brown, "a

3. Pishey Thompson, *The History and Antiquities of Boston, [England]* ... (Boston, Eng., 1856), 418, quoting John Cotton.

4. Winthrop, "Reasons to prove a necessitye of reformation from the Corruptions of Antechrist which hath defiled the Christian Churches, and yet without an absolute separation from them, as if they were no Churches of Christ," *ca.* Mar. 1631, *Winthrop Papers*, III, 12-13.

man of very violent spirit"—clung to their belief and ultimately brought about a schism in the congregation. Once more the Bostonians rode out "to settle peace, etc." A procedural question immediately arose: Did they come as magistrates of the state, or as members of a neighboring congregation offering their help? Once the Bostonians established their position as mere neighboring church members, the conference proceeded not to a resolution of the question but a reconciliation of the factions and a "solemn uniting."[5]

All the while, too, the leaders were building upon the crude outlines of congregationalism which had been laid down during the discussions of the summer of 1630. But they proceeded with trepidation, only gradually accepting the new polity as complementary to their religious ardor. The Reverend John Wilson, for example, had accepted the call of the Boston church with reservations. Born in the English hierarchy, he had as a young man given up all opportunity of a life of preferment and ease for one of religious enthusiasm and sundry suspensions for nonconformity;[6] yet in 1630 he could not bring himself to surrender his English ordination and maintained that he held his ministry by virtue of it and only his office by the call of the Boston church. In July or August 1630, Winthrop himself dispatched a series of questions pertaining to congregationalism to John Humphrey, a leader in gathering together the Winthrop fleet but one who had stayed in England, asking him to seek the best counsel he could find. The correspondence between the two is fragmentary and neither questions nor answers have survived; but it is obvious that Winthrop was unsure both of the propriety of what had been

5. *Winthrop's Journal*, I, 66, 71-72. Only later, with still another breach of communal unity—when the disparate idea was shown to be irreparably divisive because of the caliber of the disputants—was pressure brought to bear and Elder Brown discharged of his office on the grounds of "his unfitness in regard of his passion and distemper in speech"; *ibid.*, 83, 95. Even as late as 1637 the lay leaders put unity above dogmatic truth, Cotton writing of the Hutchinsonian (or Antinomian) outbreak that Winthrop and Dudley, "in a serious Conference," told him that they "did not looke at the Differences between the Elders and me" —i.e., between Cotton and the majority of the ministers—"to be fundamental matter"; they were important only inasmuch as the "Differences of notion" might be injurious to "the peace of Churches and common-wealth." Cotton to [John Wheelwright], Apr. 18, 1640, Cotton Papers.

6. His mother, Isabel Woodhall, was a niece of Archbishop Grindal; his father was Grindal's chaplain and subsequently Canon of Windsor.

done, and of how to proceed from the rough beginnings. Humphrey sent the questions abroad, circulating them among leading English congregationalists in the Netherlands. In the meantime he dispatched a newly published work of William Ames, "wherein you will find manie thinges of especial use and singularly helpeful for present direction and satisfaction." "As wee find, and you foresaw," he added, "there will neede great wisdome, much advice earnest prayer and a total subjugation of our own judgments, wills and affections, unto the clearer light of truth shining unto us in those helpes which the lord shall bee pleased to affoord unto us." When the answers were returned—possibly framed by the Reverend Hugh Peter—Humphrey quickly sent them on to the Governor. Their contents stunned Humphrey. "I confesse plainely in divers things I was perswaded otherwise," he wrote; and while the "sound pietie and deepe judgment" of the author "might enable him to a cleare discerning of the will of god in these thinges," he suggested that Winthrop "proceede warilie and with good examination and digestion" and promised to solicit additional advice from "other godly men."[7]

Humphrey might have his doubts about the advice he was forwarding to Winthrop; others, too, might have doubts about the course being followed in the Bay. "Heare is a mutteringe of a too palpable seperation of your people from our church governement," one correspondent wrote in November 1631; "in strivinge soe sodainely to be better, [you] may prove to be starke naught."[8] Yet once having committed themselves to a congregational polity, the men of Massachusetts of necessity pushed on, hammering out proper procedures and practices as they went, seeking advice as to God's truth among themselves and from England.

As they proceeded, the leaders sought additional ministers.

7. John Humphrey to John Winthrop, Dec. 12, 1630; Humphrey to Winthrop and Isaac Johnson, Dec. 18, 1630, Winthrop Papers, II, 331-34, 335-36. That the questions pertained to events of July and early Aug. 1630—i.e., the founding of the churches—is implicit in the chronology. In the second letter, Humphrey refers to the questions being sent abroad and returned to him in the space of six weeks. Hence he received them from Winthrop about Nov. 1. Bills of exchange dated in Massachusetts Bay July 14 and Aug. 19 and dispatched to England were honored in London on Nov. 4; ibid., 301, 310. The Ames work: De Conscientia et eius Jure vel Casibus Libri Quinque (Amsterdam, 1630).

8. Edward Howes to John Winthrop, Jr., Nov. 9, 1631, Winthrop Papers, III, 54-55.

Only four had arrived in 1630, two with the Winthrop fleet and two with the Dorchester settlers; only five were in the commonwealth during the winter of 1630-31, too few to serve all the towns established during the dispersal. One ministered at Salem, one at Boston-Charlestown, one at Watertown, two at Dorchester, but such towns as Saugus and Roxbury were served from neighboring churches or by lay preachers. Indeed, a critic complained as late as December 1632 "that fellowes which keepe hogges all the weeke preach on the Saboth." The Boston church itself had no regular minister through most of 1631, since the Reverend Mr. Wilson returned to England in the spring following settlement, leaving the care of the church to lay leaders to whom he "commended . . . the exercise of prophecy in his absence."[9]

The search for additional ministers was similar to that which had unearthed Phillips and Wilson earlier, though the times were increasingly more propitious. Clergymen who had been solicited in 1629 had been reluctant to hazard themselves in an uncertain venture; but with settlement effected and every day more prosperous, they were more amenable to leaving England. Furthermore, the "able and sufficient Ministers" desired by the leadership were frequently the objects of ecclesiastical discipline as the result of the movement to enforce conformity upon the English churches. John Humphrey, in England, wrote in December 1630, presumably in response to a request for churchmen, that "divers godly lecturers and ministers dayly are put by." Actively soliciting for the New England ministry, he noted that "Mr. Weld of Essex is now upon the stage and expects his doome"; consequently, "hee will bee easilie for us." There is an air of improvisation about this which denies a calculated attempt to obtain certain ministers, or ministers of a certain persuasion, one confirmed later in the same letter. Among those Humphrey approached on behalf of the Bay were some who insisted that

9. Edward Howes to John Winthrop, Jr., Nov. 28, 1632, *ibid.*, 100-101; *Winthrop's Journal*, I, 60. Wilson's departure was resented by some of the church and he was criticized upon his return for leaving "the whole Congregation above twelve moneths together without their consent." Similarly, his empowering lay readers to act in his absence was subsequently disapproved. See *A Coppy of a Letter to Mr. Cotton of Boston . . . Directed to a Friend* [ca. *1637*] (London, 1641), 1-6.

they could not go without a specific "call" from a church there; Humphrey, to satisfy those who "sticke at that knot," suggested that "it were not amisse there were some blanke call" sent over "for such, as providence shall offer."[10]

Responding to direct solicitation, to the prosperity of the Bay, and to events in England, the ministers came: Roger Williams aboard the *Lyon* in February 1631; John Eliot later that year; Thomas Welde and Thomas James in 1632; John Cotton, Thomas Hooker, Samuel Stone in 1633; Nathaniel Ward, Thomas Parker, James Noyes, Zachariah Symmes in 1634. And by mid-decade, solicitation was no longer needed; ministers such as Thomas Shepard and Hugh Peter, silenced by the bishops and forced abroad or into hiding, gravitated toward New England because of the religious ardor to be found there.

As they appeared, Boston attempted first to obtain a replacement for Wilson, then, after Wilson's return to the commonwealth in May 1632, a companion to join him in the ministry. Roger Williams, who arrived before Wilson's departure, had been approached by the Boston congregation; but Williams, who advocated disavowing the English churches—outright separatism —refused them, writing later that he "durst not officiate to an unseparated people." John Eliot, arriving in November, seems to have stayed with the Winthrops for a year and presumably preached in the First Church. But committed to joining friends coming from England, he refused to assume office despite the fact that the Bostonians "labored all they could" and protested "their want of him." Wilson's return in 1632 was followed closely by the arrival of the Reverend Thomas Welde, and the First Church attempted to combine the two in the ministry. But others sought Welde's services and "after many imparlances and days of humiliation"—the advice of both the Lord and those of Plymouth being solicited—he went to Roxbury, where that fall Eliot (his friends having arrived and settled there) joined him. Four months later, in October, Winthrop and Wilson appealed directly to John Stoughton, rector of Aller, Somersetshire, having heard "of the disposition of your thoughts toward us" and giving him

10. John Humphrey to John Winthrop and Isaac Johnson, Dec. 18, 1630, *Winthrop Papers*, II, 336.

in the name of the Boston church "what firme Assurance we may, of our stronge desires towards you." But Stoughton did not come to New England, and Wilson remained alone in the Boston ministry until September 1633, when John Cotton arrived and, after some discussion, settled in Boston.[11]

A product of Trinity and Emmanuel College, Cambridge, and formerly vicar of St. Botolph's Church, old Boston, John Cotton was a proud addition to the roster of Massachusetts ministers and to Boston's First Church in particular. He was a zealot in God's work, holding out "to the men of this world . . . such meanes and helps of seeking after the Lord" as he could; a purist, ardent to reform the services of the churches of England in the light of what he deemed God's will. For twenty years he had been able to serve as a nonconforming minister in old Boston, living and officiating (as he wrote) "by mine own faith" in all things "pertaining to God and his worship," protected by his reputation as a strenuous and effective preacher and scholarly theologian, by his casuistry in arguing away the charges occasionally brought against him, and, all else failing, by his friends in and out of the hierarchy. Indeed, Nathaniel Ward, a friend and an equally nonconforming minister, once complained that "of all men in the world I envy Mr. Cotton of Boston most, for he doth nothing in way of conformity, and yet hath his liberty, and I doe everything that way and cannot enjoy mine." Solicited by the leaders of the Winthrop migration in 1629, he had preferred to stay in England, although a few of his St. Botolph's parishioners—William Coddington among them—had traveled with the fleet and Cotton himself had given his blessing to the venture. But in the early 1630's, with conformity to the established forms demanded of all, Cotton's friends had been unable to help him. By October 1632 he had been forced from his pulpit and was in hiding. "That lively and Christ piercing, Christ powerfull Quickening, wherewith the heavenly word of your Ministry was wont to awaken your Peoples hearts, Now is turned into

---

11. Roger Williams to John Cotton, Jr., Mar. 25, 1671, James Hammond Trumbull et al., eds., The Complete Writings of Roger Williams, 7 vols. (N. Y., 1963), VI, 356; Winthrop's Journal, I, 84, 94-95; Mather, Magnalia Christi Americana, I, 529-31; John Winthrop and John Wilson to John Stoughton, Oct. 1632, Winthrop Papers, III, 88. That Eliot did not officiate further than preaching is indicated by the absence of baptismal entries in First Church Records for the period he was alone in the town.

a *silent Deadnesse*," a communicant wrote him; "the comfortable
Sabbaths which were wont to give Rest unto your Peoples Soules,
what Greife . . . and Anguish of Hearte doe they now yeild to all
your well Hearers." By June of 1633 he had resigned his vicarage
and was on his way to Massachusetts and Boston.[12] Welcomed
eagerly for his name and authority, his settling was facilitated by
both commonwealth and town. The former augmented Boston's
area so that those who followed him from old Boston could have
land for their crops and cattle and promised Cotton compensation
from the public treasury inasmuch as he agreed to continue his old
Boston practice of delivering regular lectures in addition to his
work within the church, a promise of compensation which was not
kept. For its part, the town seems to have promised that "such as
were to come over, who were of his charge in England" would be
"comfortably provided for." Subsequently his followers received
town lands and were admitted both to the church and to office in
the church, Thomas Leverett, "an ancient, sincere professor, of
Mr. Cotton's congregation in England" being installed as a second
lay, or ruling, elder, joining Thomas Oliver, the town physician,
who had been elected to the office in 1632.[13]

On his arrival, Cotton saw the results of the hammering out of
a congregational polity which had been proceeding for three years,
for he clearly affiliated with an established institution well grounded
in the community and marked by set forms and practices. Re-
nowned as he was, he was still subjected to "testing" by the Boston
congregation, on the question of his admission both to membership
and to church office. Propounded for membership on the Saturday
following his arrival, he subsequently "signified his desire and

12. William Twisse, *A Treatise of Mr. Cotton's, Clearing Certaine Doubts
concerning Predestination: Together with an Examination thereof* (London,
1646), 207; J[ohn] C[otton] to John [Williams], Lord Bishop of Lincoln,
May 7, 1633, Hutchinson Papers, Mass. Archives; Samuel Whiting, "Concerning the life of the famous Mr. Cotton . . . ," in Hutchinson, comp., *Collection of
Original Papers Relative to Massachusetts*, 246-47; [?] to [John Cotton], n.d.
but 1633, Cotton Papers. There are a number of contemporary and near contemporary sketches of Cotton: an autobiographical sketch in his *The Way of
the Congregational Churches Cleared* (London, 1648); Whiting's sketch cited
above; John Norton, *Abel Being Dead Yet Speaketh . . .* (London, 1658); and
Cotton Mather's *Magnalia Christi Americana*, I. Ziff's *The Career of John Cotton*
is interesting, but avowedly not a complete biography.

13. *Winthrop's Journal*, I, 108-9, 110, 111. Oliver had replaced Increase
Nowell when the Charlestown church separated from Boston.

readiness to make his confession according to order" and was admitted following the communicants' approval of his confession of faith.   His wife, Sarah, after indicating her desire to join the church and consenting to the confession made by her husband, was similarly admitted.   In this regard, Cotton attempted an innovation by requesting that the elders examine her in private inasmuch as an open confession "was against the apostle's rule, and not fit for women's modesty"; obviously the church did not agree and asserted its right to hear the confession of all would-be members, even if cursory.   Once admitted, Cotton presented his ocean-born son for baptism, affirming it to be no more than the act of a father "for the help of his [own] faith."

The manner of Cotton's installation into church office was to become traditional.   He was invited to speak twice by way of testing, once in open discussion and once to "exercise," after which the communicants fasted, then met to call him to office by unanimous consent.   Because Wilson had already been established as pastor of the church in November 1632, Cotton was chosen to the office of teacher.   Before the approving congregation, the pastor invited Cotton to the pulpit and queried him as to whether or not he would accept their call to minister to them, to which Cotton answered that while "he knew himself unworthy and insufficient," he had "observed all the passages of God's providence, (which he reckoned up in particular) in calling him to it"; hence, "he could not but accept it."   The officers of the church laying their hands upon his head in the name of the whole body of members, the pastor prayed.   "And then, taking off their hands, laid them on again, and, speaking to him by his name, they did thenceforth design him to the said office, in the name of the Holy Ghost, and did give him the charge of the congregation, and did thereby (as by a sign from God) indue him with the gifts fit for his office; and lastly did bless him."[14]

In these ceremonies, the fact that past difficulties had been at least in part resolved is implicit.   The first shock of Salem's refusal of communion to all but members or to baptize the child of a non-

14. *Ibid.*, 107ff.   All of the ceremonies are in evidence earlier—for example, Wilson's installations in 1630 and 1632—but only with regard to Cotton do we find them described so elaborately.

member was in the past. Now it was taken for granted that Cotton could not be invited to the communion table before his formal admission, and his child was baptized only after the admission of one of his parents. Cotton himself was specific "in declaring his faith about baptism," undoubtedly forced to it during his testing because of his open denunciation of Salem's particularism in 1630. Upon hearing of Salem's refusal, he had written that he doubted "the Lawfulness of that practise" of refusing the sacraments to non-members, "thinking then, that the Faithful and Godly men coming where the seals were to be dispensed" had a right to the seals. Now he indicated, however obliquely, that he had been in error—an error he was openly to renounce at Salem in 1636.[15]

Cotton's installation as teacher also marked the end of an extensive discussion about the proper ministerial officers of the church which a First Church query of July 1632 implies was in progress: "Whether there might be divers pastors in the same church?" The lawfulness of two pastors had been doubted by all concerned, but the problem was resolved by the division of functions between the minister who instructs—the teacher—and the minister who exhorts —the pastor.[16] Similarly, the fact that Cotton was installed (as was Wilson in the pastorate before him) without mention of his English ordination indicates that question, too, had been resolved; indeed, the resolution was in effect a denial of the efficacy of ordination, for Cotton went out of his way to acknowledge that "a minister hath no power to give the seals but in his own congregation," while the church officers, in their laying on of hands, announced that it was only by virtue of his installation within the congregation that Cotton received "the gifts fit for his office."[17]

The congregation's refusal to allow the elders to hear Sarah Cotton's confession of faith in private and Cotton's election by unanimous consent demonstrate the position of power which the congregation had come to hold, one which Winthrop was subsequently

15. Ibid., 107; Cotton, Sermon Preached at Salem, [June] 1636, 1.
16. Winthrop's Journal, I, 83. To Cotton, while he was in England, there was no necessity for both teacher and pastor: "The Difference ... inferreth a difference in their ministrations.... But yet I deny not, if god hath given to any the gifts of both, he may reasonably dispense both." Letter to [Herbert Palmer], Nov. 8, 1626, Hutchinson Papers, Mass. Archives.
17. Winthrop's Journal, I, 107.

to express formally: "Our Churches are governed by Pastors, Teachers ruling Elders and Deacons, yet the power lies in the wholl Congregation, and not in the Presbitrye further then for order and precedencye."[18]   The congregation's undertaking a few days after the installation to raise funds by voluntary contribution to provide Cotton a house in Boston and to pay part of the expenses of his journey (60*li*) and for the maintenance of both Cotton and Wilson during the coming year (100*li*) indicates the nature of the financing of the church—a sharp change from the first year when Wilson, having been engaged by the Massachusetts Bay Company, was compensated by the commonwealth government, which had to all intents and purposes succeeded the company that had originally employed him.   Before the year was out, Cotton was "to make it clear by the scripture, that the minister's maintenance, as well as all other charges of the church" should be met by "weekly contributions."[19]   Finally, the independence of the individual churches within a voluntary but loose consociation of all the churches, and the involvement of the magistrates in church activities were well established.   While Cotton's settling in Boston was partly determined by the governor and Assistants meeting with "the ministers and elders of all the churches" and even though the neighboring ministers attended his installation, observing and giving him "the right hands of fellowship" at its conclusion, the Boston church alone called him as teacher and empowered him with the "gifts" of that office.[20]

The coming of the ministers—particularly as their numbers and quality increased during and after 1633—effected changes in the Bay.   Bringing with them those deep religious feelings which had, in the main, separated them from their conforming brethren in the English establishment, the ministers augmented the already high religious tone of the commonwealth.   In old Boston, Cotton had precipitated "a great *reformation* . . . . *Profaneness* was extinguished, *superstition* was abandoned, *religion* was embraced and practised among the *body* of the people."   Now, in new Boston,

18. Winthrop to Sir Nathaniel Rich, May 22, 1634, *Winthrop Papers,* III, 167.

19. *Winthrop's Journal,* I, 114, 116.   See also Cotton to Herbert Palmer, cited above, n. 16, Cotton's position being one he had argued in England earlier.

20. *Winthrop's Journal,* I, 108, 111.

he did the same. From the town and nearby communities the people crowded into his public lectures each Thursday, abandoning their work for the word of God. By October the Court of Assistants was to observe that the morning lectures were in "dyvers wayes prejudiciall to the common good" inasmuch as they brought about "the losse of a whole day" and "other charges and troubles"; henceforth, no lecture was to begin before one o'clock in the afternoon. A year later, lectures being given by the ministers were found to be "over burdensome" to both the people and the ministers, and an attempt was made to reduce their number and frequency, but to no avail.[21]

The Sabbath services were crowded too, and the number of communicants was steadily increasing. The idea of conversion was strong, the process being explained as an awakening of God-implanted "grace," in order to maintain adherence to a form of Calvinism. But this rationalization did not imply an attempt to recognize God's own "saints"; as yet no more than one's outward behavior and testimony as to one's knowledge of the true faith (as determined and taught by the ministers) were accepted in assessing conversion and consequently fitness for membership in the church. Thus Edward Howes could send John Winthrop, Jr., four wild dogs "with an Irish boy to tend them" and assure him that although the boy was a Roman Catholic, "with gods grace he will become a good convert." The elder Winthrop, in describing the first six months of Cotton's ministry during which sixty-three persons—newcomers for the most part—joined the church, could write of "Divers profane and notorious evil persons" confessing their sins and being "comfortably received into the bosom of the church." "More were converted and added [to the Boston church], than to all the other churches in the Bay . . . . Yea, the Lord gave witness to the exercise of prophecy, so as thereby some were converted, and others much edified."[22]

The ministers brought with them, too, an air of supreme self-confidence, a belief—even though they formally renounced the

21. Mather, *Magnalia Christi Americana*, I, 260; John Cotton to the Church at old Boston, *ca.* 1649, prefacing his *Of the Holinesse of Church-Members* (London, 1650); *Assistants' Records*, II, 37; *Winthrop's Journal*, I, 135, 143.

22. Edward Howes to John Winthrop, Jr., *Winthrop Papers*, III, 134; *Winthrop's Journal*, I, 116; First Church Records.

belief—that they could read God's will in His word and in His creations.   As they arrived they looked upon the churches of Massachusetts and termed them not merely good but godly.   Cotton, for example, although he might have doubts about the lawfulness of some of the practices of the New England churches—in his later life he was to describe how he struggled for two years after his arrival before coming to accept congregationalism fully— seemed to be approving all, both by his actions in conforming to First Church practices and by his words.   Invited during his testing to speak his mind about the validity of the church, he chose his text from the Song of Solomon: "There are threescore queens, and fourscore concubines, and virgins without number.   My dove, my undefiled is *but* one; she is the *only* one of her mother, she *is* the choice *one* of her that bare her."[23]   To his listeners the "doves" were the churches of Massachusetts.   Winthrop made the most of this approbation and wrote to England in response to criticism of the way of the churches and with reference particularly to Cotton: "The Lords holy and wise servants (suche as he hath vouchsaffed to bestowe upon us both formerly and now of late) doe approve of, and accordingly doe joyne with us in the same Course."   Very quickly, too, the laymen assumed the ministerial consent to be an affirmation of perfect godliness.   Winthrop, in writing to England in 1633, had not been able to avow that the Massachusetts way was God's way perfectly: "We cannot professe a perfection . . . (which is not to be looked for in this worlde)."   But less than a year later to the same correspondent, he was to allude to a perfect conformity to God's will: "For your counsell of Conforminge ourselves to the Ch[urch] of E[ngland] though I doubt not but it proceeds out of your care of our wellfare: yet I dare not thanke you for it; because it is not conformable to Gods will revealed in his worde . . . our case heere is otherwise: being come to clearer light and more Libertye."[24]

Again indicative of the shift—the new affirmation of perfect

23. Song of Sol., 6:8-9; *Winthrop's Journal,* I, 107.   Ziff, *John Cotton,* 83, 263, suggests that the sermon had been delivered earlier in old Boston and is that subsequently published in *A Brief Exposition of the Whole Book of Canticles . . .* (London, 1642).

24. Winthrop to Sir Simonds D'Ewes, Sept. 26, 1633, July 21, 1634, *Winthrop Papers,* III, 139, 172.

godliness—is the marked change in tenor between the original
covenant of the First Church and the renewed covenant of 1636.
The first had expressed a hope of following God's will; the second,
while containing a "deep acknowledgement of our great unworthy-
nes," nevertheless quickly established that the body of the church
was the Lord's "Covenant people" bound together to walk "as a
right Ordered Congregation, and church of Christ, in all wayes of
his worship according to the holy rules of the word of God."[25]

The ministers brought with them, finally, their great concern
for theology and polity, their reputations for scholarship, and their
pedantry. The laymen who had been directing the affairs of the
commonwealth, towns, and churches turned to them increasingly
for advice and counsel, particularly on matters regarding the church
and morals, and the ministers, for their part, eagerly assumed the
role of counselors. They were confident of their abilities in such
matters. But more: Like the laymen who had ridden out to con-
front Elder Brown, the ministers were anxious to retain that unity
which was so much a part of the medieval world—for them, only
a step in the past.

There was a difference, however. The laymen had concerned
themselves with outward communal unity and had sought it at
times at the expense of leaving questions unresolved, considering
dissension even in the interest of truth to be disruptive. In March
1634, for example, an argument broke out in the Boston lecture
about the wearing of veils by women; Winthrop, "perceiving it to
grow in some earnestness, interposed" and brought the discussion
to an end. But to the ministers unity with regard to "fundamental
and principall points" could only be established on the basis of
God's pure truth, ascertained from the Bible and nature.[26]

In England the ministers, for the most part, had been limited
by the necessity of remaining true to their medieval commitment
to a single and unified society and its one church; their nonconformity, pushed upon them by their desire to follow God's truth
as they individually saw it and by what they considered errors

25. Cf. the First Church covenant in First Church Records and the renewed
covenant in *Winthrop Papers*, III, 223-25. Cf., too, the Salem covenant of 1629
and the enlarged covenant of 1636 in Walker, ed., *Creeds and Platforms of
Congregationalism*, 116ff.
26. *Winthrop's Journal*, I, 120.

propounded by the establishment, was consequently limited, for to deviate too far from the establishment was to hazard the sinful pit of outright separation. When accusing Salem's Samuel Skelton of separation in 1630, Cotton had asked, "What is more anti-christian than to set up two churches?" But New England offered the ministers a "wide door of liberty."[27] There was no longer need to temporize, for truth and unity could be effected within the new society—the ministers, like Winthrop, were utopians of a sort —while casuistry would make the point that the new society and its churches had not separated from the old. "Follow the truth we must," Thomas Hooker was to write; and for Cotton truth was to become "so cleare" that a dissenter could not "but be convinced in Conscience of the dangerous Error of his way" once it was pointed out to him. Even with regard to "thinges of lessre moment," where dissent "in a spirit of Christian meeknesse and love" —though not with "boisterous, and arrogant Spirit to the disturbance of Civill Peace"—might be tolerated, it was only until "god may be pleased to manifest his Trueth" to the dissenter.[28]

The basic structure of the Massachusetts churches conformed to God's truth as the ministers saw it, but the surface unity which had been achieved by the laymen displayed too many half-hidden disparities for their tastes. Too many "of weake Judgments" had found their way into the churches, a correspondent in England wrote in March 1633: "I verilie perswade my self you have many ...amongst you, on whome it were good your ministers took a little paines, that they might be rectified." Cotton perforce agreed. Noting the lack of ministerial direction, he wrote on behalf of himself and Thomas Hooker that their work in the Bay was "enough, and more than enough to fill both our handes, yea and the hands of many brethren more." This was the case even in

27. John Cotton to Samuel Skelton, Oct. 2, 1630, in Harris, *Memorials of the First Church in Dorchester*, 56; Miller, *Orthodoxy in Massachusetts*, 102.

28. Thomas Hooker, "Touchinge the Crosse in the Banners," n.d. but *ca.* 1635; [John Cotton to Roger Williams] in answer to "The Question you putt, is, whether Persecution for Cause of Conscience, be not against the Doctrine of Jesus Christ," n.d. but *ca.* summer, 1636, both in Hutchinson Papers, Mass. Archives. The latter is, with minor variations, "The Answer of Mr. John Cotton ... To the aforesaid Arguments against Persecution for Cause of Conscience," in Williams' *The Bloudy Tenent, of Persecution, for Cause of Conscience, Discussed* ... (London, 1644).

regard to the general polity of the Bay, for not all the churches of
the commonwealth had come to the same conclusions with regard
to various problems.   Before the end of 1633, the ministers began
to meet periodically "at one of their houses by course" to debate
and presumably establish a common position on "some question
of moment."   Orthodoxy was in the making, for although the
ministers maintained that "no church or person can have power
over another church" and that they did not "exercise any jurisdiction" by virtue of their meetings, the fears of Roger Williams
and Samuel Skelton that "it might grow in time to a presbytery
or superintendency to the prejudice of the churches' liberties" were
to prove prophetic.[29]

Yet orthodoxy was not to be established overnight, nor disparity to disappear.   The latter was still rampant in 1635, when
the General Court entreated "the elders and brethren of every
church" to "consult and advise of one uniforme order of discipline
in the churches, agreeable to the Scriptures, and then to consider
howe farr the magistrates" might act "for the preservacion of that
uniformity and peace of the churches."   The newly arrived Hugh
Peter noted it a year later, when, before the Boston church, he
suggested that Cotton go through the Bible "and raise marginal
notes upon all the knotty places of the scriptures" and that "a form
of church government might be drawn according to the scriptures."[30]

Neither plea could be acted upon at the moment.   The ministers were in actuality not of a single mind as to God's truth,
and while they sought unity they regularly introduced dissent
among themselves. The English correspondent of March 1633 had
noted this, as well as the "weake Judgments" among the laymen:
"I have heard ... that your ministers preach one against anothers
doctrine; which I conceive to be a great scandall to your societieis,
and if not reformed in tyme, may prove ... fatall."   The case of
Roger Williams is familiar, the brash young separatist lighting
fires of dissent everywhere he passed, challenging the validity of

29. Edward Howes to John Winthrop, Jr., Mar. 18, 1632/33, *Winthrop
Papers,* III, 112; John Cotton to "Reverend and Beloved Brother," Dec. 3, 1634,
Hutchinson, comp., *Collection of Original Papers Relative to Massachusetts,* 56;
Winthrop's Journal, I, 112-13.
30. *Colony Records,* I, 142-43; *Winthrop's Journal,* I, 179.

the charter, the authority of the magistrates in questions of morals, the advising of one church by another, the presence of unregenerates at church services. John Eliot at Roxbury questioned the validity of the ministers' part in negotiating an Indian treaty and had to be brought "to acknowledge his error in that he had mistaken the ground of his doctrine." In Charlestown, the Reverend Mr. James and his congregation fell to squabbling, and it grew "to such a principle of conscience among them" that the other ministers were asked to give their advice; after two meetings the ministers themselves were divided.[31]

And it was not only the ministers. Much of the fiery controversy was emerging from the congregations, for the conversion and edification which Winthrop commented upon following Cotton's installation in Boston was but a part of a religious enthusiasm running rampant through the commonwealth. In Salem, the congregation turned on the "King's colors," defacing them on the grounds that "the red cross was given to the king of England by the pope, as an ensign of victory, and so a superstitious thing, and a relique of antichrist." In Dorchester, a church was to be gathered to replace that which had left the commonwealth for the Connecticut River, but it was forestalled when it was found that some of the would-be members "had builded their comfort of salvation" upon "dreams and ravishes of spirits by fits; others upon the reformation of their lives; others upon duties and performances."[32]

It was in Boston, however, that both dissent among the ministers and popular enthusiasm reached their highest peak. The first was presaged early in 1636 when the Reverend Thomas Shepard, having attended Cotton's Thursday lecture, returned home to Newtown in consternation. Cotton had spoken of faith and sanctification in terms which seemed to contradict Shepard's teachings, and Shepard wrote to ask a series of questions: "It is the earnest desire not only of my selfe, but of diverse of our members, whose harts are much endeared to you, that for the further clearing up of the truth, you would be pleased to give us Satisfaction by way of writing rather than by speech for this one time to these par-

31. Edward Howes to John Winthrop, Jr., Mar. 18, 1632/33, *Winthrop Papers*, III, 111; *Winthrop's Journal*, I, 121, 142.
32. *Winthrop's Journal*, I, 137, 177.

ticulars . . . . I have plainly writ my hart unto you, being perswaded that in the spirit of meeknes, you will not thinke I have thus writ to begin or breed a quarrell; but to still and quiet those which are secretly begun."[33] Cotton had responded in kind: "As for difference, and Jarres, it is my unfeigned desire to avoide them with all men especially with Brethren; but I doe not know, I assure you, any difference, much less Jarres between me, and any of my Brethren in our Publique Ministery."[34] Yet he was in error. There was a fundamental difference.

To such as Shepard, the holy church of Christ as an institution among men was all important, and feeling that sanctification—the moral behavior of the individual—was the principal sign by which man and the churches could hope to recognize God's elect, they were content to build their churches upon visible morality, calling their listeners to a reformation of their lives and inviting those of moral appearance to apply for church membership. True, the reprobate could not be transformed into a saint, nor could a man profit by his good works, storing up credits in heaven which would be counted in his favor at the Judgment, for those whom God would save were already known to Him. But the saint, living in sin, could be awakened (if it were God's will) to follow his duty toward God, while a man who could look upon his total life and say "I have lived as God would have me live according to His revealed word" could take comfort in the possibility that he was of the elect, for God's saints (by virtue of their election) would abide by God's commandments and ally themselves with the true church.

Cotton, concerned more with the individual than the institution, more with salvation than morality, would go further. He had earlier introduced the idea that admission to the church should be dependent not merely on the outward behavior and knowledge of the faith of the applicant, but on the church's evaluation of the applicant's profession of the working of Christ within him—a subtle but profound change in the admission procedure, in time transforming the church from a gathering of the professedly godly to a gathering of the professed visible saints.[35] Other churches in

33. Shepard to [John Cotton], *ca.* Apr. 1636, Cotton Papers.
34. J[ohn] C[otton] to [Thomas Shepard], *ca.* Apr. 1636, Cotton Papers.
35. Morgan, *Visible Saints*, 97ff.

Massachusetts were adopting the profession of grace as part of the admissions procedure, the would-be members being required to acknowledge "the great mercy and grace of God, in receiving them to his grace: and changing their heart and life by such or such means." But in most it remained secondary to the formal confession of knowledge of the faith and the evidence of good conduct; that the profession of grace was "weakely" and "briefly done . . . mindes not," a 1637 statement of admission procedures stipulated.[36]

For Cotton, however, the profession of grace was cardinal. It was not enough, however. Like any other minister he sought to join men to the church, urging them to accept (and declare to the congregation) what they felt to be God's help in renouncing their sins and embarking upon a reformed life. The number of conversions in the years immediately after his arrival indicates a great response to his appeal. But membership in the church was only an outward indication or, as he termed it, a "seal" of the individual's saved condition, and a slight one at that. Cotton sought to move his communicants into a pitiless self-examination, a never-ending search for a second and true seal, driving his words into the very entrails of his hearers. "It is the desire of my heart by the grace of Christ," he wrote, "to provoke Christians (in this countrye of universal professein) not to rest in any changes of graces, Deutyes or Ordinances (as Church-fellowship etc.)." "I would not wish christians to build the signes of their Adoption [by Christ] upon any sanctification, but such as floweth from faith in Christ Jesus; for all other holynesse, and righteousnes . . . may be . . . mortall seede, and fall short of perseverance: whereas the least seede of fayth, and of that holynes which floweth from it abideth for ever." Take comfort in the true ordinances of the church, but "while you enjoy them, trust not in them, nor thinke not to stand upon this. that you are blessed in regard of them." Take comfort, too, in the Word and in following its commandments, but do not let it close your eyes to the nearness of God Himself, "for it is not all the *promises* in Scripture, that have at any time wrought any gracious changes in any soul, or are able to beget the faith of *Gods Elect*." Only

36. "A relation in what manner any persons are received into the congregations of New England, [1637]," Colonial Office Papers, 1/9, 166, Public Record Office, London, on microfilm in the Library of Congress, Washington.

true faith—faith emanating directly from God, faith in the absolute perfection of God's will and the utter desirability of "closing"
with God, faith that leads one to say "here am I as you have created
me, weak, abject, yearning for your comfort yet comforted only
as it befits your will"—only such faith is "the Witnesse of the Spirit
it selfe, as it is distinguished from our Spirit." And it was such a
witness of the holy spirit within for which he would have his hearers search. "God giveth us his sonne and his Spirit in a promise of
grace, when he giveth Faith to the soule," he wrote; it infuses with
a perfect and irrevocable promise of salvation, and all other signs
of justification, while encouraging to the individual, should not
assure him of God's intention.[37]

As abstract theology, Cotton's doctrine was not dangerous. But
transferred through his teaching to the public mind there was
danger indeed, and this was what worried Shepard. To stress to
such an extent the personal quest for evidence of God's grace, to
dismiss the ordinances of the church as comforting but ineffectual,
to preach God's spirit rather than the moral law, absolute faith
rather than conduct, was to unleash an individual approach to God
undermining all formal religion.[38]

This was what Cotton was doing in Boston, first among those
who had followed him from old Boston to new—the Leveretts,
Haughs, Hibbenses, Heatons, Hutchinsons, Coddingtons, Quincys
—then spreading through the town. Anne Hutchinson, who had
followed her beloved teacher to the New World, was a logical
vehicle for translating the teacher's doctrine into language which
the everyday townspeople could understand.[39] Of brilliant mind

37. J[ohn] C[otton] to [Thomas Shepard], ca. Apr. 1636, Cotton Papers;
John Cotton, *Christ the Fountaine of Life* ... (London, 1651), 22; *idem, A
Treatise of the Covenant of Grace, As It is Dispensed to the Elect Seed* ...
(London, 1659), 200; *Severall Questions of Serious and Necessary Consequence,
Propounded by the Teaching Elders unto M. John Cotton* ... *With His Respec-
tive Answer to Each Question* (London, 1647), 1.

38. The implications of this doctrine in the England of the Puritan Revolution are suggested in Geoffrey F. Nuttall, *The Holy Spirit in Puritan Faith and
Experience* (Oxford, 1946).

39. The best study of Anne Hutchinson and the ensuing controversy—replacing all earlier accounts—is Emery Battis, *Saints and Sectaries: Anne Hutchinson and the Antinomian Controversy in the Massachusetts Bay Colony* (Chapel
Hill, 1962), this despite the fact that Battis, by virtue of the limitations of his
sociological method, is forced when considering the nature of Anne's followers
to proceed on the basis of artificial and occasionally erroneous assumptions and

and rapier-like wit, educated far above the average woman of the time, Anne began explaining and elaborating upon Sabbath and lecture-day sermons for the other women of the town shortly after her arrival in 1634. In the enthusiasm of the time, her meetings were considered only a "profitable and sober carriage of matters" and a fit expression of the injunction in Titus "that the elder women should instruct the younger."[40] But by 1636 her meetings included both men and women, and Anne was holding forth twice a week to between sixty and eighty persons. Her intellectual fare was drawn from Cotton's discourses, though the master's words gained something in the retelling: "The person of the Holy Ghost dwells" in the elect; "no sanctification can help to evidence to us" our own election, only the knowledge of the spirit within; without the union of spirit and flesh, one "remains dead to every spiritual action, and hath no gifts or graces," the pretences of such being mere hypocrisy.[41]

By October, Mrs. Hutchinson's activities had come to the attention of the other ministers of the Bay, and they appeared in Boston to investigate and, "if need were," remonstrate with the Boston church about them. But it was too late. In the rarified religious atmosphere, Anne's views had swept up the greater part of the church and town, from Harry Vane, "a young gentleman of excellent parts" who had eschewed preferment at the court of Charles II to savor "the power of religion," to William Dinely, the barber-surgeon. Vane, arriving late in 1635 and well regarded for his high birth, had been elected governor in May 1636 and had carried Anne's views into the council chamber. Dinely dispensed

---

to discount the rampant religiosity which led even solid and sane Bostonians into rank mysticism.

40. [Thomas Welde], *A Short Story of the Rise, Reign, and Ruine of the Antinomians, Familists & Libertines, That Infected the Churches of New England* ... (London, 1644), [vi] — a work frequently attributed to Winthrop; "The Examination of Mrs. Anne Hutchinson at the court at Newtown [Nov. 1637]," in Thomas Hutchinson, *The History of the Colony and Province of Massachusetts-Bay*, ed. Lawrence Shaw Mayo, 3 vols. (Cambridge, Mass., 1936), II, 368. Subsequently the court was more correct in its interpretation of Titus 2:3-5: "The aged women likewise, that *they be* in behavior as becometh holiness, not false accusers, not given to much wine, teachers of good things; That they may teach the young women to be sober, to love their husbands, to love their children, *To be* discreet, chaste, keepers at home, good, obedient to their own husbands, that the word of God be not blasphemed."

41. *Winthrop's Journal*, I, 195-96.

them in a more plebeian way: "So soone as any were set downe in his chaire," wrote the orthodox Edward Johnson later, "he would commonly be cutting of their haire and the truth together." To such as these, the ministers—including Wilson but excluding Cotton and the Reverend John Wheelwright, Anne's brother-in-law and a new arrival to the commonwealth—were among those with "no gifts or graces." Without the spirit themselves, they could not preach the spirit to their hearers; hence, they were but "legal teachers," drawing their congregations to hypocrisy by holding out obedience to the moral law as the way to salvation. Less than a week after the ministers met in Boston, the Hutchinson faction was openly working to have Wheelwright called to be a third minister in the Boston church.[42]

Wheelwright's bid for office in the First Church was blocked on the basis that he was desired by those who sought to gather a church at Braintree. But this was not the end of the dissension. The debate over Wheelwright thrust the Hutchinsonian opinions and their origins in Cotton's teachings into the limelight, precipi- tating almost two years of confused, chaotic conflict involving Bos- ton and the whole commonwealth. The terminology of the argu- ment was theological, and all sides displayed the exuberant right- eousness which only a theological dispute among persons convinced that heaven and hell await the results can have. Yet at stake were the community itself, Winthrop's "Citty upon a Hill," and the ministers' godly truth.

Anne Hutchinson was disruption personified. Where Win- throp would find his way to God by living a godly, useful life in an orderly society committed to God, the Hutchinsonians found their way by direct and personal revelations. They divided men into believers and non-believers, saints and damned, and took them- selves alone for saints. Ministerial authority was denounced as men of Wilson's and Shepard's and Peter's caliber were castigated as false teachers, undeserving of even polite attention. They walked out when Wilson rose to speak, or, if they stayed, heckled him with comments and questions; not content, they streamed out of the town to public lectures elsewhere, heckling and questioning

42. *Ibid.*, 162, 195-96, 240; "The Examination of Mrs. Anne Hutchinson," Hutchinson, *History*, 370; *Johnson's Wonder-Working Providence*, 192.

again, badgering all whose doctrines disagreed with theirs. They
followed Cotton, but twisted his words. When he spoke of sanctification being a natural concomitant of election but not a sign of it,
they heard (and repeated) only his denunciation; when he spoke
of faith and spirit they heard only spirit and declared faith to be
as erroneous a ground for assurance of election as sanctification.
Indeed, they dismissed Cotton, however inadvertently, by their
anti-intellectualism, for by pronouncing the personal discovery of
the Holy Ghost within as the only "infallible certaine evidence of
our Justifyed [or elect] estate" they effectively discarded the
church (and Cotton) as mediator between themselves and God.[43]
For them, truth was a lightning flash in the night sky, illuminating God's world to the elect, not a painful searching out of Scripture. To one Hutchinsonian, Anne was "a Woman that Preaches
better Gospell then any of your black-coates that have been at the
Ninneversity." "For my part, saith hee, I had rather hear such
a one that speakes from the meere motion of the spirit, without any
study at all, then any of your learned Scollers, although they may
be fuller of Scripture."[44]

Church, state, all the orderly processes of society were required
to bow before the revealed truth of the Hutchinsonians. "When
enymies to the truth oppose the way of God," John Wheelwright
told the Bostonians in a fast-day sermon early in 1637, "we must
lay loade upon them, we must kille them with the worde of the
Lorde." And if this were to "cause a combustean in Church and
Commonwealth," then so it must, for "did not Ch[rist] come to
sende fier upon the earth?" The sermon frightened the Winthrops and Wilsons of the Bay, for they remembered the bloody
swath such enthusiasm had cut in Germany. Wheelwright was
tried by the General Court and found guilty of sedition. But the
Hutchinsonians would not rest. A remonstrance in Wheelwright's
favor was prepared and distributed. Winthrop sought to curb it:

43. "Fyve propositions given by some of the Brethren of Boston to some of
the Brethren of Newtowne at a Conference betwixt them at Boston," n.d. but ca.
Dec. 1636, Winthrop Papers, III, 326. Cotton subsequently defined the position
of the minister in a debate with Roxbury's John Eliot: "The spirite of God
delighteth to concurre with such Ministers as doe Intend and Endeavor to apply
the Doctrine of the Gospell to humbled Souls." "Notes on Justification," n.d.
but ca. Mar. 1638/39, Mather Papers, Prince Collection, Boston Public Lib.
44. Johnson's Wonder-Working Providence, 127.

"You invite the bodye of the people, to joyn with you in your seditious attempt against the Court, and the Authority here established against the rule of the Apostel, who requires every soule to be subiect to the higher powers and every Christian man, to studye to be quiet, and to meddle with his own business."[45] Anne herself best expressed the challenge to authority. "You have power over my body but the Lord Jesus hath power over my body and soul," she told her judges when brought to trial in 1637: "If you go on in this course you begin you will bring a curse upon you and your posterity, and the mouth of the Lord hath spoken it."[46]

Such views provoked the wrath of the commonwealth. "Antinomian," "Familist," "Erronist," "this red Regiment"—so the Hutchinsonians were termed as magistrates and ministers alike moved to break their hold on Boston. It was traumatic. "Your complaynt of the want of Brotherly love, I needes say is too just," a friend wrote Cotton in March 1637; "I [have] found soe much Strangenes, alienation, and soe much neglect from some whoe would sometimes have visited me wth diverse myles going, (yett here, will passe by my dore, as if I were the man that they had not knowen)." And Margaret Winthrop, writing to her husband John: "Sad thoughts possess my spirits, and I cannot repulse them, which makes me unfit for anything, wondering what the Lord means by all these troubles among us."[47] But it was easily done, for despite the appearances of strength the Hutchinsonians did not form a strong party. They were but a mob scrambling after God, and like all mobs, quickly dispersed once their leaders were dealt with.

Vane was excluded from the government in a tumultuous election in May 1637, and sailed for England in the late summer, his

45. "A Sermon Preached at Boston in New England upon a Fast Day the XVIth of January. 1636" [sic, though the fast was January 19, 1636/37], Mass. Hist. Soc., *Proceedings*, 1st Ser., 9 (1867), 266-68; John Winthrop to William Coddington, John Coggshall, and William Colborne, Jan. 15, 1637/38, *Winthrop Papers*, IV, 9. Though there is a doubt that Winthrop's letter referred to the Wheelwright remonstrance—the date suggesting its applicability to a later document—there is no doubt that the sentiments expressed would accurately describe the Governor's sentiment toward the remonstrance.
46. "The Examination of Mrs. Anne Hutchinson," Hutchinson, *History*, 384.
47. Pet[er] Bulkeley to [John] Cotton, Mar. 25, 1637, Cotton Papers; Margaret to John Winthrop quoted in Darrett B. Rutman, "My beloved and good husband," *American Heritage*, 13 (Aug. 1962), 96.

reputation on both sides of the Atlantic temporarily darkened.[48]
By a series of astute maneuvers Boston's political leaders—almost
to a man committed to the Hutchinsonians—were, if not silenced,
rendered ineffectual. Cotton, whose views, "too obscurely" stated,
continued to be used to support their position as the conflict raged
in 1637,[49] was weaned away in a succession of conferences with his
fellow ministers and the commonwealth's lay leaders. The con-
ferees did not change his views, but they brought him to see the
extreme position of those who claimed him for their master and
the shattering effects of their doctrines on the churches, the ministry, and the state.[50] With Cotton neutralized, the ministers met
in synod in August to catalogue and denounce the Hutchinsonian
errors. All the while the First Church was being barraged with
lectures and sermons, John Davenport, for example, expounding
on "the nature and danger of divisions, and disorders."[51] Finally,
the more vocal Hutchinsonians were brought to trial before the
General Court. Their conviction in November was assured, for the
commonwealth leaders had already agreed "that two so opposite
parties could not contain in the same body" and determined "to
send away some of the principal." Anne herself was convicted of
"traduceing the mi[niste]rs and their ministery in this country"
and committed to custody until the Court should enforce an order
banishing her. Wheelwright, his sentencing postponed since
March, was ordered to leave the commonwealth within fourteen

48. Emmanuel Downing to John Winthrop, Nov. 21, 1637, *Winthrop Papers*,
III, 512; Lord Say and Sele to [John Cotton?], n.d. but *ca.* Mar.-Apr. 1639,
Cotton Papers.

49. "The Autobiography of Thomas Shepard," Col. Mass. Soc., *Publications*,
27 (1932), 385; J[ohn] C[otton] to [Samuel] Stone, Mar. 27, [1638], Cotton
Papers.

50. The Mass. Hist. Soc. Library copy of *Severall Questions of Serious and
Necessary Consequence* includes manuscript addenda in Cotton's hand, which,
together with the printed text and *A Conference Mr. John Cotton Held at Boston
with the Elders of New England . . .* (London, 1646), constitute the fullest
exposition of the argument between Cotton and the other ministers of the Bay
and of its partial resolution. The former, in addition to the questions propounded by the ministers and Cotton's answers, contains "The Elders Reply" to
the answers, "Mr: Cotton's Rejoynder," and "Mr: Cotton's Revisall." The
Conference picks up where Cotton's "Revisall" ends. In point of time, the conferences extended from Dec. 1636 to *ca.* June-July 1637. See also, Mather,
Magnalia Christi Americana, I, 267; and J[ohn] C[otton] to [Samuel] Stone,
Mar. 27, [1638]; John Cotton to [John Wheelwright], Apr. 18, 1640, both in
Cotton Papers.

51. *Winthrop's Journal*, I, 230.

days. Others were penalized, the list spanning Boston's social spectrum and including two deputies, three selectmen, and a deacon of the church: John Coggshall, disfranchised and "enjoyned not to speake any thing to disturbe the publike peace, upon pain of banishment"; William Aspinwall, disfranchised and banished; William Baulston, disfranchised, barred from public office, and fined twenty pounds; Edward Hutchinson, disfranchised, ousted from office, fined forty pounds, and committed "dureing the pleasure of the Courte"; Richard Gridley, disfranchised; William Dinely, disfranchised; John Underhill, disfranchised and ousted from his militia captaincy. Ten others, threatened with the same penalties, signified their submission by denouncing their part in the Wheelwright remonstrance.[52]

The humbling of Boston followed. Fifty-eight of the townsmen were required to give up their arms and ammunition, not to receive them back again until they "acknowledg their sinn in subscribing the seditious libell" contained in the remonstrance. It was a demand for a symbolic and conscious surrender and the Bostonians knew it. But while the order "troubled some of them very much," as Winthrop wrote, "especially because they were to bring them in themselves," they meekly obeyed. A few tried to continue the struggle within the church, attempting to have the Governor called to account before the congregation for his actions during Anne's trial. The effort was easily turned aside.[53]

By ones and twos, then in groups, the Bostonians appeared before the magistrates to acknowledge their previous errors. Those who would not recant—William Coddington and his family, for example—left. More than twenty families followed Wheelwright north beyond the Merrimac River; an equal number traveled south to Narragansett Bay, first to attempt an absolute theocracy, then to split into voluble, argumentative sects.[54] In March 1638 Bos-

---

52. *Ibid.*, 239; *Colony Records*, I, 207; Wheelwright had apparently been advised by the Court to depart voluntarily before his banishment, but he refused, preferring martyrdom as a way of proclaiming "a strong Argument of ... Innocency to all the world." John Cotton to [John Wheelwright], Apr. 18, 1640, Cotton Papers.

53. *Colony Records*, I, 212; *Winthrop's Journal*, I, 241, 256-57.

54. Edmund M. Wheelwright, "A Frontier Family," Col. Soc. Mass., *Publications*, 1 (1895), 271-303; Irving Berdine Richman, *Rhode Island: Its Making and Its Meaning* (N. Y. and London, 1908), 117ff.

ton's humiliation was completed as Anne, for "divers Errors. and unsound Opinions," was brought before the people she had once moved so deeply to be dealt with "in a church way." Cotton, Wilson, Shepard, Eliot, Welde, Peter, Davenport—all the leading ministers of the Bay were there to go through the formality of attempting to bring her to see the truth of God. For some in the congregation it was too much: Thomas Savage, Edward Gibbons, and one of Anne's sons. But it was a sporadic, divided opposition, easily overborne by the assembled ministers. At one interruption Wilson shouted, "Should one mans scruple or doubt hinder all the rest of the Congregation, which are satisfied, to crye out, that the Lord is God, the Lord is God, and the Lord only is the Lord?" In the end Anne was excommunicated, the majestic but horrible phrases rolling from Pastor Wilson: "In the name of our Lord Jes[us] Ch[rist] and in the name of the Church ... *I doe cast yow out ... I doe deliver you up to Sathan* ... I doe account yow from this time forth to be Hethen and a Publican .... *I command yow* in the name of Ch[rist] Je[sus] and of this Church *as a Leper to wthdraw your selfe.*"[55]

Religious enthusiasm had given rise to the disturbances of 1637 and 1638; a statement of religious orthodoxy was to emerge from it as the ministers combined to declare truth and the magistrates sought to uphold it. Yet orthodoxy in Massachusetts was to be a curious thing. It involved no great statement of creed or belief. Truth in such matters was defined in negative terms by virtue of the condemnation of Anne's multitude of errors: Thou shalt not believe "that those ... that are united to Ch[rist] have 2 Bodies, ... [Christ's] and a new Body"; "That the first Thinge we receave for our Assurance is our Election," that revelations "are to be beleeved as well as Scripture because the same holy Ghost did indite both."[56] But what one should believe as credo was left unstated.

Undoubtedly there was no other way to unite the ministers against the challenge of enthusiasm except through such a negative

55. "A Report of the Trial of Mrs. Anne Hutchinson before the Church in Boston, March, 1638"—an excerpt from one of the lost journals of Robert Keayne—in Mass. Hist. Soc., *Proceedings*, 2d Ser., 4 (1889), 161, 167, 190-91.

56. *Ibid.*, 162-63. The full catalogue of errors is in [Welde], *A Short Story*, 1-17—82 errors in all.

approach. Cotton, meek and loving, "yet one that held his owne stoutly . . . what himselfe judged to be the truth," had not been brought to see error in himself, only error in his followers. "The difference of judgment and Profession" between himself and the other ministers of the Bay was "still the same," he wrote to one of the exiles who accused him of acting Samson for the ministers' Delilah. "If you thinke I condescende to the opposite part, because I beare Witnesse against a more opposite Part (to wit against our [brethren]) . . . . I wish you a better Spirit of Discerning." "It is one thing to Invert a Branch or [twig] of the [Covenant] of Grace (by letting the Light of [Works] before the Light of Christ:)"—an allusion to the stressing of good conduct by the majority of Massachusetts' ministers. It is a more reprehensible thing "to subvert the Covenant of Grace, by blotting out the [moral] Law written in our hearts and bring in (instead thereof) the . . . life of the Sonne of God . . . . and so make all New Creatures" as the Hutchinsonians had done.[57]

Thomas Shepard realized that "Mr Cotton: repents not: but is hid only . . . he doth stiffly hold the revelation of our good estate still, without any sight of woord or woorke." John Eliot knew it too, and went to great pains to translate Cotton's doctrine into one more palatable to himself and suitable for his Roxbury congregation. When Cotton taught that "the spirite of God . . . Declareth and wittnyseth to me the grace and favour of God in Christ Jesus," Eliot carefully explained that the spirit acted through the ministry, "for ministers are witnesses of Christ."[58] The ministers being rational and learned men, reasonable disagreement between them could be tolerated, indeed had to be tolerated if such as Cotton were not to leave the commonwealth. But the congregations, in their enthusiastic outbursts at Salem, Dorchester, and, climactically, Boston, had proved irrational and unlearned. They had seized upon a direct and individual communion with God and rejected man's institutions, threatening the

57. Whiting, "Life of Cotton," Hutchinson, comp., *Collection of Original Papers Relative to Massachusetts*, 246; [John Cotton] to "Beloved Brother" at Aquidneck, June 4, [1638], Cotton Papers.
58. "Autobiography of Thomas Shepard," Col. Soc. Mass., *Publications*, 27 (1932), 386n; "Notes on Justification," *ca.* Mar. 1638/39, Mather Papers, Prince Collection, Boston Public Lib.

very foundations of society. Challenging magistrates and ministers alike, they had opened the door to a thrusting aside of all
distinctions of birth, wealth, education. To the internal peril they
had added an external danger, for they had made it more difficult
to present a united front to renewed English criticism; at the very
height of the Hutchinsonian struggle a group of English ministers had written to their New England brothers accusing them
of having "embraced Certaine new opinions" since their removal
overseas, separatist opinions "such as you disliked formerly."
Similarly, the religious upheaval had endangered the settlements
at a time of Indian peril, for while the dispute raged, war had
broken out with the Pequots of Connecticut, and the Bostonians,
called to serve in an expedition into Pequot country, at first refused
to comply on the grounds that Pastor Wilson was to go as chaplain
to the force.[59]

The congregations, therefore, not the ministers, were to be
curbed by an orthodoxy asserting that the minister's voice within
the church was the voice of God. (No more would a Wilson be
harassed in his own pulpit!) "Christ's sheep ought to hear his
voice," Richard Mather of Dorchester wrote at the end of the first
decade; they ought "to obey them that speak unto them in his
name."[60]

Boston's First Church and its teacher, as they emerged from
the dissensions of the 1630's, reflected this orthodoxy. Teacher
Cotton still provoked men to go beyond outward morality and
search their souls for the spirit of God; but more and more, in
writings dealing with the nature of God's church, he was a spokes-
man for orthodoxy. Within the church itself, the officers assumed
precedence, sitting apart from the congregation on raised benches,
meeting privately as the presbytery to prepare what was in effect
an agenda for the church. The process had begun earlier. During

59. William Bourne and others to "Reverend and Beloved," n.d. but summer
1637 (with variations the same is published in Simeon Ash and William Rathband,
*A Letter of Many Ministers in Old England, Requesting the Judgement of Their
Reverend Brethren in New England concerning Nine Positions* . . . [London,
1643]), and John Cotton to John Dod[d], Dec. 19, 1637, both in Cotton Papers.
See also, Battis, *Saints and Sectaries*, 156.

60. [Richard Mather], *Church-Government and Church-Covenant Discussed,
In an Answer of the Elders of the Severall Churches in New-England to Two
and Thirty Questions, Sent over to Them by Divers Ministers in England* . . .
(London, 1643), 58.

the controversy over Roger Williams, the officers had considered and answered a letter from the Salem church without referring it to the congregation, brushing aside Salem's complaint that it was only the prelatical who considered the people "weak . . . giddy and rash" and hence incapable of dealing with such matters.[61] But by 1640 the power which Winthrop had earlier ascribed to the congregation was formally redefined by the ministers as: "Libertie to enter into the fellowship of [the] church . . . to chose and call well gifted men to office . . . to partake in sacraments . . . to joyn with officers in the due censure of offenders and the like." Real authority was in theory vested only in the assembled elders. "The Gospel alloweth no Church authority (or rule properly so called) to the Brethren, but reserveth that wholly to the Elders," Cotton wrote in 1644.[62]

It was emerging orthodoxy which Thomas Lechford saw in Boston during a sojourn in the town at the turn of the decade and which he described on his return to England.[63] Morning and afternoon on a Sabbath (at nine and two) the people gathered in the meetinghouse to the tolling of the town bell. Pastor Wilson standing "above all people in a pulpit of wood, and the Elders on both sides," opened the morning service with a "solemn prayer" of a quarter-hour or more, followed by Teacher Cotton reading and expounding upon a chapter of Scripture, then a psalm, the congregation singing unaccompanied as the ruling elders lined out the words for them to follow:

> The Lord to mee a shepheard is,
> want therefore shall not I.
> Hee in the folds of tender-grasse,
> doth cause mee downe to lie.[64]

61. "The Church of Jesus Christ at Salem, to our dearly beloved and much esteemed in Jesus, the Elders of the Church of Christ at Boston," n.d. but *ca.* Sept. 1635, Trumbull *et al.*, eds., *Writings of Roger Williams*, VI, 73. The original, much mutilated, is in the Cotton Papers.

62. John Cotton, *The Keyes of the Kingdom of Heaven, and Power Thereof, According to the Word of God* . . . (London, 1644), 9, 12.

63. In his *Plain Dealing*. Cotton's descriptions in *The Doctrine of the Church, to Which Are Committed the Keys of the Kingdome of Heaven* (London, 1643) and *Way of the Churches of Christ in New-England*, agree on all principal points.

64. *The Whole Booke of Psalmes Faithfully Translated into English Metre*, ([Cambridge, Mass.], 1640), psalm XXIII.

In the stillness following the last phrases of the tune, the pastor
rose again to begin the sermon. Sometimes Wilson would add an
exhortation based on recent happenings in the town; sometimes he
would call on a visiting minister to speak. A final prayer by the
teacher, a blessing, and the congregation filed out. Once a month,
however, the morning session was extended as the Lord's Supper
was celebrated. The non-members having withdrawn, a table was
brought to the center of the meeting and the ministers and ruling
elders took seats around it; the bread was broken and laid on a
"charger" and the wine poured into a chalice, Cotton and Wilson
alternating the service. As the people watched—standing on their
seats and crowding the aisle—first the bread, then the wine were
consecrated and passed around the table to the seated elders. Later
they were circulated by the deacons to the people as one of the
ministers droned on in prayer. A psalm, joyous,

> O Give thee thanks unto the Lord,
>   because that good is hee[65]

and a blessing ended the service.

In the afternoon, the meetinghouse was filled again. The
worship was shorter, an opening prayer, a psalm, and Cotton's
sermon. But the meeting ran on into the evening, for the business
of the church had to be taken care of. Baptisms followed the sermon, the pastor or teacher descending from the elders' bench to
stand by the deacons' seat, "the most eminent place in the church,
next under the Elders," as a single parent, a member of the church,
carried the child up to be sprinkled "into the name of the *Father*,
and of the *Sonne*, and of the *holy Ghost*." As the minister finished,
one of the three deacons rose: "Brethren of the congregation,
now there is time left for contribution, wherefore as God hath
prospered you, so freely offer." Pastor and teacher at times
pressed "a liberall contribution, with effectuall exhortations out of
Scripture," and the people—"Magistrates and chiefe Gentlemen
first" and including "most of them that are not of the church"—
filed down the aisle to bring their offerings to the deacons' seat,
putting money into a wooden box set out for the purpose, or, if

65. *Ibid.*, psalm CXVIII.

they brought goods, laying them down before the deacons. The admission of new members and the disciplining of those who had slid from righteousness, together with the resolution of various church problems followed and continued on until dusk, the ruling elders propounding the questions and leading whatever discussion there might be (for it was they who "*open the doors of speech and silence* in the assembly"), the members signifying their consent by their silence. If time allowed—and in winter, after shivering through hours in the unheated meetinghouse, there was seldom time—the congregation joined in a final psalm, Pastor Wilson prayed, and the meeting broke up with a final blessing on all.[66]

The "inconsequentials" of the services might vary from church to church, but the proceedings invariably reflected the transformation which was taking place. From being the font of church power, the communicants were coming to be viewed as but silent partners to their officers. "Elders be in a superior order, by reason of their office," Cotton declared; "the brethren (over whome the Elders are made Overseers and Rulers) they stand also in an order, even in orderly subjection, according to the order of the Gospel." Christ himself had ordained the structure of the church, designating its parts and duties: The "*Elders who Labour in the Word and Doctrine*" to preach "*of the word with all Authoritie*" and offer the sacraments in God's name; ministerial and lay elders to administer the affairs of the church "with an audible and lively voyce, in the open face of the Brethren of the Congregation"; the deacons to collect and dispense the funds of the church and to attend on the ministers, "wayting" on them "as their servant." The role of the members was to "readily yeeld obedience to their Overseers, in whatsoever they see and hear by them commanded to them from the Lord," for while they choose their officers, "the office itself is ordained immediately by Christ, and the rule annexed to the office, is limited by Christ only." Cotton used a metaphor drawn from the sea to explain the relationship between the congregation and its officers: "A Queene may call her servants, her mariners, to pilot and conduct her over the Sea to such an Haven: yet they

66. Lechford, *Plain Dealing*, 45, 46, 48, 49; John Cotton, *The True Constitution of a Particular Visible Church, Proved by Scripture* ... (London, 1642), 6; *idem, Keyes of the Kingdom of Heaven,* 21.

being called by her ... shee must not rule them in steering their course, but must submit herselfe to be ruled by them, till they have brought her to her desired Haven. So is the case between the Church and her Elders."

The queen should not question the crew. Hence the questioning of points of doctrine so rampant in the Hutchinsonian outburst was considered, if not unlawful, then unnecessary. The decisions of the crew, though presented to the queen, were to be consented to by her without hesitation. Hence, questions of church administration—including admissions and discipline—were presented to the communicants. But the elders had already pondered and decided the questions. The would-be member applied first to the presbytery, made his confessions of faith and of the workings of grace within him before the assembled officers, and was subjected to their scrutiny; the member feeling aggrieved by another brought his grievance before the elders, who considered "whether the offence be really given or no, whether duely proved, and orderly proceeded in," and who had the authority to dismiss "causelesse and disorderly" charges or "propound and handle just complaints." The application for membership or the grievances were presented a second time to the whole church—though it should be noted that in the case of women applying for membership Cotton had his way and their confessions were merely read in the open meeting. But consulting the congregation was to all intents and purposes a mere formality, the elders declaring "what the *Law* ... of *Christies*" might be, and the church of necessity concurring. Indeed, there could in theory be no dispute among the saints. The truth of God on any question, once pointed out, was instantly recognizable to those to whom Christ had promised "godly concord and agreement" and "his owne gracious presence." Dissent might arise, but it would emerge from the "corruptions and distempers of men," and if by argument the dissenters would not yield, they could be admonished for their error (as those dissenting to the excommunication of Anne Hutchinson had been) and, standing under censure, their voices would not count. The will of God, found in the Word and expounded by the elders, would be unanimously affirmed.[67]

67. Cotton, *Keyes of the Kingdom of Heaven*, 11, 20, 22, 23, 34, 37; *idem,*

Yet differences of opinion remained and disputes arose both within the single church and between churches. Robert Keayne's occasional notes on the discussions within the First Church[68] indicate that the members did not always accept the ministerial will humbly and meekly but regularly violated the ministers' orthodoxy by their contention. The definition of "inconsequential" with regard to proceedings in various churches bothered some. Thomas Allen of Charlestown, for example, sought Cotton's advice as to whether "some things be Arbitrary to doe them or not, or to doe them thus or otherwise?" How far did the effects of excommunication extend? To forbidding the faithful to eat and drink, converse and deal in business with the excommunicant? When should the sacraments be offered? "The Time of Administration of the L. Supp; we here doeing it in the morning; and suppose others should doe it in the evening"? Peter Bulkley of Concord asked Cotton's advice on the proper role of women in church affairs: May a woman seeking guidance ask advice in a private assembly, or should a man undertake to ask for her?[69] How should the ministers be maintained? Cotton had long held that Scripture demanded their maintenance by the congregation, citing Timothy's injunction to "let The elders that rule well be counted worthy of double honour, especially they who labour in the word and doctrine," and interpreting "double honour" as meaning not "reverence only, but maintenance" for both ministerial and ruling elders. Yet he consistently held that the purity of the ministry demanded voluntary contributions; "lands, or revenues, or tithes," he argued, "have always been accompanied with pride, contention, and sloth." And his opinion prevailed in the Boston church, although other ministers thought differently and sought an edict from the magistrates establishing a set tithe to be collected from members and non-

Doctrine of the Church, 9; Nathaniel Mather to Increase Mather, Feb. 13, 1677/78, "Mather Papers," Mass. Hist. Soc., Collections, 4th Ser., 8 (1868), 11; Mather, Church-Government and Church-Covenant Discussed, In an Answer of the Elders of the Severall Churches, 61, 78.

68. Only two of Keayne's journals of the proceedings within the First Church have survived in their entirety, one volume, 1639-42, in the Mass. Hist. Soc. Library, another, 1643-46, in the Rhode Island Historical Society Library, Providence.

69. Thomas Allen to [John Cotton], Nov. 24, 1642, Hutchinson Papers, Mass. Archives; Pet[er Bulkley] to [John Cotton], Feb. 1641/42, Cotton Papers.

members alike. In September 1639, the General Court responded
by enacting a law compelling "every inhabitant who shall not vol-
entarily contribute" to pay such assessments as might be levied "for
upholding the ordinances in the churches."[70] But the First Church
appears to have refrained from using the law, relying upon voluntary payments throughout the period.

There were other questions. What recourse did a church have
against an ungodly elder? On what day did the Christian Sabbath
fall, on the first day (Sunday) or the seventh (Saturday)?[71] More
serious were those problems associated with admissions and baptisms, for here and there in the commonwealth—and increasingly
as the 1640's opened—sharply dissenting views arose. Some
would have "all that dwell in the same town, and will provess
their faith in Christ Jesus" admitted, doing away with the elaborate
formality which had grown up within the church; others would
have "all baptized ones" automatically admitted. Some decried
the rule which limited baptism to the children of a member and
sought to expand it to include the grandchildren of members;
others would have all children baptized, regardless of the affiliation of the parent.[72]

To the ministers the peaceful resolution of such questions had
of necessity to remain in their own hands, and in curbing the congregations, they elevated the power of the presbyters assembled in
synods such as that which had condemned the Hutchinsonian
errors. Their model was the synodical system among the English churches in the Netherlands;[73] their rationale was the exten-

70. I Tim. 5:17; Cotton, *Way of the Church of Christ in New England*, 25;
Winthrop's Journal, I, 299; "Positions about the Maintenance of the Church
Ministery in New England: The Elders being called by the General Court to
express their judgments from the word doe Answer," n.d. but *ca.* 1638, Miscellaneous Bound Manuscripts, Mass. Hist. Soc. Lib.; *Colony Records*, I, 216, 240.

71. For example, the Shepard-Cotton correspondence of 1646 about Shepard's
Theses Sabbaticae: or the Doctrine of the Sabbath ... (London, 1649), then in
preparation, in Hutchinson Papers, Mass. Archives.

72. *Winthrop's Journal*, I, 286, 292; John Cotton, Thomas Oliver, Thomas
Leverett, "In the Name of the [First] Church" to "our Reverend and Beloved
Brethren the Elders with the rest of the Church of Dorchester," Dec. 16, 1634,
in Increase Mather, *The First Principles of New-England Concerning the Sub-
ject of Baptisme & Communion of Churches* ... (Cambridge, Mass., 1675), 2-4;
Lechford, *Plain Dealing*, 56.

73. See Raymond P. Stearns, *Congregationalism in Dutch Netherlands: The
Rise and Fall of the English Congregational Classis, 1621-1635* (Chicago,
1940), *passim*.

sion of the idea of the single congregation as a community of believers dependent upon one another in living the life God commanded into the idea of the community of interdependent churches. *"In multitude of counsellers is safetie,"* Cotton was fond of saying. Hence, if one member felt himself slipping away from God, he should seek the advice and counsel of others; and if a member did slip, it was the duty of the assembled church to point out error to him, and, *in extremis,* cast him out that his sin would not involve them all. Similarly, if one church lacked "light or peace at home," it should ask "the counsell and helpe" of other churches; and if one church "lyeth under scandall, through corruption in doctrine and practise," it should be dealt with by the assembled churches, their presbyters serving as their representatives. The power of the synod over the single church was considered, therefore, as extensive as the power of the church over an individual, even to the extent of commanding and enjoining "the things to be believed and done" upon pain of the churches' withdrawing their communion from an error-ridden church.[74]

It was a razor's edge the ministers were walking in putting forward the synod, for jealous of the liberties of the churches (which were in reality their liberties within their respective churches), they feared synodical power. Having in mind the episcopacy of England and that drive for conformity from which so many of them had fled, they hedged. Indifferent things could not be commanded, nor could a synod compel anything more than that which Christ commanded. Cotton's examples reveal a cautious distinction, for they bound the communicants and not the ministers: Christ commanded that Christian duties be performed "decently and orderly"; hence the synod could enjoin against "men with long haire, and women to speak in open assemblies, especially to pray with their haire loose about them," for these are indecent; but it could not command the ministers to "preach in a gown," for while a gown is decent, the minister in a cloak "preacheth decently enough."[75] In the end, however, the ministers were more afraid of an errant congregation than the possibility of an errant synod, dominated as it would be by the ministers themselves. To the

74. Cotton, *Keyes of the Kingdom of Heaven,* 55, 25.
75. *Ibid.,* 28.

synod, as to the presbytery, the ministers imputed divine origins: "*A Synod . . . is the first subject of that power and authority whereby error is judicially convinced and condemned, the truth searched out, and determined, and the way of truth and peace declared and imposed upon the Churches,*" Cotton wrote. Hence, "as a truth of the Gospel taught by a Minister of the Gospel . . . bindeth to faith and obedience, not only because it is Gospel, but also because it is taught by a Minister," so the truth as proclaimed by the ministers assembled in synod is the truth because it is drawn from the Word and proclaimed by "the authority of the Synod."[76]

How far the churches had come in a single decade! Fearfully, hesitantly, the lay leaders had taken the first step in deciding for congregationalism during the confused days following their landing. And on their rough beginnings, the ministers—learned, scholarly, self-assured, knowledgeable about all the theories and speculations of the time concerning the structure of God's one and true church—were attempting to build an elaborate edifice. They could do no other, driven as they were by their quest for truth and the defense of their rational, sophisticated approach to God against the ardent mysticism of such as the Hutchinsonians. In Boston and elsewhere in the commonwealth, the ministers, and to a lesser extent the lay officers of the church, were proclaiming themselves God's guardians, the Levites of a New Jerusalem.

76. *Ibid.*, 25, 47.

VI

DIVERSITY AND DIVISION

ABOARD THE *Arbella,* contemplating his "Citty upon a Hill," Winthrop had envisioned a truly united society. He had spoken of the human body as a single entity, each part accepting its role and quietly performing its proper function that the body itself might live and flourish. His ideal society was a similar entity, each individual accepting his place and quietly contributing to the welfare of the whole. In the New World, however, men argued over the rich land and the truth of God; Boston's developing land policy increasingly acknowledged the necessity of giving opportunity for fulfillment of personal aspirations; emerging orthodoxy reflected, in the ministerial attempt to limit contention, the contentious nature of man. And all the while artificial distinctions were arising between the inhabitants of Winthrop's "Citty," dividing the populace which Winthrop on the *Arbella* would have so firmly "knitt together."

Initially there were few prerequisites and no formal bars to admission to town or commonwealth, or to participation in public affairs. The moving force which had brought the first settlers together had been a small group in England—Winthrop, his brother-in-law Emmanuel Downing, Isaac Johnson, Sir Richard Saltonstall, Dudley, John Humphrey (like Johnson, a brother-in-law of the Earl of Lincoln), Increase Nowell, and others. Among friends, neighbors, acquaintances, they had circulated descriptions of New England and various arguments for the plantation; where necessary, they had specifically solicited the participation of persons whose occupations were indispensable to the success of the settlement: ministers, carpenters, stonemasons, soldiers, a surgeon, a midwife.[1] Winthrop, for one, had established a rough standard which prospective settlers had to meet, one involving no peculiar creed or belief, but simply "honest conviction" toward the godliness of the venture and faithfulness and diligence to one's work or "calling." He wanted none who would prove disruptive or obstinate, who would not accept his own "unitie bond, and waie of pietie, and devocion" to the enterprise.[2] The screening process had continued in the New World, and, like the men of Plymouth, the Bay leaders had adopted in the first years the policy of accepting into the settlement "only of shuch as come to dwell, and inhabite, whether as servants or free men; and not soujourners which come but for a seasone." But they moved even farther in this direction. When the sixty passengers aboard the ship *Handmaid* arrived in New England in 1630 and expressed their desire "to plant" in the Bay area, the authorities "would not receive them," "having no testimony" as to their character and godliness.[3]

Given this regular, though informal, screening and Winthrop's optimism—that he could effect his ideal community among those with him in the 1630 fleet—it is not surprising that there was no general exclusion from participation in public affairs (other than the usual exclusion of women and servants). To the contrary, Winthrop and his cohorts had thrown open the door to participation in commonwealth government almost as soon as they arrived, calling together the whole body of settlers in the first General Court of October 1630, and resolving issues "by the generall vote of the people, and erreccion of hands." Quite naturally, however, the leaders had attempted to retain their own paramount position by limiting the activity of the generality they were inviting into the government. Thus the Court ordered at this first meeting that

1. The Dorchester group, gathered under the auspices of John White, is an exception, although John Humphrey was a link between White and those around Winthrop and the Earl of Lincoln. Frances Rose-Troup, *John White* ... (N. Y. and London, 1930), 108 ff. Another exception was the group aboard the ship *Lyon* mentioned in Appendix I.

2. Henry Hazard to Winthrop, *ca.* Feb. 1629/30, Nathaniel Ward to Winthrop, Jan. 16, 1629/30, and Arthur Tyndal to Winthrop, Nov. 10, 1629, all in *Winthrop Papers*, II, 202, 192, 166. See, too, the sundry letters and documents relating to the solicitation, *ibid.*, *passim*.

3. The Governor and Assistants of Plymouth to the Governor and Assistants of Massachusetts, Feb. 6, 1631/32, *Winthrop Papers*, III, 64; *Winthrop's Journal*, I, 54.

the Assistants, to be elected by the Court, "should have the power of makeing lawes and chuseing officers to execute the same" rather than the Court itself as specified in the charter.[4]

Yet practicality decreed that the generality in its broadest sense could not be admitted precipitously to the public affairs of the commonwealth even in this limited fashion, just as they could not be admitted en masse and immediately to the church without putting it in danger of degeneration. The leaders had met the problem of the church by turning to a congregationalism which required assurances of godliness and character from the would-be member. They met the problem of participation in commonwealth affairs— or commonwealth citizenship—in the same way. In May 1631, at the second General Court, participation was made contingent upon admission to freemanship as defined in the charter, thus giving the leadership a device whereby it could be assured of the caliber of those joining in the government. At the same time, 116 men were admitted to freemanship, apparently on the basis of their earlier requests and their proven characters as judged by the leaders. For the most part the new freemen were relatively prominent and well-to-do, although not necessarily members of the church. Among the dozen-odd from Boston, for example, were William Colborne, Robert Harding, Samuel Cole, William Hudson, John Underhill, William Baulston, Edward Gibbons, the Reverend Mr. Blackston. (Such men as Winthrop and Coddington were already freemen by virtue of their prior investment in the company.) Provision was made by which others from among newcomers and those already in the commonwealth—by no means all of the adult males were included among the 116—could apply for and be admitted to freemanship and participation. But the test of character was to be made within the local congregations rather than by the government itself, the Court voting to insure the participation of none but "honest and good men" by providing "that for time to come noe man shalbe admitted to the freedome of this body pollitick, but such as are members of some of the churches within the lymitts of the same." In effect commonwealth

4. *Colony Records*, I, 79; Morgan, *Puritan Dilemma: The Story of John Winthrop*, 90-91; B. Katherine Brown, "Freemanship in Puritan Massachusetts," *American Historical Review*, 59 (1954), 869.

citizenship was further defined in terms of the church.[5] For the
moment, too, participation remained limited to voting for officers—
governor, deputy governor, assistants—in whose hands full power
rested, for not until 1634 would the freemen, through a representative General Court, insert themselves into the legislative process.

The establishment of criteria for commonwealth citizenship
did not affect Boston immediately. As a result of the gathering
together of the first settlers through the personal solicitation of a
small group, the rough screening, and a natural screening inherent
in the necessity of traveling across a dangerous ocean to an unsettled and forbidding land, there was a homogeneity about the first-
comers to the town.[6] It was imperfect, Winthrop aboard the
Arbella having spoken of the settlers coming together from many
miles apart. Yet of those persons aboard the ships of the Winthrop
fleet who settled on Shawmut in 1630 and whose origins are known
(a total of 141) forty were from villages immediately surrounding
Winthrop's manor at Groton out of a total of eighty-three from the
East Anglian counties of Suffolk and Essex, and the rest were scattered in origins among ten counties, the city of London (fourteen),
and the English community in the Netherlands (three). This first
population was generally young, the emigrants from the fleet
including thirty-one childless couples out of forty-eight family
groups.[7] Some among the settlers were servants, eight persons
(including single men and women and even couples) being readily
identifiable as such, though the number was presumably greater.

5. *Colony Records*, I, 87, 366. While the normal course was to be admission
to a church, followed by freemanship, followed by participation in government,
it was not to be rigidly adhered to, for note such cases as Nicholas Willis, admitted
to the First Church in May 1634, to participation in the General Court of May
14, and to freemanship in Nov. 1634; John Coggan, admitted to freemanship
but never a church member; Charlestown's John Harvard, admitted a freeman
Nov. 2, 1637, and to the Charlestown church on Nov. 6. Only by considering that
the primary factor initially was not church membership per se but the desire to
limit participation to "honest and good men" (using the churches to discover
such qualities when the individual was unknown) do such cases fit into a general
pattern.
6. The discussion of Boston's population here and on the following pages is
based upon the close examination of the extant Boston records described below
in "A Note on Sources and Methods."
7. The figures given include those who died or moved away from Shawmut
shortly after settlement and therefore exceed the figures given above, chap. 3,
pp. 57-58, of 131 adults and 45 families remaining for any length of time.

For the most part the emigrants had been associated with agriculture and small household manufactures.

In view of this homogeneity—augmented during the early years by the inclusiveness of the church and the synonymous nature of town and church government—formal prerequisites for admission to the town would have been superfluous and there is no indication that they existed. The privileges and duties associated with residence within the community were conferred across-the-board. All adult males (servants excepted) participated and held office when called upon; all shared in the distribution of land and grazed cattle on those lands which the town held in common; over all was extended the protection of the community in sickness or want; all contributed to the support of the commonwealth, town, and church.

Servants constituted a separate group, but one integrated into the early society. The term as used at the time was a broad one, embracing voluntary servants working for wages ("hired servants" or "labourers"), apprentices whose servitude was a form of education, and bound servants, largely those committing themselves to so many years' service to cover the cost of their trip from England. The hired laborer was only semantically a servant, however; technically free, he might be a "setled housekeeper" with a family and permanent residence, hence a part of the free community. Bound servants and apprentices (and henceforth the term servant will be applied only to these) were assimilated into the society through the church, which was open to them with regard both to attendance and membership—between 1630 and 1640 the First Church was to admit sixty-one men and women identified as servants—and through their affiliation with particular families, partaking of the protection and moral discipline of the head of the family much as did women and children. Winthrop, for example, referred to his servants as "my family" in reporting their health and prosperity to his wife in 1630, while a law of 1631 provided that even the hired laborer, unless maintaining his own home and family, be engaged for no less than a year and incorporated into the family of his employer during that time.[8] The individual serving his master

8. *Assistants' Records*, II, 15; First Church Records; John to Margaret Winthrop, Sept. 9, 1630, *Winthrop Papers*, II, 312; Edmund S. Morgan, *The Puritan Family: Essays on Religion and Domestic Relations in Seventeenth Century New England* (Boston, 1944), 62-63, 69.

well and truly during his term of service would ultimately merge into the homogeneous free society, obtaining land, a family, and the freedom of the town.[9]

However, the town was growing, the population becoming more complex; homogeneity was giving way to heterogeneity. The nature of the incoming settlers changed as the difficulties of the first settlement were overcome and relative stability appeared. Family groups became larger, and the presence of elderly persons within a family, if not common, was not unusual. In 1633 the Leveretts arrived—Thomas, his wife Anne, and three children. In 1634 the huge Hutchinson clan made its appearance in the town, as did the Heatons and the Freeborns—William, aged forty, his wife Mary, thirty-three, and two children, aged seven and two. The same year, Robert Wing of Lawford, Suffolk, aged sixty, arrived. The Tuttles—an aged mother of seventy, two sons, their wives, and a total of seven children—came in 1635, as did George and Alice Griggs, both forty-two, with their children, Thomas, fifteen, William, fourteen, Elizabeth, ten, Mary, six, and James, two. A greater variety of occupations was indicated. The Northamptonshire Tuttles were both "husbandmen," as were the Webbs, the Newcombs, the Meareses; but "mercer," "draper," "carpenter," "joiner," "tailor," "glover," "miller," "shoemaker," "tanner" were common occupational designations. Increasingly, the later emigrants were from the towns rather than the villages—Norwich, Boston, London.

The number of unattached men and women rose, increasing the number of hired laborers. Servants brought into the community to serve a limited number of years began completing their obligatory service in the third and fourth year of settlement, swelling the ranks of free laborers even more. Some could not wait to complete their terms and either bought their freedom or otherwise convinced their masters to dispense with their services—despite the laws forbidding the freeing of servants before-time. All the while, additional servants were arriving. Many were actively solicited from England, for the task of building in a wilderness was an enormous one and labor was always scarce. Those soliciting looked for servants of "good towardnes," yet those solicited were interested

9. Such cases were not at all infrequent in Boston.

not in the venture, but in "what shal be the most of their employment there, whether dayrie, washing, etc. and what should be the
Wages, and for how many yeers tyed"; once in the commonwealth
they would seek only their freedom and a share of the New
World.[10] The number of children arriving without parents grew
noticeably as the decade progressed, many of them apparently
attached to families as servants at the time of their arrival. For
example, Stephen Beckett, aged eleven, was attached to the Pepys
family, which settled in the Reverend Mr. Blackston's old home
after that gentleman departed for Rhode Island; Mary Fuller,
Richard Smith, and Richard Ridley (aged fifteen, fourteen, and
sixteen respectively) were attached to the Saunders family. But
many of the children were gathered from the London streets and
shipped over en masse to be put out to families already in the
country, children such as Katherine, "one of the maids brought
over on the countryes stocke" early in the second decade, for whose
services John Winthrop paid five pounds.[11]

The pressure of both numbers and complexity broke the unity
of congregation and town. The early church was open to the
newcomers, Cotton calling for personal reformation and conversion, and precipitating that enthusiastic religion which would cul-
minate in the Hutchinsonian outburst. But not all came to hear
him. By March 1635 there were enough absenting themselves
from the churches everywhere on a Sabbath to warrant the attention of the General Court, and attendance was made mandatory
upon pain of fine or imprisonment. To maintain a unity which
was fast slipping away, town citizenship was made contingent upon
membership in the church, as commonwealth citizenship had been
earlier, the General Court in September 1635 placing conditions
upon participation in town affairs for the first time by ordering that
"none but freemen shall have any vote in any towne, in any accion
of authority . . . as receaveing inhabitants, and layeing out of lotts."
Before this act was passed, the general government had been proceeding upon the assumption that only freemen were involved in
land distribution, and in December 1635 the town itself had re-

10. Henry Jacie to John Winthrop, Jr., June 12, 1633, *Winthrop Papers*, III,
126; *Colony Records*, I, 186; *Assistants' Records*, II, 84, 94, 100.
11. *Colony Records*, III, 48.

solved that none should receive town lands unless they were "likely
to be received members of the Congregation." Bound servants
were specifically excluded from receiving town land by an act of
the General Court of 1636.[12]

The net effect of these regulations, ideally carried out, would
have been the maintenance of the earlier homogeneity. On the
one hand, the church—and hence freemanship—was not yet a closed
body, for, as has been suggested, the idea of conversion was strong.
On the other hand, the belief that all free families of the town
should share in the land was clearly indicated, "all the inhabitants"
being directed on one occasion to plant in a given area and the
acreage of every "able man" established. Consequently, since
town practice held that all free inhabitants should receive land,
specifying only that they be actual or obviously potential church
members, and commonwealth law established church membership
as a prerequisite to freemanship and participation in town affairs,
then the implied hope was that the whole body of male inhabitants
exclusive of servants would eventually be freemen, participating
citizens of the town, property holders, and church members.[13]

But such an ideal was impossible to realize. The number of
newcomers was far too great to be readily absorbed; the variety of
backgrounds, outlooks, desires, and personalities was too much to
be pressed into a common matrix, the newcomers ranging from the
intensely devout Anne Hutchinson and urbane, acquisitive William
Tyng, through shopkeepers, farmers, artisans, free laborers, and
servants, to Samuel Maverick's Negroes—he had three in 1638,
one claiming to have been "a Queen in her own Countrey."[14]

The church was fundamental to the ideal, for its role was to
mold "honest and good men" that they might take their places in
town and commonwealth. Yet the church failed. Unable to cope
with the growing, variegated population, it came to accept a disparity between church and town, one indicated in the division of

12. *Ibid.*, I, 140, 161; *Assistants' Records*, II, 45; *Winthrop's Journal*, I, 122;
"Boston Records," 5.
13. "Boston Records," 3; Rutman, "God's Bridge Falling Down," *Wm. and
Mary Qtly.*, 3d Ser., 19 (1962), 411-12.
14. John Josselyn, *An Account of Two Voyages to New-England...*, 2d ed.
(London, 1675), reprinted in Mass. Hist. Soc., *Collections*, 3d Ser., 3 (1833),
231.

land to the male inhabitants of 1635—that division ostensibly limited to those who were or were likely to be members of the church —when one-quarter of the recipients were non-members.[15]

In part, the failure lay in the caliber of the newcomers themselves, their decadence being deplored in letters passing among the leaders. "Our Towne of late but somewhat too late have bene carefull on whome they bestowe lotts," Nathaniel Ward of Ipswich wrote Winthrop Jr. in 1635, "being awakned therto by the confluence of many ill and doubtfull persons, and by their behaviour since they came in drinking and pilferinge.... We conceive the lesse of Satans kingdome we have in our Towne, the more of Gods presence and blessinge we may expect."[16] In part it was the material opportunities of the New World which were bringing men to think less of heaven, and the land system which was dispersing them to pursue material gain. The dispersal provoked the law of 1636 restricting men's habitations to within a half-mile of the meeting house, a futile injunction, as indicated by Plymouth's plaintive letter of 1639 soliciting advice on how to counteract the dispersal of its people and by the repeal of the law in 1640. The all-too-apparent materialism was evident to a friend in England. "Many in your plantacions discover much pride, as appeareth by the lettres we receave from them, wherein some of them write over to us for lace ... cuttworke coifes ... deep stammell dyes; and some of your owne men tell us that many with you goe finely cladd," he complained; "if once Pride, Covetousnes, opposicion and contention etc. destroy the [power] of holines among you ... there will soone grow a strangenes betweene you and God."[17]

But in part the failure of the church to encompass all men rested with the church itself—the traumatic schism of the late 1630's and its aftermath. The proud piety of the Hutchinsonians, their conceit in their personal knowledge of the saved and damned,

15. Cf. "Boston Records," 22 ff., and First Church Records.

16. Nathaniel Ward to John Winthrop, Jr., Dec. 24, [1635], *Winthrop Papers*, III, 216.

17. [?] to John Winthrop, *ca.* May 1637, *Winthrop Papers*, III, 402-3. On the half-mile law, see above, chap. 4, n. 49. John Reyner and William Brewster "in the name and with the consent of the rest" of the Plymouth Church to the "reverende Brethren the church of Christ in Boston to the Elders there," Aug. 5, 1639, Cotton Papers.

kept those of lesser faith away from the church. (Like Roger
Williams, the Hutchinsonians would have left Winthrop's "weake
Christians" to their own fate and would not have stooped to help
them.) At the same time, the conflict brought about a cessation
of admittances, both sides being fearful that new members would
espouse the cause of their enemies; between January 9, 1637, and
December 29, 1638, not a single new member was admitted. Indeed, in the three-year period from January 1637 to December
1639, when more than 1,000 people poured into the town, the
church added only 76 communicants, an increase canceled out by
the withdrawal of the exiled Hutchinsonians. Close scrutiny of
the extant town and church records has indicated 362 families resident in the town in 1639; 70 were represented in the church by
both husband and wife, and 95 by either one or the other, but 197
families—over one-half the town—had no formal tie.[18]

Even after the Hutchinsonians were downed, the effects lin-
gered. The ready acceptance of new members was a thing of the
past. "Be verye carefull in admission of members," Winthrop
wrote to his son at Ipswich. "There be some of these newe opinions that will simulare and dissimulare beyond expectation, to gett
into our churches: ... I hope the sad experience of the effects of
such spiritts in other churches wilbe caution enoughe to them and
others, to beware and knowe men well ere they admit them."[19]
In Boston, the would-be members were required to speak exten-
sively of their *"knowledge* in the principles of religion, and of their
experience in the wayes of grace, and of their *godly conversation*
amongst men"; those found *"ignorant, and graceless, or scandalous"* were refused. How many applied and were rejected cannot
be known, but there were some. "We have had much experience
of it," the ministers wrote to England; "men of approved pietie in
the judgement of some have been found too light not onely in the
judgement of others, but even of their own consciences, when they
have come to triall in offering themselves to be members of
Churches." Certainly, too, many who might have otherwise sought
membership were dissuaded by the piercing, grueling examinations

18. See above, n. 6.
19. Winthrop to John Winthrop, Jr., Jan. 31, 1637/38, *Winthrop Papers,*
IV, 10-11.

which came to be a part of the formality of entering the church, the "high stiles for hypocrites" as Cotton called them. Thomas Lechford, early in the 1640's, was to observe that "here is required such confessions, and professions, both in private and public, both by men and women . . . that three parts of the people of the Country remaine out of the Church." The percentage was exaggerated, but the onerous nature of the procedure was not.[20]

The church continued to grow through the 1640's, but the gap which had opened between it and the town did not close. From 1639 to 1642 many whose membership had been delayed by the Hutchinsonian controversy joined. Others, both newcomers and longtime residents of the commonwealth, joined. The religious force, so powerful on the seventeenth-century mind, drew some, for in that sacramental age it was difficult to accept exclusion from holy communion, and even those willing to accept the risk of hell for themselves undoubtedly hesitated before leaving their children in jeopardy for want of baptism.[21] Ropemaker Alexander Baker and his wife Elizabeth, for example, arrived in town in 1635 but were not accepted into the church until a decade later, October 4, 1645; on the day following they brought their Boston-born children to be baptized, Alexander, Samuel, John, Joshua, and Han-

20. Cotton, *The Way of the Churches of Christ in New-England*, 54, 56; Ash and Rathband, *Letter of Many Ministers in Old England concerning Nine Positions*, 50; Lechford, *Plain Dealing*, 150-51. Compare for the earlier and more lax standards of admission, *A Coppy of a Letter of Mr. Cotton of Boston . . . Directed to a Friend*, 1-6, written *ca.* 1637: "We refuse none for weakenesse, either knowledge or grace, if the whole be in them, and that any of the Church can give testimony of their Christian and sincere affections."

21. Perhaps this is one reason for the slight tendency for women to outnumber men in the church (although the more important reason was undoubtedly the greater propensity of the men to place the affairs of this world before those of the afterworld), a tendency which began at the turn of the decade as the following chart of church admissions for the years 1630 through 1649 indicates:

Year	Men	Women	Total	Year	Men	Women	Total
Prior to Jan.							
1633/34	119	89	208	1642	21	23	44
1634	50	42	92	1643	15	31	46
1635	17	15	32	1644	37	25	62
1636	18	17	35	1645	9	21	30
1637	1	1	2	1646	8	15	23
1638	1	2	3	1647	11	30	41
1639	29	44	73	1648	2	8	10
1640	21	18	39	1649	0	1	1
1641	20	29	49	Totals	379	411	790

nah, the eldest almost ten years of age.[22]   And there were other considerations.   Church membership was a necessary prerequisite to success in the community; until the latter years of the second decade no major officeholder or leading merchant residing permanently in the town remained outside, the single exception being merchant John Coggan, and even he was connected to the church through his wife, nephew, and daughter.[23]   The church drew its members from all walks and levels of life—merchants and coopers, farmers and laborers; even Negroes and Indians were not excluded.   But only the upper class, the economic and political leaders, were so inclusively represented; those outside the church were most often of low status, the "unregenerates" being largely holders of minimal or no property and designated "laborer," "wheelwright," "housecarpenter."

The outsiders eventually constituted a considerable part of the town's population, however.   Of 421 families identifiable as resident in 1645, 128 were represented in the church by neither husband nor wife, while of the 481 families of 1649, 156 were unrepresented.   The figures can only be approximations, inasmuch as the records for the 1640's are scant and not every family left an imprint on what little has survived.   Yet the nature of the extant material would indicate that error would lie only in an understatement of the number of families outside the church, for while the later church records contain the names of virtually all members, the town and land records by which the number of nonmember residents is ascertained are far less complete.   Moreover, computation by families does not take cognizance of Boston's enlarged servant population, which was almost entirely excluded from church membership following the Hutchinsonian disturbances, the number of servants admitted declining precipitously from one-third of all those admitted in 1634 to less than one-tenth of those of 1639, from 62 of the 445 admittances during the first decade to 29 of the 345 of the second.   By extrapolation, one can estimate that by the end of 1649 the 484 communicants of the First Church

22. First Church Records; Banks, *Planters of the Commonwealth*, 155; "Boston Births, Baptisms, Marriages, and Deaths, 1630-1699," 22.

23. Cf. Robert F. Seybolt, *The Town Officials of Colonial Boston, 1634-1775* (Cambridge, Mass., 1939), the gentry as identified in chaps. 4 and 9, and First Church Records.

represented certainly no more than two-thirds of the town's families and less than one-half of the town's total adult male population.[24]

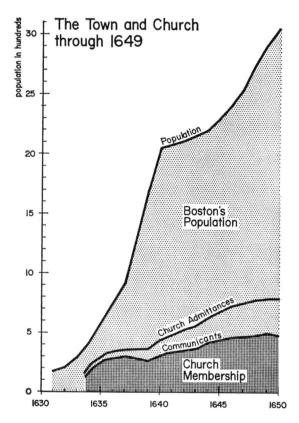

Most serious for the future, however, was the failure of the children of church communicants to follow their parents into membership, particularly the children born in the Bay area and baptized in the First Church. Within certain families, notably those prom-

24. The accompanying graph visually depicts the divergence of the community and church by comparing the estimated population of the town, the total number of admittances to the church from 1630 to 1649, and the estimated number of communicants at any one time. See below, chap. 7, the chart of "Estimated Population of the Commonwealth and Town, 1630-50" with regard to the first; the admittances are computed from First Church Records; the communicants are estimated on the basis of admittances, plus those recommended to the Boston church from elsewhere, less those dismissed from the First Church to another, voluntarily withdrawing, excommunicated, or dying.

inent in public affairs, the church quickly became traditional. Thus, Thomas and Anne Leverett, who joined the church on their arrival in 1633, were followed by their English-born son and daughter in 1639, and a second grown daughter in the 1640's. John and Margaret Winthrop, together with their children Mary, Stephen, and John Jr. joined in the 1630's, while another son, Adam, his wife, Stephen's wife Judith, and Sarah, the wife of Deane Winthrop, joined in the 1640's. Thomasine Scotto, a widow, joined in 1634; in 1639 her sons Joshua and Thomas joined and in the 1640's their wives Joan and Lydia were added. Of the Hutchinsons and Olivers there were twenty-four members enrolled during the two decades. Yet more frequently the opposite was the case, the grown sons and daughters remaining outside. Of 47 adult children (over 16 years old) found living with their parents in 1639, but 5 were members; of 32 in 1645, only 7 had joined; while of 53 in 1649, only 6 were communicants. Of children born in the commonwealth and baptized in the First Church, only one, Elizabeth Wilson, the daughter of Pastor John, sought and obtained full membership in Boston during the two decades under consideration.

In the face of the continuing discrepancy between church and town, the church turned inward. To the tendency toward formality and ministerial domination which followed the Hutchinsonian disturbance was added that toward "tribalism," so named by historian Edmund S. Morgan: the church's accenting itself and its own to the exclusion of outsiders.[25] The notion of the church as an assemblage of visible saints—inherent in the confession of grace first introduced by Cotton—was increasingly stressed. At the same time the idea of a general conversion was lost, Cotton in 1641 teaching out of Revelation, "none could enter into the temple until, etc." and delivering the doctrine "that neither Jews nor any more of the Gentiles should be called until Antichrist were destroyed, viz. to a church estate, though here and there a proselyte."[26] In essence, the church ceased to appeal for souls; it

25. In his *Puritan Family*. See also his *Visible Saints*, 114ff.
26. *Winthrop's Journal*, II, 30. The reference is to Rev. 15:8: "And the temple was filled with smoke from the glory of God, and from his power; and no man was able to enter into the temple, till the seven plagues of the seven angels were fulfilled."

became simply a vehicle, traveling in a godly direction and filled with passengers whom God had put aboard.

The ministers from their pulpits still called upon all to live the good and pure life, while urging individual church members to reform their families, servants, and neighbors. But the purpose was not the salvation of the subjects of this zeal; rather, it was a Christian obligation, an act of devotion on the part of the believer. "When we undertake to be obedient to him," Cotton wrote, we undertake not only "in our owne names, and for our owne parts, but in the behalfe of every soule that belongs to us . . . our wives, and children, and servants, and kindred, and acquaintance, and all that are under our reach."[27] The sinner might be brought to better conduct as a result, yet reformation did not bring salvation. Only God could grant that. "It is not in the power of men to ordaine or provide meanes or helps to such ends; but onely for him that can worke upon the Soule and Conscience." More and more intent upon divining those most probably saved through an increasingly sophisticated evaluation of the would-be members' conduct and confessions of grace and faith, the church did not call the reformed sinner to communion, but merely waited until God moved him to seek its comfort. "Wee have nothing to doe to bring them to the Church," Edward Winslow wrote in his *New-Englands Sala-mander.*[28]

The catechizing of children exemplifies the tendency. Formal catechism was notably weak from the beginning, there being neither opportunity nor inclination for it during the early years. The informality of the church and the time-consuming work of building and planting, as well as the prejudice against set prayers and forms, such as established questions and answers for imparting religious instruction, all worked against formal catechizing. When the ministers arrived in force, they elaborated a theology in which catechizing had little place. Their parents might love and dote upon them, but children were born in sin; they shared with man-

27. Quoted by Morgan in his introduction to "The Diary of Michael Wigglesworth," Col. Soc. Mass., *Publications,* 35 (1951), 317.

28. Cotton, *Doctrine of the Church,* 9; Edward Winslow, *New-Englands Salamander, Discovered by an Irreligious and Scornfull Pamphlet, Called New-Englands Jonas . . .* (London, 1647), reprinted in Mass. Hist. Soc., *Collections,* 3d Ser., 2 (1830), 122.

kind in general the damnation consequent on Adam's fall and were obligated by their natures to do evil. Christian parents could set them on the road to salvation by offering them for baptism, but as with the zeal to reform one's neighbors, it was not for the sake of the child but for the parent: "A beleever bee not in Gods account baptized himselfe, till his seed bee baptized."[29] The parents could, and indeed were obliged to, discipline the children, to restrict their propensity to sin and so prepare them to take their places in society. It was not at all uncommon in the 1640's for a child to be sent to live with another family on the grounds that the discipline of a stranger would be more efficient than that of a loving parent, lesser families sending their children to serve as maids and servants in the homes of more prominent families.[30] Parents also could put their children in the way of God by bringing them to the church to hear His word. But they could do no more. God alone could impart grace and save the children from inevitable sin and damnation, and only when He saw fit to place His mark on them would they enter the church and so come under its purview. Until then, there was nothing the assembled saints could do. Theology of this sort left little room for catechizing.

To a limited extent, Cotton's practice was an exception, for from the mid-1630's he was meeting Boston's children to "goe over the Principles of Religion in way of Cathechisme" and presenting "the Principles of Church Government" to them. Yet even he avoided formality, and when a catechism appeared in print under his name in England, he wrote to deny authorship.[31] Only as the church as a whole formalized, as its failure to attract the children into membership became obvious, as the absence of regular religious training drew criticism in the 1640's from the populace, magistrates, and opponents of the "New England Way" alike, did the church openly accept the Biblical injunction to *"Traine up a childe*

29. John Cotton, *The Grounds and Ends of the Baptisme of the Children of the Faithfull* . . . (London, 1647), 194.

30. Morgan, *Puritan Family*, 36-37.

31. J[ohn] C[otton] to John Dod[d], Dec. 19, 1637, Cotton Papers. Cotton's practice of catechizing probably began in old Boston, and the work in question might well have been an early form of his *Spiritual Milk for Boston Babes in Either England.*

in the way he should goe."[32] Cotton's *Spiritual Milk for Boston Babes in Either England. Drawn out of the Breasts of Both Testaments for Their Souls Nourishment.* circulated widely after 1646:

> *Quest. What is the wages of sinn?*
> *A.* Death and damnation.
> *Quest. How look you then to be saved?*
> *A.* Onely by Jesus Christ. . . .
> *Quest. How doth Christ redeem and save us?*
> *A.* By his righteous life, and bitter death, and
> glorious resurrection to life again.[33]

Weekly classes under ministerial auspices made their appearance. But notably, such formal catechizing was mandatory only for the "Children of the Church"; children of non-members attended voluntarily, if at all.

By the end of the decade, too, Cotton was ascribing a sanctity to the children of the church which was denied to those outside. Sinful by birth, they were nevertheless under Christ's protection by virtue of the accident of their parentage: "There is a double state of grace, one adherent . . . signifying to the pacifying of the flesh . . . another inherent . . . . In respect of the adherent or federall grace, all the [baptized] children of a believing parent are holy, and so in an estate of grace." They could fall away from God, and many of them did, but it was the responsibility of the church to cause them to cling to it as God's holy institution and so to their salvation. "God gave thee the ordinance of baptisme," Thomas Shepard of Cambridge wrote for his son; "god is become thy god, and . . . when ever thou shalt returne to god, he will undoubtedly receive thee."[34] For the rest, the church assumed no responsibility.

32. Lechford, *Plain Dealing*, 53; *Colony Records*, I, 328; *Johnson's Wonder-Working Providence*, 255; *Good News from New-England: with An Exact Relation of the First Planting that Countrey* . . . (London, 1648), reprinted in Mass. Hist. Soc., *Collections*, 4th Ser., 1 (1852), 213.

33. Quoted from the Cambridge, Mass., 1656, ed., 6-7.

34. Cotton, *Grounds and Ends of the Baptisme of the Children*, 43; "The Autobiography of Thomas Shepard," Col. Soc. Mass., *Publications*, 27 (1932), 355; Manuscript Sermons, Ipswich, Mass. Hist. Soc. Lib., under date of Sept. 8, 1645; "Note-Book of Rev. John Fiske," Mass. Hist. Soc., *Proceedings*, 2d Ser., 12 (1899), 319-20. Cf. Albert Matthews, "Early Sunday Schools in Boston," Col. Soc. Mass., *Publications*, 21 (1920), 259-85.

The non-members could, and probably in some measure did, attend services in the church, though regularity was undoubtedly lacking in the great majority and the number absent from any given service large. Indeed, it could not have been otherwise, for the single church building in the town could not possibly have held the town's populace, even discounting the young and old and those necessarily detained elsewhere. Even with the construction at the beginning of the second decade of a new meetinghouse— large for the time and place and boasting a balcony for the town's youngsters—it is difficult to envision its holding many more than the four to five hundred actual communicants of the years after 1643. Nevertheless, the law required the attendance of all, and the religious aura of the time prompted at least occasional attendance. And to Cotton, non-members, even heathens and Indians, were welcome; God's word might enrich and better their lives, and there was always the possibility that He might use the minister's oratory to awaken a spark and impart the knowledge of salvation to one who, unknown to himself or the church, had been chosen. Yet the easy intermingling of communicant and non-communicant which marked the early years disappeared. During Anne Hutchinson's trial before the First Church, for the first time in the records, members and non-members were separated as Elder Leverett announced that he was required "to request those that are Members of the Congregation, that they would draw as neare togeather as they can and into such places as they may be distinguished from the rest of the Congregation, that whan thear Consent or Dissent is required to the Things which shall be read: we know how they doe express themselves."[35] Cotton, in his *Way of the Churches of Christ* written in 1640-41, in speaking of the election of church officers, noted that they must be approved not only by the communicants and the messengers of other churches, "but of all that

35. "A Report of the Trial of Mrs. Anne Hutchinson before the Church in Boston, March, 1638," Mass. Hist. Soc., *Proceedings*, 2d Ser., 4 (1889), 162. The act was necessary to the leadership inasmuch as the Hutchinson opinions were as rampant outside the church (particularly among newcomers blocked from membership by the temporary cessation of admittances) as they were within, and to allow the participation of the non-members might have been to hazard defeat even at that late date. The non-members seem to have participated to the extent of speaking during the proceedings, however, for note (p. 190) the contribution of a "straynger" to the debate—the word being a synonym for non-member.

stand by; because *an Elder is to be a man of good report to them that are without.*" But subsequently he was to write and publish *The Keyes of the Kingdom of Heaven,* announcing that "wherein the *Book of the Way* is diferant from that of the *Keyes,*" his judgment should be sought in the latter. Here, among several changes, the teacher was clear in limiting the power of election to "the brethren of the church."[36]

Similarly, the purity of the church became all important. During the formative years, the status of baptized children was unclear. The way to God was open to them, "but whether they should . . . be admitted to all other priviledges when they come to age," notably holy communion, "without any personall profession of Faith, or entring into Church Covenant, is another Question, of which by Reason of the Infancy of thse Churches, we have had no occasion yet to determine what to judge or practise one way or other." As the children grew and displayed their secular proclivities, however, and as the church institutionalized and turned inward, the question was answered. When agitation arose for a broadening of the church and a lessening of the gap between church and town by the automatic admission of baptized children to communion and active membership, Cotton was adamant in advocating that system by which "all the Infants of the Church-members bee baptised; yet none of them are received . . . unto Communion at the Lords Table, nor unto liberty of power in the Government of the Church, untill they doe approve themselves both by publick Profession before the Church, and also by their Christian conversation, to take hold of the Covenant of their Fathers." By "this primitive practise," he argued, "there will bee no more feare of pestering Churches with a carnall Generation of members baptized in their Infancy." "Either the Lord in the faithfulnesse of his Covenant, will sanctifie the hearts of the baptized Infants to prepare them for his Table; or else hee will discover their hypocrisie and profanenesse in the presence of his Church, before Men and Angels, and so prevent the pollution of the Lords Table, and corruption of the Discipline of the Church."[37]

36. Cotton, *Way of the Churches of Christ in New England,* 40; Increase Mather, *The First Principles of New-England,* 7-8; John Cotton, *The Keyes of the Kingdom of Heaven,* 12-13.

37. [Mather], *Church-Government and Church-Covenant Discussed, in an*

Turning inward, the church eschewed its social function.   It
no longer screened men for society; rather it was becoming an end
in itself, a society within the total society.   In the early years, it
had been the guardian of public morals throughout the town, both
directly by dealing with offenders in a church way, and indirectly
by advising the magistrates and people of the proper course to be
taken in public business.   Church and town had to all intents and
purposes been but two facets of the same society and a crime
against one was a moral offense within the jurisdiction of the other.
Disputes between town residents had been settled amicably by
arbitration within the church, without recourse to law and courts.
It was in this atmosphere that a general meeting of the town in
1635 ordered that "none of the members of this congregation or
inhabitants among us shall sue one another at lawe before that Mr.
Henry Vane and the twoe Elders Mr. Thomas Ollyver and
Thomas Leveritt have had the hearing and desyding of the cause
if they cann"; that Cotton and his fellow ministers, at the behest of
the magistrates, debated a written code for the commonwealth and
proceeded to frame one which envisioned the towns of Massachusetts as the tribes of Israel reincarnate.[38]

In subsequent years, the church still gave advice.   But a fine
line was being drawn between sacral and secular: "The government
of the Church is as the Kingdome of Christ is, not of this world,
but spirituall and heavenly," Cotton wrote in 1640; "the power
of the keyes is far distant from the power of the sword."   Church
and state in Massachusetts were set about the same task: "The
Establishment of pure Religion, in doctrine, worship, and government, according to the word of God: As also the reformation of
all corruptions in any of these."   Hence the ministers, in whose
care the word of God was placed, could and did press for "sweet
and wholesom laws" and "civil punishments upon the willfull opposers and disturbers" of the church; an observer could laud
"Moyses and Aaron ... magistrate and minister, in church and
common[wealth]" walking "hand in hand, discountenancing and

Answer of the Elders of the Severall Churches, 20; Cotton, _Grounds and Ends of
the Baptisme of the Children_, 161-63.
    38. "Boston Records," 5; "How Far Moses Judicialls Bind Mass," Mass. Hist.
Soc., _Proceedings_, 2d Ser., 16 (1902) 280-84; John Cotton, _An Abstract of Laws
and Government_ ... (London, 1655), _passim_.

punishinge sinne in whomsoever, and standinge for the praise of them that doe well." But for the things of this world—"the disposing of mens goods or lands, lives or liberties, tributes, customes, worldly honors, and inheritances"—"in these the Church submitteth, and referreth it self to the civill state."[39]

The arbitration of disputes within the church continued throughout the period, an elaborate machinery being erected for that purpose. Indeed, Cotton continued to teach that to go to law against a member of the church was "a defect of brotherly love." "*Know ye not* (saith he)," quoting Corinthians, "that *the Saints shall judge the world? yea the Angels?* how much more the things of this life?"[40] Yet the church did not, could not, extend its jurisdiction to non-members; its arbitration was of necessity confined to disputes between members, and even members tended to ignore the facilities of the church, or dissatisfied by its decisions they appealed to law. And while the church continued to enforce morality, its effectiveness was limited to its communicants. Robert Keayne was admonished for overpricing his goods, but John Coggan was not; Richard Waite was excommunicated for excessive drinking, but his partner in wine, Lesly Gunton, did not come under the purview of the church; Ann Hudson was beyond the church's displeasure, though Henry Dawson, excommunicated for his "wanton dallyance" with her, was not. So adamant was the church in enforcing morality on its members that in 1645 it sent for William Letherland, a Hutchinsonian exile who had not been formally dismissed from the First Church, to answer charges of committing adultery with his maid in Aquidneck, excommunicating him when he failed to appear. But a murderer about to be

39. Cotton, *Way of the Churches of Christ in New England*, 19, 50; *idem*, *Keyes of the Kingdom of Heaven*, 50; *idem*, *A Brief Exposition of the Whole Book of Canticles*, 251; John Wiswall to George Rigby, Sept. 27, 1638, Historical Manuscript Division, *The Manuscripts of the Duke of Roxburghe; Sir H. H. Campbell, bart.; The Earl of Strathmore; and the Countess Dowager of Seafield* (London, 1894), 56. The line was not always observed, yet its trespass by the ministers brought sharp reaction from laymen such as Winthrop. See below, chap. 9, pp. 258-59.

40. Cotton, *Way of the Churches of Christ in New England*, 18; *idem*, *Keyes of the Kingdom of Heaven*, 46; I Cor. 6:20. In 1640 there was an attempt to obtain a law giving the church original jurisdiction over civil cases between church members and criminal actions against a member. The effort failed. See Lechford, *Plain Dealing*, 34-36; *Winthrop's Journal*, II, 15.

turned off the gallows' ladder received neither censure nor comfort from the church he had not joined; he was only an example of the sinful depths to which an unregenerate might sink. "There is not any minister or any of our Churches can usurpe Pastorall authoritie" over the stranger resident among us, Cotton wrote; "nor can such a man expect any Ministers watchfulnesse over him as his Minister unless . . . he give himself to them [the church] and professe his subjection to the Gospel of Christ amongst them."[41]

The church might meet the challenge of a rapidly growing and heterogeneous population by maintaining artificial signs of conformity—conversion and church membership—and disregarding all who failed to comply. So too, from the standpoint of political activity, could the commonwealth, which attempted to adhere to church membership as a prerequisite for freemanship despite the growing disparity between the number of freemen and the number of adult males. But the town of necessity had to establish a framework by which it could deal with those who, newly arrived or newly freed from obligatory service, demanded its rights and privileges while refraining or being barred from church membership. Hence the town gradually assumed to itself the right to judge the character of would-be residents in line with that English tradition which refused to allow a newcomer "to take up his dwelling in the vill, without the express permission of the community."[42]

As early as 1635 the town began screening newcomers, a town ordinance of that year requiring the approval of the town's authorities for any sale of land from an established settler to a "stranger." In March 1636 the town empowered the newly created selectmen to oversee "all Comers in unto us," the selectmen subsequently prescribing that "noe Townesman shall entertaine any strangers into theire houses for above 14 days, without leave" from them. At the same time the pressure of an ever-growing population brought about the abandonment of the fiction that linked land and church membership. Commonwealth law recognized in 1635, as it had not in 1634, the ownership of land by non-

41. First Church Records under dates of Nov. 26 and Jan. 13, 1639, July 6, and Aug. 3, 1645; Cotton, *Way of the Churches of Christ in New England*, 63.
42. C. F. Adams, "The Genesis of the Massachusetts Town," Mass. Hist. Soc., *Proceedings*, 2d Ser., 7 (1892), 202n; Haskins, *Law and Authority in Early Massachusetts*, 78.

freemen, while in 1636 the town gave up the policy of granting land only to those who were, or would eventually become, church members, making it available to newcomers and freed servants "upon the usual Condition of inoffensive Carryage." Similarly, the transfer of land from established settlers to newcomers was being approved on the basis of the "inoffensive Carryage" of the purchaser.[43]

These acts in effect created a new status, that of "inhabitant," a resident who was not necessarily a church member or freeman, but nevertheless possessed the broad rights and privileges of a citizen of the town. At its inception, inhabitantship was tied to the land—indeed, it was conferred initially by virtue of the grant of land itself[44]—the town attempting to preserve at least a part of the earlier equating of citizenship, church membership, and land ownership. All admitted during the early years were expected to receive from the town or by purchase plots both on and off the peninsula and to make use of them, building their houses on one and cultivating the other. Yet just as some men preferred to live on the land and thus gave rise to the peripheral villages, some men preferred to avoid large holdings. An artisan such as carpenter Thomas Joy was too busy with his trade to assume the responsibility of farm lands; he was content with house, workshop, and sawpit on the peninsula, from which base he led his crews of hired and indentured servants to all the towns around the harbor to work. Laborers such as William Herrick, out of design or financial necessity, refused even a house lot on Shawmut and rented their houses, or lodged in the homes of others.[45] For a while the town attempted to enforce the tie between the land and its residents, the selectmen ordering in 1638 that "none shall sell their houses, but with some parte of their great Allottments," and as late as 1640, in the case of carpenter John Palmer, they made admission to inhabitantship conditional on obtaining "an house, or land to sett an house upon" on the basis that it was "not proper to allowe a man an Inhabitant Withou[t] habitation." Landless laborers were

43. "Boston Records," 5, 9, 10, 15.
44. For example, the case of William Mawer, *ibid.*, 12, 31, 51.
45. *Ibid.*, 16, 37; "Boston Book of Possessions," 176, 177; *Lechford Notebook*, 283-85, 286.

discouraged by the enforcement of earlier laws forbidding the townsmen's hiring any who had no settled place of residence.[46]

Just as the attempt to maintain a unity between town and church had been futile, so too was the attempt to maintain a correlation between town and property owners. The growing segment of the population without land could not long be excluded. Herrick, for example, still a renter, was admitted an inhabitant in January 1639; laborer Henry Dawson, who was co-renter of Owen Roe's house, lot, and three acre garden for nine pounds a year, was admitted in January 1641.[47] As the second decade advanced, as the town land diminished and less and less was available for distribution, as the town became more and more a place for crafts and merchandising, the link between land and town citizenship disappeared entirely. Men were admitted "an inhabitant," "a townesman," or "to dwell in the town"—and the three terms were used interchangeably—without regard to house or holdings. Yet even though divorced from the land, inhabitantship was still a special status, one formally conferred by the selectmen in a specific act entered into the records after a due consideration of the character and quality of the applicant. At times, such consideration could take months; Edward Arnold, for example, was "taken into Consideration" in January 1641 and finally admitted in November.[48]

Having emerged in connection with the land, inhabitantship brought to the individual (in early theory) no other privilege than, as John Cotton expressed it, the "freedome of commerce and inheritance of such land as the generall courte or the severall townes wherein they dwell shall allot unto them."[49] But in actuality various adjuncts to the right to hold land were initially conferred with inhabitantship. Most directly associated was the privilege of

46. "Boston Records," 34, 51; *Assistants' Records*, II, 79.

47. "Boston Records," 37, 58; *Lechford Notebook*, 286; "Aspinwall Notarial Records," 35-36. Cf. the inhabitants admitted and lands granted in "Boston Records," augmenting the latter with indications of land in "Boston Book of Possessions" and *Suffolk Deeds*.

48. "Boston Records," 58, 63.

49. Cotton, *Abstract of Laws and Government*, as reprinted in Hutchinson, comp., *Collection of Original Papers Relative to Massachusetts*, 165. Hutchinson printed the work under the heading "An Abstract of the Laws of New England," the erroneous title of the London, 1641 ed.: *An Abstract of the Lawes of New England, as They Are Now Established* . . . .

grazing cattle on town land—"commonage"—and until 1646 all "those who are admitted . . . to be inhabitants" were considered to "have equall Right of Commonage in the towne." The right to gather hay from the ungranted marshes of the town was originally included, but the scarcity of marshland quickly forced a limitation. From 1637 on, only a few specified inhabitants were given permission to mow town land, and by 1646 the town was openly renting its marshland on a yearly basis.[50] Participation in town government was clearly associated with inhabitantship, too, though the commonwealth law limited such to freemen.

Confusion marks the freemanship law on the town level. Despite the fact that church and town were no longer synonymous, that a distinct town citizenship was emerging, the general government continued to view the body politic in terms of church members and freemen. The law of 1635 restricting the town electorate to freemen was followed by others. In September 1636 the General Court established representation on the basis of the number of freemen in the towns; the following month, the Court gave the freemen of the towns control over workmen's wages and bound all non-freemen to their decisions. The "Body of Liberties" of 1641 —the commonwealth's first code of laws—placed in the freemen's hands "full power" to choose deputies to the General Court and selectmen of the town and "make such by laws and constitutions as may concerne the wellfare of their Towne," the non-freemen being bound to abide by their laws and decisions.[51] When it became clear that freemanship did not offer enough privileges to compensate for the onerous duties entailed—for officeholding was time consuming and occasionally expensive and in law only freemen were to hold office—the commonwealth attempted to force the qualified but recalcitrant church member to assume his responsibilities. In May 1643 the General Court ordered that with regard to "members that refuse to take their freedom, the churches should be writ unto, to deale with them"; subsequently, in 1647, inasmuch as there were "within this jurisdiction many members of churches who, to exempt themselves from all publike service in the common

50. "Boston Records," 16ff, 88ff.
51. Colony Records, I, 178, 183; "The Body of Liberties. 1641," in William H. Whitmore, A Bibliographical Sketch of the Laws of the Massachusetts Colony from 1630 to 1686 (Boston, 1890), 47-48, hereafter cited as "Body of Liberties."

wealth, will not come in to be made freemen," it ruled that all adult male church members, except servants, be considered free-men and required to take office when called upon.[52]

And yet there was a clear and regular ignoring of the law. The Court itself, in 1636, empowered "the inhabitants" of the towns—not just the freemen—to demolish houses built without local permission; "the Townes . . . by orderly agreement amonge themselves" (no mention of freemen) were charged with the election of certain judicial officers in the "Body of Liberties." That code, again, implied that town meetings consisted only of freemen, one section stipulating that "if any man shall behave himselfe offensively at any Towne meeting, the rest of the freemen then present, shall have power to sentence him for his offence"; but in another section it recognized that any man, "Inhabitant or for-reiner, free or not free," could attend any court, council, or town meeting and propose measures "in convenient time, due order, and respectful manner." Among the militiamen there was an outright expansion of the suffrage, the Court enfranchising both freemen and non-freemen for the selection of trained-band officers in 1637.[53] A general failure to maintain the division between free and non-free within the town is shown in the Court's penalizing of towns-men for participating in illegal elections. Newbury's freemen were fined six pence apiece in 1636 "for chuseing and sending to this Court a deputy which was noe freeman"; Concord's freemen and "those that were not free, which had a hand in the undewe election of Mr Flint" were fined six shillings eight pence each in 1638; a general law of 1643 established a standard fine of ten pounds to be levied upon "any man that is not free, putting in any vote" for "the choyce of any officer." George Bowers of Cam-bridge, haled before the General Court "for putting in a vote on the day of election for Governor (he being no freeman)," readily acknowledged his guilt, but added that he had been voting "every yeare since he came into these parts."[54]

Boston's town meeting throughout the period gives every indi-

52. *Colony Records,* II, 38, 208; Winslow, *New-Englands Salamander,* in Mass. Hist. Soc., *Collections,* 3d Ser., 2 (1830), 139.

53. *Colony Records,* I, 168, 188; "Body of Liberties," 35, 45; Brown, "Free-manship in Puritan Massachusetts," *Amer. Hist. Rev.,* 59 (1954), 870.

54. *Colony Records,* I, 174, 221, II, 48, III, 279.

cation of being an open body. Participation of non-freemen was not at all uncommon, although the town records, by their nature, indicate only cases of officeholding. William Hibbens, for example, arriving in Boston late in 1638, was admitted an inhabitant in May 1639 and elected a selectman in December, yet he was not admitted a freeman until May 1640, and merchant Thomas Fowle, admitted to inhabitantship in 1639 and elected a selectman in 1645, was never recorded as a freeman.[55] That non-freemen were a part of the periodic gatherings of the town in the meetinghouse, contributing to the discussion and voting, can be assumed from the success of such non-freeman candidates in the balloting, and from isolated entries in the records, that of 1636, for example, whereby the secession of Mount Wollaston was declared to be dependent upon "the consent of this Towne's inhabitants." Moreover, the usual description of a town meeting was that of "a Generall meeting upon Publique notice or Warning," a phrase which takes on added meaning when the exceptions are considered. For example, the town in describing the meeting of November 6, 1637, and fearing that any technical error in the election would result in the exclusion of its Hutchinsonian deputies from a hostile General Court, carefully noted in the record that "att a meeting this day, upon particular notice, the Freemen" met for the election.[56] Thomas Lechford, whose descriptions of the conduct of affairs in the town at the turn of the decade are invaluable, summed it up. No friend of a mass electorate, he lashed out against the "electorie courses" in the commonwealth, lauding the possibilities of riches in New England "if that popular elections destroy us not."[57]

As it so often does, the law trailed the fact and it was not until 1647 that the commonwealth formally acknowledged the political activity of the town inhabitant (though the matter had been considered in 1644 and again in 1646). "Taking into consideration the useful ... abilities of divers inhabitants amongst us, which are not freemen, which, if improved to publike use, the affaires of this common wealth may be the easier carried on end, in the serverall

55. Cf. the admission of inhabitants and elections to office in "Boston Records" and the freemen lists in *Colony Records*.
56. "Boston Records," 14, 20, 35.
57. Lechford, *Plain Dealing*, 131, 143.

townes," the Court declared that henceforth it would be lawful for the freemen of the towns "to make choyce of such inhabitants ... to have their vote in the choyce of the select men for towne affaires, asseasment of rates, and other prudentials proper" and to hold certain town offices, including that of selectman although a majority of the selectmen had always to be freemen. The only restrictions were that those admitted to town suffrage must have taken the "oath of fidelity to this government," must have reached the age of twenty-four (reduced to twenty-one by the following year), and that they must not be under sentence "for any evil carriage against the government, or commonwealth, or churches."[58] Participation in commonwealth elections, as distinct from town elections, was still limited in law to freemen, and non-freemen continued to be barred from major offices. But the fine distinction drawn could not be held to; the town meeting—at which, until the 1650's, both town and commonwealth officers were chosen— retained its air of openness. A committee of the General Court protested in 1655 that everyone, including "scotch servants, Irish negers and persons under one and twenty years," was voting.[59]

Participation in public affairs, the right to live and work in the town, and, until the mid-1640's, land and commonage—these were the privileges of the town, and they were shared alike by Boston's freemen and inhabitants, church members and non-members. But the freedom of the town did not, in law, include the freedom of the commonwealth. The general government, concerned with the purity of the state, clung steadfastly (if not always effectively) to a definition of commonwealth citizenship in terms of the church, attempting to enforce the laws which limited commonwealth suffrage and office to the freemen while encouraging the sometimes reluctant church members to seek the privilege of freemanship. Nor did the freedom of the town include the freedom of the church. Concerned with its internal purity and that of its visible

58. *Colony Records*, II, 197; *Winthrop's Journal*, II, 163-64, 271-72; Max Farrand, ed., *The Laws and Liberties of Massachusetts; Reprinted From the Copy of the 1648 Edition in the Henry E. Huntington Library* (Cambridge, Mass., 1929), 50-51.

59. Dan[iel] Gookin, Rich[ard] Russell, Thomas Savage, Francis Norton, and Roger Clap to the General Court, *ca.* 1655, MS Photostats, Box 7, Mass. Hist. Soc. Lib.

saints, tending more and more to formality, the church and its Levitical guardians were a part of, but apart from, the total community. The result was a tripartite division of the town, some men being inhabitants, freemen, and church members; others being inhabitants and church members; still others being mere inhabitants. In these distinctions was a denial of that fundamental unity which Winthrop had spoken of aboard the *Arbella,* the one community to which all belonged "as members of the same body."

VII

"BOSTON IN NEW ENGLAND"

IF THE CRUMBLING of the Winthropian ideal is to be seen in roughly the first decade of settlement—in the dispersal, the land system, the church, and in the legal distinctions arising—it is even more clearly discernible in Boston in the second. The very fact of the town's central position in the commonwealth with a concomitant prosperity and commercial activity, a preoccupation of the Bostonians with their own town rather than the community of towns which made up the commonwealth, and an internal fragmentation completed the destruction of the ideal, at least in this one town. And while no one of these factors was unique to the second decade—indeed, each had its origins in the first—the full force of each and their cumulative impact were features of the forties.

From the very beginning, the geographic position of Shawmut separated Boston from the other towns of Massachusetts. William Wood had noted it: the peninsula thrust out into deep water, the focal point of the major waterways along which most of the commonwealth's first towns were built. Merchantmen visiting the new settlement realized it too, and made Boston (and to a lesser extent its sister town Charlestown) their port of call. The commonwealth government was aware of it, noting in 1632 that the town was "the fittest place for publique meeteings of any place in the Bay."[1] Economically and politically Boston was to become the capital first of the commonwealth and subsequently, to all intents and purposes, of New England as a whole. In consequence it was to have a vitality and excitement, a wealth and prosperity which other towns lacked.

1. *Assistants' Records*, II, 28.

The paraphernalia of government were very quickly lodged in the town, for from the first year—when Winthrop moved across the river from Charlestown—the governor almost invariably resided there. During the nineteen-year period before his death, Winthrop was governor for eleven years, and for only five years of this period was the office held by a resident of another town.[2] And inasmuch as the commonwealth lacked a statehouse, the political center was the governor's home. In it the lay and ministerial leaders gathered for informal conferences, as on May 1, 1632, when they met through the day and on into the night discussing the agenda of the forthcoming General Court and anticipating the problems which might arise. To it came celebrated visitors: barbaric Indian chieftains such as Miantunnomoh of the Narragansetts, who visited Governor Vane in 1636 (Winthrop carefully noting that the chief and his sachems "dined by themselves in the same room where the governor dined" while his retinue were "sent to the inn"); prisoners such as Rhode Island's self-styled "Professor of Christian Mysteries," Samuel Gorton, led in chains through Boston's streets to an audience in Winthrop's great hall; the elegant representatives of Charles D'Aulnay, Lieutenant General of French Acadia, who wandered about Winthrop's gardens and read the Governor's books during a moment away from affairs of state in 1646. From the governor's home in the early years, a great part of the commonwealth's funds were disbursed; prior to 1633, for example, Winthrop as governor spent more money on commonwealth business than did the Bay's treasurer.[3] Even on those few occasions when the governor resided elsewhere, public business remained centered in Boston: "I did hope upon the discharge of my place, to have good leysure," Winthrop wrote an English correspondent in 1634, "but our new Governor (my brother Dudley) dwelling out of the way" in Cam-

2. Thomas Dudley (1634, 1640, 1645); John Haynes (1635); John Endecott (1644).

3. *Winthrop's Journal*, I, 76ff, 192-93, II, 286; Samuel Gorton, *Simplicities Defense against Seven-Headed Policy. or Innocency Vindicated, Being Unjustly Accused* ... (London, 1646), reprinted in Peter Force, comp., *Tracts and Other Papers Relating Principally to ... the Colonies in North America* ..., 4 vols. (Washington, 1836-46), IV, 62; William Pynchon, "My account of Receipts and Payments while I was in the Treasurer's Office, Anno 1632 and 1633," "Pincheon [*sic*] Papers," Mass. Hist. Soc., *Collections*, 2d Ser., 8 (1819), 230-35.

bridge "I am still as full of Companye and business as before."[4]
By the 1650's so well established was Boston as the official residence of the governor that the General Court ordered that who-
ever might be elected to the office must make his home in or within
"fowre or five" miles of the town "so he may be the more serv-
iceable to the country in gen[era]ll, both in respect of straungers
and other wise."[5]

Following the governor came the Court of Assistants—the
governor's council, the commonwealth's sole legislative body before 1634, and its busiest judicial body throughout the period. It
was both court of appeals and superior court and, in the latter role,
tried all major criminal and civil actions. Not all the assistants
lived in the town, for almost immediately it became a mark of distinction for a community to boast an assistant, and the competition to attract them to take up residence in a given town was fierce.
But the majority had their homes either in Boston or immediately
around the Bay, and from the early 1640's those nearest the town
constituted a special commission to handle affairs which were
beyond the authority of the governor and yet needed action before
the next regular meeting of the full body or the General Court.[6]
The "beadle," a company officer whose duty it was to serve the
governor's needs, followed Winthrop to Boston, too, and soon the
office was transformed into that of marshal with broad duties involving all phases of commonwealth life, from police work and
process serving to tax collecting and road mending.[7]

As the commonwealth evolved, so too did Boston's public
function. Vital news from abroad was first made public in the
town. Thus William Hibbens, returning in 1642 from a commonwealth errand to England, presented "a public declaration to the

4. Winthrop to Sir Simonds D'Ewes, July 21, 1634, *Winthrop Papers*, III,
171; *Winthrop's Journal*, I, 125.
5. *Colony Records*, III, 373-74.
6. Samuel Whiting and Thomas Cobbett to John Winthrop and Thomas
Dudley, Jan. 8, 1638/39, *Winthrop Papers*, IV, 94-95; *Colony Records*, II, 31,
32, 46; *Winthrop's Journal*, II, 176. The Court of Assistants met in Charlestown in Aug. and Sept. 1630, thereafter in Boston and only occasionally elsewhere until June 1634 when it followed Governors Dudley and Haynes to
Newtown (Cambridge). By June 1636 it was back at Boston where it remained
except for a brief interlude during the Hutchinsonian affair.
7. The evolution of the marshal's office can be traced in *Assistants' Records*,
II, and *Colony Records*, I and II.

church in Boston, of all the good providences of the Lord towards him in his voyage to and fro"; the Reverend John Knowles, sent to Virginia to organize a church, returned in 1643 with letters from his congregation "which were openly read in Boston at a lecture."[8] The commonwealth prison was built in the town, and the gallows; levies collected by the various towns at the behest of the general government were made payable to the commonwealth treasurer there; a central location for dispatching or receiving letters from across the sea was established; and provision was made for advertising lost articles in the town's marketplace. Public records were kept in Boston, the General Court in 1647 providing "a stronge presse" six feet high, five feet long, and three feet broad, "well bound, with 3 strong locks" for their safekeeping.[9] The commonwealth's notaries public were there, Stephen Winthrop, William Aspinwall, and (unofficially at the turn of the decade) Thomas Lechford. When counties were formally established in the early 1640's, Boston became the shire town for Suffolk and the seat of government for those areas claimed by the commonwealth to the southward—Shawomet and Pawtuxet in Rhode Island, as well as Block Island; consequently more courts and records and officers were located there, including (until 1648) those for nearby Middlesex County, which was separate from Suffolk in little more than name.[10]

But the excitement and vibrancy which went with being the capital were associated above all with the General Court, the commonwealth's legislative body after 1634 and a judicial body having jurisdiction in cases in which justice could not be obtained "in any other Court."[11] Two, three, and four times a year, sometimes more frequently, it convened in the town, bringing with it a host of members, petitioners, litigants, and witnesses from all over the Bay.[12] At first it met as a single body in the First Church, the

8. *Winthrop's Journal*, II, 71, 94.
9. *Colony Records*, II, 208.
10. *Ibid.*, I, 217, 281, II, 214, 227, III, 201, 275; *Winthrop's Journal*, I, 235, 236, 300; *Assistants' Records*, II, 27; Richard Le Baron Bowen, *Massachusetts Records* (Rehoboth, Mass., 1957), 39.
11. *Colony Records*, II, 17.
12. The General Court first met at Boston Oct. 19, 1630, and stayed there until Dudley was elected governor. It met at Newtown from Sept. 1634 until May 1636, when it returned to Boston with Governor Vane. It moved to Newtown

governor and assistants assuming the elders' and deacons' seats, the deputies, from each of the towns, in those of the congregation. Boston's own deputies—elected earlier in town meeting[13]—took places near the front, for the towns assumed precedence according to their "antiquity." To the side, but in places of honor, sat the ministers, Cotton and Wilson from Boston and those of other towns observing and advising. Much of the actual work of the Court was done in closed committees and private gatherings at the Winthrop home or elsewhere. But often during the early years the Court met in public session and carried on its business while spectators watched from every corner. Scandals, both public and private, brought gasps from the audience, as in 1639 when Nathaniel Eaton took his place at the long table "where all offenders do usually stand" to answer charges of malfeasance in his administration of Harvard College: scholars cudgeled, whipped "twenty and thirty stripes at a time," and fed "nothing but porridge and pudding, and that very homely." Public debates evoked partisan feelings: How far did the authority of the assistants extend? Should the commonwealth have a written code of law, or should crime and punishment depend upon the extempore judgments of the magistrates? Should the commonwealth intervene in the squabbles between rival Frenchmen for hegemony in what was to become Nova Scotia? After 1644 the public debates were less frequent, the Court having separated into its component parts— deputies and assistants—and forming two distinct houses. Occasionally the two met together to hear exceptional cases: in 1645, for example, when before "a great assembly of people," they held public hearings to ascertain the truth or falsehood of charges brought against Winthrop for exceeding the authority of his office, a trial which ended with Winthrop's exoneration and his "little speech" on liberty. For the most part, however, the two houses met separately and all-too-often behind closed doors, the

again in May 1637, remaining through the Hutchinsonian controversy. In May 1638 its meetings were returned to Boston. By a law of 1636 (*Colony Records,* I, 170) the Court was to meet twice a year—May and October—but until the end of the period under discussion the law was ignored.

13. Before 1642 the deputies were elected immediately preceding each General Court; thereafter they were normally elected in the spring and served in all courts for the next twelve months. The change can be followed in *Colony Records,* I and II, and "Boston Records," *passim.*

deputies in the meetinghouse and the assistants in a nearby home or tavern. But rumors of legislative din and strife seeped out.[14]

If it was the Easter Court, the excitement was even more intense, for that was the Court of Election, when commonwealth officers were selected. There were no political parties or campaigns, but there were factions energetically at work.[15] There was the election sermon, a high point of the year's oratory although it sometimes degenerated into political caviling.[16] And there were the crowds, not just the deputies and assistants, the ministers, and the comparatively few out-of-town visitors who appeared for the General Court, but freemen from all parts of the Bay, come to cast their ballots. Not all made the trip. Many were kept away by their everyday affairs, for this was the planting season, and men who made their living from the land had much to do; others were uninterested, the trip to Boston by horse or boat from the outlying towns being hard and costly. And from the mid-1630's, one could vote by proxy, casting one's vote at home and having it carried to Boston by the town's deputies. The proxy system, permissive at its inception, appealed to the leadership, to whom the crowds and disorders accompanying the election in Boston were a constant source of annoyance, and there were periodic attempts to make the use of proxies mandatory during the 1640's. But all were unsuccessful; "an infringement of their liberties," the townsmen said.[17] Hence, however many stayed at home and quietly voted in their country towns, enough came to Boston to create a circus air on election day.

The Bostonians themselves had no need for proxies and joined the throng to vote individually. Thomas Lechford described the scene.[18] The magistrates, ministers, and simple freemen lined up

14. *Winthrop's Journal*, I, 312-13, II, 233ff; *Colony Records*, I, 145, II, 98, III, 2, 7, 158; Israel Stoughton to John Stoughton, *ca.* May 1635, endorsed "A relation concerning some occurences in New England," Mass. Hist. Soc., *Proceedings*, 1st Ser., 5 (1862), 138.

15. For example, *Winthrop's Journal*, I, 302ff, II, 3, 36, 49, 323.

16. Lindsay Swift, "The Massachusetts Election Sermons," Col. Soc. Mass., *Publications*, 1 (1895), 388-451. See the 1638 sermon in *New England Historical and Genealogical Register*, 24 (1870), 361-66; others in *Winthrop's Journal*, II, 36-37, 97-98.

17. *Winthrop's Journal*, II, 327. The evolving election procedures can be followed in *Colony Records*, I, II, III.

18. In his *Plain Dealing*, 59-61. There is no indication that Boston made use of proxies before 1653.

before the side door of the meetinghouse and one by one entered to deliver their votes for governor, carefully laying the paper ballots upon the table before the incumbent. The law was quite specific: "open or once folded, not twisted or rolled up, that so they may be the sooner and surer perused."[19] Silently, tensely, the crowd followed the count as it progressed, the ballots cast at Court being added to the proxies handed in by the deputies. Sometimes the contest was close, as in 1641 when Richard Bellingham won by a majority of six,[20] and at such times the jubilation of victory and dejection of defeat followed the proclamation of the new governor. But there was more to do; celebration and consolation must wait. Once again the voters lined up at the side door and entered to cast ballots, this time for deputy governor. Again the process was repeated as the old governor propounded the name of each candidate for assistant, the freemen entering to submit either a blank ballot signifying nay to the name called, or a marked ballot signifying approval. (White and black beans respectively were used in the 1640's.)[21] There was little contest over the assistants, for but a single slate was offered the voters— normally the existing members of the Court. And until the turn of the decade, no provision was made for formal nomination, the old governor merely propounding those names he thought best and stopping when the requisite number had been elected. Thereafter, although an elaborate "primary" system was devised in which the candidates were chosen in advance by the freemen meeting in their towns, only that number of candidates to be elected (usually seven) were nominated, and the law specified that none but these could be propounded on election day. Not until 1649 was provision made for the nomination of more candidates than offices, and even then those incumbents receiving any number of ballots in the primary were declared nominated and given "precedency of all others ... on the day of election." Consequently, the regular re-election of the leaders was assured.[22]

19. Farrand, ed., *Laws and Liberties of Massachusetts*, 20-21, quoting a 1647 statute.
20. *Winthrop's Journal*, II, 36.
21. *Colony Records*, II, 42.
22. *Winthrop's Journal*, I, 150; *Colony Records*, I, 293, 308, II, 21, 37, 87, 175, 210, 286-87, III, 86, 177.

Lastly the secondary officers were chosen—secretary, treasurer, major general of the militia, commissioners to represent Massachusetts in the New England Confederation. The list of such officers steadily lengthened as government expanded.[23] The sense of contest returned, for nomination and election to such lesser offices were subject to the political jockeying of the commonwealth's cliques and counter-cliques, as that of governor and deputy governor had been. Yet the prizes were smaller, and the excitement less. Perhaps some of the visitors and townsmen were already drifting away as the day's last act was played, the new governor rising to deliver a short speech, and the successful candidates who were present being solemnly inaugurated into their offices, each taking suitable oath before his immediate predecessor, or, in his absence, "the fittest instrument at hand": "You do here sweare by the liveing God, that you will truely indeavor (according to yor best skill) to carry and demeane yor selfe in yor place for the said time, according to the lawes of God, and of this land, for the advancement of the gospell, and the good of the people."[24]

The spring dusk would be settling as the last oaths were administered, for the voting, beginning about noon, was a lengthy process; quickly what was left of the crowd would disperse, some to their homes, others to the taverns, the leaders to a traditional supper at the old governor's. Undoubtedly there were sighs of relief as the leaders sat over their Madeira, the pungent, full-bodied wine they loved so dearly. Another election was over! Then to business, for the General Court would commence its regular meeting the next day.

For Boston, being the capital meant not just excitement, but prosperity as well, since money from all sections of the Bay commonwealth—a part of the toll which government exacts from its citizens for services rendered—poured into the town and the pockets of its people. The magnitude of this toll and its diffusion

23. In 1649 the General Court noted "that the multiplication of the choyce of officers on election day" was growing "to such a number as may proove burthensome." *Colony Records,* II, 285.

24. From the 1645 Assistants' oath, *Colony Records,* I, 356; [Mather], *Church-Government and Church-Covenant Discussed, In an Answer of the Elders of the Severall Churches,* 67.

through the town can be sensed only in the multitude of petty transactions found in public and private records.[25]

As a matter of policy, no official was required to bear his own expenses while on public business; hence the deputies and assistants attending General Court were reimbursed from the treasury, assistants receiving 3s 6d per day "for their dyot and lodging" from the time they left their homes until their return, deputies receiving 2s 6d.[26] The small sums accumulated into large totals. In 1645, for example, the General Court met from May 14 to July 10 (with but a one-week adjournment), approximately forty-five days at a cost to the commonwealth of 291li 7s 6d. So prolonged a session was extraordinary, but even a more normal ten-day session during the late 1630's and 1640's involved payments of about 65li to the participating members, between 150 and 250li a year. Most of the money was expended for food, the deputies and magistrates organizing formal "messes" in various establishments in the town at which they might eat. In the early 1640's, the mess was kept at Robert Turner's "Sign of the Anchor," the treasurer being ordered to pay him 100li for his services during a General Court session of 1644. For a brief period at mid-decade, James Penn operated the mess, but from 1647 through 1650 deputies and assistants dined separately, the lower house at Hugh Gunnison's King's Arms Tavern, the upper at William Phillips' wine shop. The lodgings of the members of the Court were similarly paid for. In 1645 the Widow Webb was ordered paid 5s 6d for lodging one deputy during the session; Goodwife Sherman, for lodging three deputies and three attendants (servants attending on the personal needs of their masters) was to be

25. The examples following in the text have been drawn for the most part from *Colony Records*, I, II, III; *Assistants' Records*, II, III; *Lechford Notebook*; "Aspinwall Notarial Records"; *Suffolk Deeds*; *Winthrop's Journal*; *Winthrop Papers*; miscellaneous financial reports such as that of William Pynchon in "Pincheon Papers," Mass. Hist. Soc., *Collections*, 2d Ser., 8 (1819), 230-35; sundry manuscripts in Mass. Archives; Misc. Bound and Photostat MSS collections of the Mass. Hist. Soc.; and among the holdings of the Office of the Clerk of the Supreme Judicial Court for Suffolk Co., Boston. Monetary expressions are used throughout but only as a convenience, for while taxes, fines, honoraria, expense payments, commercial transactions, and the like were recorded in pounds sterling, after 1640, when specie was scarce, the sums almost invariably represented the value of produce to be paid or exchanged—i.e., commodity money.

26. "Body of Liberties," 47; *Colony Records*, I, 228.

paid 1*li* 12*s* 6*d*; Goodwife Hagborne, 20*s*. Nor were the members of the General Court very close with commonwealth money. They regularly voted gratuities to the servants employed about their messes and lodgings, the "helpers" in Mrs. Sherman's house receiving 1 noble (6*s* 8*d*) in 1645, while the same year 20*s* were distributed among James Penn's "servants and helps," the Court specifying that "the present cook" receive 10*s* in recognition of their esteem for her art.[27]

It was not only the General Court. The governor initially received money to cover the extraordinary expenses of his office and from the mid-1640's an honorarium as partial compensation —1,549*li* 16*s* 8*d* during the years from 1630 through 1649, of which governors residing in Boston received 1,134*li* 3*s* 4*d*. Winthrop alone was voted payments of over 1,000*li* for his years in office. In addition, the governor held special meetings around the dinner or supper table at Turner's or one of the other inns, the commonwealth bearing the charge: 1*li* 11*s* 6*d* "for a dinner for the Magistrates and Elders, and some of the Deputies" at the conclusion of the May Court in 1643; 1*li* 5*s* 7*d* for a dinner for the governor, magistrates, selected deputies, and distinguished French visitors and attendants.[28] The commissioners of the United Colonies were similarly reimbursed by their various governments for the expenses of their periodic meetings in the town.

Jurymen, drawn from all the towns to sit in judgment in cases heard before the Great Quarter Court—the Court of Assistants meeting in its judicial role in March, June, September, and December—received compensation for their expenditures, as did those sitting on the twice-yearly grand juries at Boston, the former 3*s* per trial in 1635, 4*s* a day in 1650, the latter commensurately more as the senior body. Again small sums accumulated into large totals; the grand jury of 1635, for example, presented over one hundred cases for judgment, while the Great Quarter Court usually remained in session fifteen to twenty days a year by the end of the second decade. The expenses of the assistants and their personal attendants at the Court were paid, too. In 1643,

27. *Colony Records*, II, 116, 139.
28. "Accounts, 1643," in "Hutchinson Papers," Mass. Hist. Soc., *Collections*, 3d Ser., 1 (1825), 19.

one day's expenses, presumably at Turner's, amounted to 1*li* 18*s*
6*d*, the assistants receiving dinner, supper, "bread and beer and
fires." Turner's total bill, exclusive of lodgings, for three Great
Quarter Courts and two grand juries that year came to 26*li* 13*s*
6*d*.[29]

Not all the expenses at court were chargeable to the commonwealth. In civil suits successful litigants added personal costs to
damages payable by those who lost. Defendants summoned to
court by plaintiffs who failed to appear were regularly awarded
from the defaulters 4 to 10*s* in damages to cover their expenses.
Witnesses appearing in court were reimbursed, sometimes by the
Court itself, sometimes by the parties engaged in the proceedings,
and, in criminal cases, out of the fines levied: an Ipswich man
receiving 10*s* for his time and expense as a witness in 1635, three
witnesses receiving 5*s* each in 1639, ten witnesses receiving 2*s* a
day for their attendance at a 1641 trial. The awarding of costs
often effected no more than a transfer of money from one Bostonian's pocket to another, for the townspeople were quick to go
to law against each other. But fully half the recorded cases heard
before the Great Quarter Court involved non-Boston people.

To expenses must be added the compensation of commonwealth and county officers resident in Boston. As early as 1630
townsmen were on the public payroll. James Penn, the marshal
of the commonwealth through most of the first decade, received
5*li* 3*s* 4*d* in 1630, 8*li* in 1632, 20*li* in 1634, 40*li* in 1636, plus fees
paid him for his work (including 6*s* from each person he committed to the prison, which was in his charge), all in addition to
a house built at the public expense. Captain John Underhill,
one of three military advisors maintained at commonwealth expense through most of the 1630's and a Boston resident, received
the first year provisions, "howseroome," and a 31*li* 4*s* annual stipend, in addition to 6*li* 8*s* "to buy . . . howsholde stuffe, and for
helpe to washe brewe and bake." A second military advisor,
"surveyor of the ordinanc and cannouneere" Joist Weillust, received 10*li* annually until his return to Holland.[30] Similarly,
high public officials living in Boston (in addition to expenses and

29. *Ibid.*, 17.
30. *Assistants' Records*, II, 4, 5-6, 11.

honoraria) were rewarded for their service by grants of land; in 1646, moreover, governor, deputy governor, and assistants were partially exempted from public rates and in 1648 from all rates except those for the maintenance of the ministry, thus making available to them money they would normally pay in taxes.

Annual stipends became less important after the first few years, lesser officials receiving compensation in the form of established fees paid to them directly by the recipients of their services. Postmaster Richard Fairbanks received 1*d* for every letter left in his charge; the jailer (Richard Brackett in the late 1630's when the office was separated from that of marshal, William Wilson during the early 1640's, and George Munnings for the remainder of the period) was voted 13*li* 6*s* 8*d* a year in 1637, 15*li* in 1646, plus the fees to be collected from the prisoners for a variety of services, including supplying their food. Another Bostonian (Alexander Beck) was paid for caring for infirm inmates, while by 1647 two guards were found to be necessary and hired from the town at 3*s* a day. The public executioner (Thomas Bell in the 1640's) received fees for executing punishments according to the sentences of the courts. By 1637 fees accruing to the marshal were so lucrative that his stipend was reduced to 10*li*; a schedule of legal fees of that year provided that he could collect a minimum of 3*s* for each execution for debt, the maximum dependent upon how much he collected, 2*s* 6*d* for each attachment, and the same for every commitment to the prison. Should he have to travel beyond Boston to perform his duties, he could collect an additional 1*s* per mile in travel money (subsequently reduced to 6*d*). By the 1640's a deputy marshal was necessary, the jailer undertaking the duties and receiving the appropriate fees. The recorder was compensated on a similar fee basis, Stephen Winthrop, then William Aspinwall, receiving 6*d* or more for each will, inventory, or administration of estate recorded in the public records, 1*d* for each birth or death listed, and 6*d* for each deed or lease entered into the land records. Until the emergence of counties such fees were received in payment of legal actions or recorded entries from all parts of the commonwealth. But even as county administrations evolved, the fees of the deputy marshal and recorder at Boston were received from towns and villages throughout Suffolk County (southeastern Massachusetts as far as the Plymouth border) and Middlesex (central Massachusetts); only the northern towns—Salem, Ipswich, Newbury—escaped Boston's exactions in this regard. Demi-officials, too, received a part of the annual toll: Thomas Lechford, acting as a copyist and notary, collected 38*li* for his work during his first two years in the colony and was owed another 9*li*; notary William Aspinwall received two, three, and four times as much per year as the volume of commercial paper in need of notarization rose through the decade. Lawyers drifted into the town to settle near the primary courts throughout the 1640's. And there was the "Governor's Guard," a special body of six men attending his person at General Court until 1637, when a permanent guard of two men was established, to be maintained "at the charge of the country."[31]

Expense money paid directly to Boston's tavern and innkeepers, housewives, and servants, fees and stipends allowed Boston residents for public duties and so put into circulation in the town's economy, all amounted to only a part of the town's toll. Public buildings—the prison, the jailer's house, the fortifications on Castle Island in mid-harbor, which commonwealth funds built and in part maintained—were forever in need of repair, and Boston's carpenters and masons were generally given the task, at a price. And for every person attending a General or Great Quarter Court whose expenses were paid, there were others who received no money for their pains nor compensation for tavern bills at Gunnison's or Turner's—unsuccessful litigants, petitioners at the General Court, simple onlookers. Some of the money spent in the town originated there and was paid to the commonwealth government in the form of taxes and by the government in the form of stipends and expenses. But Boston got back far more than it gave.

How much was the aggregate of the flood of pounds, shillings, and pence? One can only estimate. Certainly it amounted to as much as 1,500*li* a year by the mid-1640's, less at an earlier date, more by 1650. The figure is conservative, but in terms of present-day purchasing power it can be compared to well over $150,000 a year channeled into the economy of a town numbering never more

31. *Colony Records,* I, 142, 209.

than three thousand people during the period, over $50 annually for every man, woman, and child.

Combined with its political position in quickening the economic life of the town and the tempo of its people was Boston's central place in the economy of the whole commonwealth, one based during the first decade upon the crowd of newcomers entering from England and in the second on the development of trade and commerce.

What the men of the Winthrop fleet anticipated in regard to the economy is vague. How were they to maintain themselves in New England? For over a century the northwestern waters of the Atlantic had been a thriving fishing area for Europeans of diverse nationalities, and fishing equipment was loaded aboard the vessels of the 1630 fleet. A profit from the fur trade could be expected, and in the first three years more than six hundred pounds of furs were gathered and sold. But dependence for success could not be put on either fish or fur, and when some in England objected to the venture on the grounds that "the place affordeth not comfortable meanes," Winthrop could only answer in terms of the land itself. "Whatsoever we stand in neede of is treasured up in the earth by the Creator, and to be fetched thense by the sweate of our browes: We must learne with Paull to want as well as to abounde; if we have foode and rayment (which are there to be had) we ought to be contented."[32]

Winthrop was, in part, prophetic, for the land was New England's greatest asset, "rich and fat" to old England's eyes.[33] During the first years the settlers found subsistence in it. They fell "to tearing up the Roots, and Bushes with their Howes; even such men as scarce ever set hand to labor before, men of good birth and breeding."[34] Before they had plows, they copied the hill agriculture of the Indians and grew corn, peas, and gourds in their garden plots; when plows arrived, they opened larger fields and planted English "corn"—barley, oats, wheat, rye. They

32. [John Winthrop], "Reasons to be considered for justifieinge the undertakeres of the intended Plantation in New England . . . [1629]," *Winthrop Papers*, II, 143-44. The reference is to Phil. 4:11-12.
33. Darrett B. Rutman, "The Pilgrims and Their Harbor," *Wm. and Mary Qtly.*, 3d Ser., 17 (1960), 168.
34. *Johnson's Wonder-Working Providence*, 85.

planted orchards and vineyards, took building material and wood
for their winter fires from the forests and marshes, grazed their
cattle on natural meadows.   Often in the first years there were
shortages and the colonists imported foodstuffs, but soon "the
Country came to feed its owne Inhabitants; and the people who
formerly were somewhat pincht with hunger, eat bread to the
full, having not onely for their necessity but also for their con-
veniency and delight."[35]   They were establishing themselves as
an agricultural people, and their towns as agricultural communities.   Dorchester was noted for its "Orchards and Gardens full
of Fruit-trees," Roxbury for its "fruitfull Fields and Gardens,
their Heard of Cowes, Oxen and other young Cattell of that kind
about 350," Ipswich as a "very good Land for Husbandry, where
Rocks hinder not the course of the Plow."   Even Boston found
its livelihood at first in the soil.[36]

By the mid-1630's, New England was a land of agricultural
surplus.   It was also a rapidly growing area as each year between
five and twenty ships arrived to unload a human cargo.   No ac-
curate figures of population growth are available, for as Winthrop
once wrote, "the number of our people, we never took any sur-
veigh of them, nor doe we intend it."[37]   But by a variety of
methods, one can arrive at fairly conclusive estimates.[38]   In 1630,
the Winthrop fleet carried about seven hundred people to the
Bay.   Other arrivals that first year made up the losses due to
deaths and desertions and, combined with the number of persons
already there, brought the total population to about one thousand.
In the succeeding three years, the arrival of newcomers was such
that the population was no larger than three thousand by the end
of 1633.   But by 1634 the difficulties of the first years—exaggerated reports of which had served to dissuade persons from
emigrating—had been largely overcome, while the Laudian attempt
to reform the English churches was well underway, driving nonconforming ministers and their most faithful followers to seek a

35. *Ibid.*, 182.
36. *Ibid.*, 69-70, 72, 96.
37. Winthrop to Sir Nathaniel Rich, May 22, 1634, *Winthrop Papers*, III,
166.
38. The accompanying chart visually depicts the growth of the commonwealth and town during the period.   See below "A Note on Sources and Methods"
for a full discussion of the methods used in compiling the data.

haven overseas. The population of the Bay swept upwards, jump-
ing to slightly over four thousand at the end of the year, then to
over six thousand by the end of 1635, when "a great scarcity of
Bread" developed "by reason of the multitude that came" and the
existing towns began to be "in some straites" to accommodate the
rush. During the ensuing year, in part because scarcities in Massachusetts revived fears in England that "the country cannot afford
subsistance for many people" and in part because of the beginning
of the exodus to the Connecticut River, there was a moderation of
the rate of growth.[39] But in 1637 it quickened again as some fifteen
hundred newcomers arrived, and in 1638 a record three thousand
swelled the total population of the Bay to just over eleven thousand.

This tremendous growth, combined with the agricultural

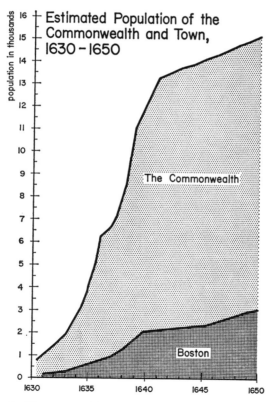

39. *Johnson's Wonder-Working Providence*, 108; Lucy Downing to John
Winthrop, *ca.* July 1636, *Winthrop Papers*, III, 279; *Winthrop's Journal*, I, 151.

surplus, engendered prosperity in the Bay.[40]   The newcomers
brought little in the way of material goods; as early as 1633,
Thomas Welde had advised his English congregation that "such
as are to come need bring no more or littele or no provision except mault."[41]   Whatever else they needed they could buy from
the already established settlers and so save themselves freightage.
There was Indian corn and wheat to see them through the first
year, timber with which to build, and seed and cattle to start life
anew.   Hence the emigrants transformed their English possessions into cash and arrived eager to transform that cash into new
possessions.   The older settlers readily obliged them and quickly
passed their cash on to English ship captains in exchange for pots
and pans, nails, cloth, plows, tools, and even luxuries.

Boston profited doubly in this cyclic economy.   It was, on the
one hand, the point of entry for the great migration from England.   The newcomers, with their baggage and goods, disem-
barked in the town; from it they set off to settle north and south
along the coast or in the interior.   It was the accepted pattern.
"I follow your Councell in coming to the Bay before I resolve
where to pitche," Emmanuel Downing wrote to Governor Winthrop as he prepared to depart old England for New in 1637; "I
pray helpe me to hire or buy some howse (soe as I may sell yt
againe if I shall remove)."[42]   Some of the new arrivals stayed
for a time before moving on.   Those from Braintree, Essex County, who arrived in 1632 as a part of Thomas Hooker's congregation, paused in Boston, temporarily took up land along the
south shore of the harbor, then moved on to Newtown; and the
250 settlers who arrived with Theophilus Eaton and John Davenport in June 1637 crowded into the homes and inns of the town
for a year's stay before leaving to found New Haven.   But most
moved quickly through the harbor area to join friends and relations already settled elsewhere, staying only a day or week in the
town.   However long they remained, wherever they went, they

40. The text following is based upon Darrett B. Rutman, "Governor Winthrop's Garden Crop: The Significance of Agriculture in the Early Commerce of
Massachusetts Bay," *Wm. and Mary Qtly.*, 3d Ser., 20 (1963), 396-415.

41. To the congregation at Terling, England, 1633, Col. Soc. Mass., *Publications*, 13 (1912), 130.

42. Letter of Nov. 21, 1637, *Winthrop Papers*, III, 512.

left a toll in Boston: a night's lodging, a meal, a first purchase in the New World. And more often than not, they returned to make additional purchases in the town. No one community being capable of meeting all the needs of its newcomers, resort had to be made to a central location where produce and cattle from all over the commonwealth were available. Boston's geographic position, the fact that it was the political capital, and the drawing power of John Cotton's Thursday lectures after 1633, all influenced selection of the town for this role, one recognized in 1634 when the Court of Assistants sanctioned a weekly "market" to be held each Lecture day.[43]

Furthermore, Boston was the entrepôt for English goods entering the commonwealth, arriving for the most part aboard the same vessels which brought the emigrants. In the spring, those in need of English goods began drifting into the town to await the first ships of the season. Each sail entering the harbor was a signal, and would-be purchasers crammed into dories and lighters, racing to be among the first aboard to enter a bid for needed items from the ship's inventory. Periodically the government tried to curb the chaos of the scene, aghast at the "loss of time, and drunkeness . . . people's running to the ships, and the excessive prices of commodities" resulting from the open bidding. In March 1635, merchants from each of the nine towns (John Coggshall from Boston) were appointed as exclusive agents to buy from the ships "all such commodityes as they shall judge to be useful for the country," selling them through a public magazine at no more than 15 per cent profit.[44] But it was futile and the act was repealed within four months. The generality objected to the scheme, the merchants appointed did not have cash enough to effect their monopoly, and the ship captains complained against the low prices resulting from the restrictions and openly disobeyed, landing their goods in the town itself for public sale. A year later an attempt was made to prohibit all trading until the ships' inventories were submitted to the governor. But this too failed.

43. *Winthrop's Journal*, I, 120; *Assistants' Records*, II, 40. Other markets would exist by 1638—Salem, Watertown, Dorchester—but by then Boston's economic leadership would be well established.

44. *Colony Records*, I, 141-42, 149; *Winthrop's Journal*, I, 152.

Not the law but the development of a merchant community in Boston ended the chaos. Men inclined toward commerce gravitated to the town because of the ships which stopped there. Thus John Coggan, brother of an Exeter merchant, abandoned Dorchester in 1633 and opened Boston's first shop, retailing directly and wholesaling to shopkeepers in the outlying towns; John Coggshall, familiar with trade through a variety of commercial activities in old England, moved to Boston from Roxbury in 1634. As residents of the town, such men avoided the expense of a specific trip to Boston, and being regularly in trade they could buy in bulk and drive out the smaller purchasers. Others arrived, some from London's commercial world, most with family ties or long-standing friendships among English merchants: the Hutchinsons (1633 and 1634), Robert Keayne (1635), Valentine Hill (1636), Edward Tyng (1636) and his brother William (1637), and Edward Shrimpton (1638). Given the prevailing economy, land was still an attractive investment; hence William Tyng was a large-scale purchaser of land in and around Boston. But the newcomers were quick to take advantage of commercial opportunities, and by their presence in Boston gave the town an additional edge in its surge to economic predominance. For men such as these could avoid the hurly-burly of the shipboard or quayside bidding, the high prices inherent in that system, the uncertainties of a cargo selected by a shipmaster or merchant who might never have been to New England and thus be ignorant of what was or was not desired. They could deal directly with their English connections, ordering the specific goods needed to maintain adequate stocks; and because they were known to their suppliers in England, they could ask for credit and obtain it, thus enlarging their operating capital effectively. As a result, by the end of the decade the ship-and-quayside auction was rapidly becoming a thing of the past. The Bostonians still bought from ships peddling their wares in the harbor; yet more and more they were relying on direct purchases from England, dispatching specie to meet their bills or, more often than not, accumulating larger and larger debts. The outlying towns, for their part, were buying their finished goods largely through the Bostonians, paying for them with cash entering the economy through the purchases of the newcomers.[45]

The commercial cycle based upon the newcomers created a "golden glow" in the commonwealth, a feverish prosperity. It was inflationary, wages and prices spiraling as demand regularly outpaced supply. But opportunity was everywhere. The New England soil gave a good return, and land stretched infinitely in all directions. Some were concerned that Massachusetts returned nothing of her own to pay for necessary imports, the ships that called in Boston sailing on to Newfoundland, the Maine coast, the Caribbean, or Virginia to fill their holds with fish, timber, tobacco. Hugh Peter, at the height of the early chaos, preached at Boston and Salem on behalf of a locally financed fishing station "as the only probable means to free us from that oppression, which the seamen and others held us under," and he wrote in 1639, "Graunt ships doe come, eyther wee are too many to bee served by so few ships; or theire supply will not bee quadrate, or we shall want money to take them off." Minister Edmund Browne, sojourning in Boston in September 1639, reported to Sir Simonds D'Ewes in England that "if the Lord put us upon some way of trading wee shall bee happy in outward injoyements." In England in the spring of 1640, John Tinker reported discontent among English shippers: "It is a very greate grievanc and generall Complainte among all the Merchants and dealers to New England that they can have noe returnes ... insomuch that if there be not some Course taken for beter payments of our Creditors our tradeing will utterly cease."[46]

Even as Tinker wrote, the Massachusetts economy was collapsing. The years immediately preceding had been tremendously prosperous, the tide of newcomers running strong in 1637 and 1638. In 1639, however, there had been a slackening, and while the momentum of the previous years kept the economy operating, fatal changes had occurred. The farmers of the commonwealth

45. Bernard Bailyn, *The New England Merchants in the Seventeenth Century* (Cambridge, Mass., 1955), 33ff.

46. *Winthrop's Journal*, I, 165; Hugh Peter to John Winthrop, *ca.* Apr. 10, 1639, and Tinker to Winthrop, May 28, 1640, *Winthrop Papers*, IV, 113, 251; "Report of Edmund Browne [to Sir Simonds D'Ewes, Sept. 1639]," Col. Soc. Mass., *Publications*, 7 (1905), 78.

found their agricultural surplus harder to dispose of as the market created by the flood of newcomers contracted; the store of cash in the coffers of the Boston merchants diminished as the specie contributions of the newcomers failed to keep pace with the outgoing payments for imports. In 1640 the ships entering the harbor from England, encouraged by "the store of money and quick markets" of preceding years, carried enlarged inventories. But the diminished supply of specie would not even cover old bills, let alone permit the contracting of new ones. Shippers found the market steadily worsening through the summer and fall and grumbled over poor profits. More important was the position of the settler. The market for his surplus, contracting since the previous year, all but disappeared. He offered his produce in payment for goods and debts, but the merchants "would sell no wares but for ready-money." In consequence, commodity prices plummeted, wheat from seven shillings a bushel in May to four shillings in October; Indian corn from five shillings to three, then, by June 1641, to nothing. Cattle prices fell from twenty and thirty pounds a head to four and five. But even at that price there was no market. The very land lost value, and holdings worth 1,000*li* in the late 1630's were worth but 200*li* in 1641 and 1642. For the moment pessimism engulfed the commonwealth. "*The times of the Unsettled Humyrs of many mens spirits to Returne for England,*" John Cotton called these years, and Thomas Hooker wrote, "Why should a man stay untill the house fall on his head and why continue his being ther, where in reason he shall destroy his subsistence." "They concluded there would be no subsisting here," Winthrop said, "and accordingly they began to hasten away."[47]

Trade—the dispatching overseas of the commonwealth's agricultural surplus, first to the Azores, Canaries, the Iberian coast, and subsequently to the islands of the Caribbean—was to be the salvation of Massachusetts.[48] The beginnings were slow. In 1640 and 1641, probably through their connections with English

47. [John Cotton] to Richard Saltonstall, *ca.* 1643, Cotton Papers; Hooker to Thomas Shepard, Nov. 2, 1640, Hutchinson Papers, Mass. Archives; *Winthrop's Journal*, II, 82.
48. Rutman, "Governor Winthrop's Garden Crop," *Wm. and Mary Qtly.*, 3d Ser., 20 (1963), 415.

merchants, a few merchants in Boston learned of the existence of a market for wood products in Spain and the Atlantic islands, George Story arranging for the shipment of 8,500 clapboards in 1640, Samuel Maverick, in 1641, dealing with William Lewis of Malaga, Spain, for the sale of clapboards. Undoubtedly it was through such contacts that the Bostonians learned of a market across the Atlantic for the cheap wheat and other grains glutting the Bay area. Edward Gibbons, a leading Boston merchant, was early in seeing the possibility, and in October 1641, at his urging, the General Court gave official encouragement to the preparation of a grain ship which presumably sailed for Spain or the islands before May 1642. Thereafter the trade grew steadily, Winthrop recording the sailing of six ships "laden with pipe staves and other commodities of this country" in the fall of 1642, and five more ships sailing in 1643, including the sixty-ton *Hopewell* of Boston with a cargo of wheat-in-bulk for the Canaries.[49] In 1645, at least five ships sailed, one carrying three thousand bushels of peas, wheat, and Indian corn, another seven thousand bushels or more. That year a total of some twenty thousand bushels of grain valued at approximately four thousand pounds sterling in Boston prices were exported from the commonwealth, so much indeed that the provisions market in the Canaries was temporarily surfeited.[50] By 1647 a second market had been found in the Caribbean Islands where planters had become "so intent upon planting sugar that they had rather buy foode at very deare rates than produce it by labour."[51] At the end of the decade the shipment of grain, packed and salted meat, livestock, and horses to the southward surpassed the exports eastward across the Atlantic. By then, too, still a third market had developed, for ships were attracted to the port by the facilities and cheap foodstuffs available there for provisioning and outfitting. Initiated in 1641 and 1642, when privateers began outfitting in the harbor before operating in the Caribbean and when storm and accidents at sea forced ordinary vessels to make port in Boston, outfitting and provisioning had

49. *Ibid.*, 401-5; *Winthrop's Journal*, II, 85.
50. Losses at sea alone in 1644 and 1645 were reputedly "at least" 10,000*li*, "yea some think twenty, or thirty thousand pound losse." John Eliot in "Roxbury Church Records," VI, 189.
51. Richard Vines to John Winthrop, July 19, 1647, *Winthrop Papers*, V, 172.

become a major industry at the end of the decade when Edward Johnson wrote of the "store of Victuall both for their owne and Forreiners-ships, who resort hither for that end."[52]

With the turn to overseas trade, prosperity returned to the commonwealth. The outward flow of grain, cattle, and other produce from any given town provided its people with the means to purchase what they could not produce themselves, while the outward flow from the whole commonwealth paid for necessary imports. Prices reflected the recovery, rising steadily through the second decade, though never reaching the inflated levels of the late 1630's. By 1652, in contrast to the dark days of ten years before, the General Court commented upon "mens outward estates . . . increasing in their hands," and one New Englander wrote soon after of his land "being grown more worth: to such value as we thought it was at the hiest."[53] However, for most of the commonwealth, the old economy remained unchanged. The depression had broken upon the towns when, as one Puritan rhymester put it,

> . . . men no more the Sea passe o're, and
> Customers are wanting.[54]

The development of trade merely substituted overseas customers for the newcomers who had earlier absorbed the agricultural surplus without changing the basically agricultural nature of the towns. As the men of Lynn phrased it: "For our selves we are neither fitted for or inured to any such course of trade but must awayt Gods blessing alone upon our Lands and Cattell."[55]

But Boston could not escape change. While in the 1630's the town had been drifting toward its function as a commercial center, it now rushed. Its merchants, and to an extent those of Charlestown, led in the search for overseas markets for the commonwealth's agricultural surplus, entering into an elaborate Atlantic

52. *Johnson's Wonder-Working Providence*, 71.

53. Draft "Declaration concerning the advancement of learning in New Engl: By the genrall Court [Oct. 1652]," and "A Replye to the resenes of Mr Philop Nelson by Richard Dommer [May 1656]," Mass. Archives.

54. *Good News from New-England*, in Mass. Hist. Soc., *Collections*, 4th Ser., 1 (1852), 204.

55. Petition of the inhabitants of the town of Lynn to the General Court, *ca.* Oct. 27, 1648, Mass. Archives.

commercial world, a criss-crossing network of affiliated merchants and agents. They established a place for themselves dispensing grains, wood products, meats, and livestock to various places and receiving wine, sugar, and manufactured goods in return. Their ties of kinship and friendship with the London commercial community stood them in good stead, for this Atlantic world was one of credit and trust, where goods were sold in one port and payment made in other goods at another port a thousand miles away, where Boston wheat, for example, might be exchanged in Barbados for sugar delivered in London and credited against an earlier purchase of cloth and metal goods made on the promise of delivering the wheat in Barbados. The same ties involved the Bostonians as factors for English houses in the carrying trade of fish from the settlements northward from Cape Ann to southern Europe, a connection which brought them still more credit, and capital to finance such endeavors as shipbuilding.

Very quickly—and largely because of the contacts with the Atlantic community which no other town was able to duplicate—Boston made itself indispensable not only in the economy of the commonwealth but in that of the whole area, as apparent in the common appellation of the late 1640's, "Boston in New England."[56] It became the hub of a vast internal trade system which stretched deep into the interior to Springfield and Hartford and west along Long Island Sound to the borders of Dutch New York, the products of the land flowing one way to the town at the head of Massachusetts Bay, imports (purchased by those agricultural products) the other way to the towns and villages of the hinterland.

The records of the system are scant but the process is clear. Settlers in the outlying towns bought goods and paid their debts and taxes in grain and other produce; local merchants were supplied with their stocks from Boston and forwarded the agricultural goods they received from their own customers as payment. The dependence upon Boston was acknowledged by simple towns-

56. John Clark, *Ill News from New-England* ... (London, 1652), reprinted in Mass. Hist. Soc., *Collections*, 4th Ser., 2 (1854), 23; Albert Matthews, "The Name 'New England' as applied to Massachusetts," Col. Soc. Mass., *Publications*, 25 (1924), 382-90.

men and governments alike. "Who ever would send any thing
to any Towne in New England," one man advised, should
send it to Boston or Charlestown "for they are haven Townes for
all New England and speedy meanes of conveyance to all places
is there to be had." In the early 1650's Captain Johnson attributed resistance to sporadic attempts of the authorities to promote
the home manufacture of cloth to a fear on the part of the farmers
that "if the Merchants trade be not kept on foot ... their corne
and cattel will lye in their hands." And in 1650 the Massachusetts magistrates drafted a letter to their agent in England:
"Wee ... have a Competencie of Cattle of all Sorts and allso of
Corne for Subsistence and Some to spare, whereby with the help
of some fish here taken wee formerly have procured Clothing
and other necessaries for our families by means of some Traffique
in bothe Barbadoes and some other place." But if this should fail,
they continued, we are undone, for then "the generallitie of
poeple are exceedingly [distressed] and in small Capacitie to
Carrie through their ocasions."[57]

To the toll collected in Boston by virtue of its being the political capital was added the toll coming to it as the economic center
of New England. The merchants' share is obvious, for they took
a profit on every bushel of grain and every head of cattle passing
through the port, on every nail and pot and cask of wine imported. In 1648, for example, shipmasters buying wheat in Boston
complained that it could be had for no less than 5s in the town,
but that it might be bought directly from nearby farmers for 4s
8d.[58]

But the toll was collected by the whole town. Ships had to
be loaded, giving employment to draymen, porters, lightermen.
The export of meat gave work to butchers, while skins were
salvaged by tanners, and made into gloves by glovers and into
shoes by shoemakers. The leather goods were sold domestically
and even exported to other New England colonies and to the
Caribbean. So great was the influx of cattle from the interior

57. John Eliot to [?], ca. spring 1650, Mass. Hist. Soc., *Proceedings*, 2d Ser.,
2 (1886), 50; *Johnson's Wonder-Working Providence*, 211; Draft of a letter
from the General Court to Edward Winslow in England, ca. 1650, Mass.
Archives.
58. "Aspinwall Notarial Records," 189.

towns that in 1648 Boston petitioned the General Court for two fairs a year, the second exclusively "for Cattle to make provisions both for our selves and shipping."[59]   Wheat was exported in bulk, but also as flour and even as bread and biscuits; hence milling and baking were profitable endeavors.   Meat and flour were exported in casks and barrels to the profit of coopers.

Ships not only took on cargo.   In port they made repairs, provisioned themselves, and fitted out for their journeys, creating more work for Boston's artisans and sales for her shopkeepers. One such ship was the *John*, bound from the West Indies to Africa for slaves in 1650, and putting into the harbor to prepare for the journey.   Its account of expenditures in Boston included 14*s* 6*d* "to goodman franklin for nailes," 9*li* 4*s* 2*d* "to goodman Clarks bill" for ironwork, 5*li* 5*s* "to goodman Ward for a boate," 9*s* 6*d* "to goodman Barlow for caske," 11*s* "to the saile maker." A ship engaged in a similar voyage the year before paid out 30*li* 5*s* 6*d* for cordage, 4*li* 10*s* for 1,775 boards, 26*li* 14*s* 3*d* for canvas and 7*li* to the sailmaker, 81*li* 6*s* 1*d* to four of the town's blacksmiths, 55*li* 14*s* 9*d* for 3,698 pounds of beef, 42*li* 5*s* for 4,200 quarter-pound loaves of bread.[60]

Shipbuilding was closely linked to outfitting.   Begun in the dark days of the depression when the commonwealth's leaders feared that English vessels would not stop at the settlement and had taken steps to encourage ship construction in a number of coastal towns, the industry centered in Boston, for liquid capital (both local and English) became more readily available there than elsewhere.[61]   By the end of the second decade over a score of ship and boatyards had been erected on the North End and were turning out pinnaces, ketches, yawls, and oceangoing full-rigged ships: the *Trial* launched in 1642, the *Seabridge, Increase, Greyhound, Malaga Merchant*.   Each represented the investment and profit of a dozen or more men who contributed ⅛th, ⅟₁₆th, or ⅟₃₂nd of the cost; each involved the labor of a multi-

59. Petition of the town of Boston to the General Court, *ca.* Oct. 1648, Mass. Archives.

60. "Aspinwall Notarial Records," 285-86, 310-11.

61. The shipbuilding of the 1630's—the *Blessing of the Bay* of 1631, for example—was only sporadic.   That of the second decade is reflected primarily in "Aspinwall Notarial Records."

tude of men and crafts—shipwrights, caulkers, rope and canvas workers, blacksmiths, laborers.

Prosperity, trickling down from trade to crafts allied to trade, quickly pervaded the whole economy. A constant coming and going of people had marked Boston in the first decade. Now the traffic increased. Boston's shops, markets, and fairs were a beacon to other towns—Dedhamites, for example, found the capital's "coyne and commodities" luring them into making "many a long walk" with their produce.[62] The number of the new arrivals to the commonwealth was less now than in the 1630's; hence fewer moved through the town on their way from England to the interior. But the twenty to twenty-five ships which arrived annually at the end of the second decade deluged the town with their crews, and every shipmaster found himself paying a fine or two in order to free overexuberant topmen or deckhands in time for sailing. Factors arrived to do business with the local merchants, stayed for a season, then left. Boston's innkeepers, taverners, vintners, and brewers profited in satisfying the needs of the transients as well as the Bostonians themselves. In 1638 there had been but two "ordinaries" in the town, Cole's and Baulston's, both limited to selling food and beer, although Cole's was regularly selling wine illegally; Richard Fairbanks' tavern alone was allowed to sell "strong waters." A decade later, however, there were five inns licensed to sell food, beer, wine, and hard liquor, at least two taverns, and eight or more "pubs" selling food and beer to those of "an inferiour ranke that wilbe content with meaner diats paying less then in other places." In addition there were numerous irregular establishments similar to that belonging to the misnamed Sister Temperance Sweete, who early in the decade was admonished by the church "for having received into house and given entertainment unto disorderly Company and ministring unto them wine and strong waters unto Drunkennesse and that not without some iniquity both in the measure and pryce thereof."[63]

62. *Johnson's Wonder-Working Providence*, 179.

63. Petition of William Davis to the governor and General Court, Oct. 20, 1643, MS Photostats, Box 2, Mass. Hist. Soc. Lib.; First Church Records under date of Mar. 8, 1639/40. Boston's taverns and inns can be traced through their licenses and offenses in *Colony Records*, I, II; *Assistants' Records*, II, and "Boston Records."

For most of the commonwealth, the ebbing of the immigrant tide at the turn of the first decade tended to stabilize the population. But while Boston's rate of growth slowed, its increase from two thousand to three thousand—largely during the years after 1644—was far out of proportion to that of the other towns, and by 1650 almost one-fifth of the Massachusetts population lived in and about Shawmut.[64] Some of the new arrivals came from England, frequently as agents for English merchants anxious to involve themselves in the town's burgeoning trade. Others wandered in from the Atlantic community, men like Thomas Breedon, who arrived in 1648 with a cargo loaded by an English house in Malaga to exchange for "wheate fish or Tobacco" and ultimately settled as a merchant in his own right, or Thomas Cromwell, a privateer out of the Caribbean, who retired to Boston to enjoy his wealth and add to it by trade.[65] Most, however, came from nearby towns—indentured servants freed from their obligations and attracted by Boston's opportunities, artisans who could practice their trades to greater advantage at the center of economic life. Among such were Nehemiah Bourne and Alexander Adams, both Dorchester shipwrights, arriving in 1640 and 1645 respectively; George Dell, shipmaster, from Salem in the mid-1640's; Christopher Holland, a lighterman, coming in the late 1640's; John Marrion, a cordwainer from Watertown, in 1646; Robert Nash, a Charlestown butcher, in 1643; Thomas Roberts, a Roxbury feltmaker, in 1644; Hezekiah Usher, arriving from Cambridge in 1645, a bookseller turned merchant. Some arrived only to fail and move out again. Others, encouraged by their success in Boston, moved into the Atlantic community—shipbuilder Thomas Hawkins, for example, entering trade in Boston and subsequently operating from London; or Stephen Winthrop, who carried a cargo of wheat to the Canaries at mid-decade, traded along the Spanish coast, then went on to London; or his brother Samuel, settling briefly in Tenerife in the Canaries, then serving as an agent for Boston merchants trading to Barbados. But in the balance, Boston gained.

64. The discussion of Boston's population on the pages following, together with the examples given, is drawn from that analysis of the identifiable residents described below in "A Note on Sources and Methods."
65. "Aspinwall Notarial Records," 137.

Steady growth and the limited amount of land on the peninsula forced property values upward, in this one area value levels coming to exceed even those of 1639.[66]

Sample Property Values

1638-40			1645-50		
	li	s		li	s
House and garden	15		House	25	
House and garden	15		"Decayed" house frame		
House and garden	16	10	and lot	45	
House	21		House, yard, garden	55	
House and lot	25	4	House	83	
House and lot	28		House, cellar, shop	94	10
House and garden	28		House	130	
House and lot	45		House	150	
House and garden	50		House	200	
			House, yard, garden	600	

The "double tenement" or duplex became common, two or more families sharing the same house and lot; so too did the division of lots into more than one houseplot, although the town at first frowned on the practice. The beginnings of row-houses appeared, as in 1645, when John Davies sold a plot ten feet wide and forty feet long to Edmund Jackson, stipulating that Jackson should "build his house equall in stud and conformable in front" to his own house, "lay his floore over the entry" even with Davies' floor, and "at his owne cost lay the gutter betweene the two houses and be at halfe charge to maintain it afterwards."[67] All the while construction steadily encroached upon lands originally allotted for gardens, entering the "fields" laid out in the 1630's for agriculture, encroaching upon the common meadow until the town voted to preserve it for public use. A building boom developed and the trades involved prospered—carpenters, brickmakers, limeworkers, masons, sawyers. Some of the houses were elaborate for the time and place—Winthrop's "mansion," which the Gov-

66. The accompanying chart is compiled from the extant land records, notably *Lechford Notebook*, "Aspinwall Notarial Records," *Suffolk Deeds*, "Boston Records," and "Boston Book of Possessions."

67. *Suffolk Deeds*, I, 61.

ernor lost for debt in the early 1640's and Valentine Hill mortgaged to Richard Hutchinson in 1650 for 600*li*; the Governor's second house, with its hall, parlor, bedchambers, kitchen, garretts, and outbuildings. But most were still on the order of the one-room house built by carpenter John Davies for William Rix: "One framed house 16 foot long and 14 foote wyde with a chamber floare[,] finisht summer and joysts[,] a celler floare with joysts finisht[,] the roofe and walles Clapboarded on the outsyde[,] the Chimney framed without dawbing[,] to be done with hewen timber."[68] A second building presumably held the tools of weaver Rix's trade.

Construction was not confined to houses. In the first decade only one small section of the waterfront along Town Cove had been wharfed, a company of fourteen being formed to finance the work (with help from the town government) and erect a crane and warehouse.[69] But in the second decade more than twenty-five separate wharves were licensed to be built. Some men combined the needs of commerce and housing. In 1641, Valentine Hill, Edward Bendall, and a group of associates received from the town the use of a large tract of "wast ground" extending from the wharf built earlier on Town Cove northeastward to the marshes dividing the bulk of the peninsula from the North End. In the succeeding five years they expended 818*li* 13*s* 4*d* improving the harborside, turning the cove into "Town Dock," obscuring the shoreline with pilings and planks. Their profit—until the property reverted to the town in 1649—came from wharfage and tonnage charged to all who used the facilities, and from the sale of lots carved out of the grant.[70] Farther northeastward another group began work—the Mill Creek proprietors, including Henry Symonds, George Burdon, John Button, John Hill, John

68. *Lechford Notebook*, 302-3.
69. *Ibid.*, 69-74; "Boston Records," 37. The fourteen: Thomas Leverett, William Hutchinson, John Coggan, John Coggshall, John Newgate, James Penn, Edward Hutchinson, Thomas Savage, Edward Bendall, William Dyar, Thomas Griffin, Richard Tuttle, [Henry?] Flint, and Ralph Hudson. In 1639 the facility, known as Town Dock or Bendall's Dock even at that time, was sold to Richard Parker for 170*li*. Apparently it was subsequently incorporated into the wharf constructed by the Hill associates of 1641, which was also known as Town or Bendall's Dock.
70. "Boston Records," 63-64, 94, 97, 98-99.

Mylam, and William Franklin. In 1643 they obtained title from the town to the cove on the northwest side of the peninsula, together with all the marsh surrounding it and a strip of marsh sixty feet wide linking the cove to the town side of Shawmut. The marsh-creek running through the strip was widened and deepened (making the North End an island joined only by a bridge to Shawmut proper) and dams were built to use the tides in such a way as to operate two grist mills, one on the creek and another on a causeway dividing the cove from the Charles River. The land itself was drained, divided among the proprietors, and by them subdivided and sold for house plots, Mylam and Franklin being the most active in this business.[71]

The newcomers arriving in the 1640's did not change the course of the town's development established in the 1630's. But they hurried it. Broad acres, vital to the agricultural village of the first years, had not been particularly important to carpenter Thomas Joy, though he had been in a minority in that regard during the first decade. They became less important during the 1640's as the flow of corn and cattle from country to Boston and out into the Atlantic community grew; the town's opportunity now lay in the marketplace, the merchant's storeroom, the artisan's shop. The difference in emphasis can be illustrated by comparing William Tyng, who arrived in the late 1630's to invest 1,300*li* in land and to trade on the side, and Thomas Breedon, arriving ten years later, to whom commerce was a way of life and land a luxury to be enjoyed. Tyng's primary interest shifted from land to trade as the economy shifted; Breedon arrived as a merchant. On a lesser level, the difference was that between William Talmage, who had sought town land for a house and farm as soon as his indentured servitude was ended in 1636, and shoemaker John Stevenson, who was content with house, yard, and shop in the 1640's.

71. *Ibid.*, 73, 74-75, 76; "Aspinwall Notarial Records," 376-77; *Suffolk Deeds*, II, 41-42; Samuel C. Clough, "Ownership of Certain Land in Boston," Col. Soc. Mass., *Publications*, 25 (1924), 44ff. Winthrop, Valentine Hill, Richard Fairbanks, Robert Turner, and James Davis began the work expecting to get the town to undertake its completion. Apparently the town rejected the idea and the original group gave way to Symonds and the others. Button and Hill dropped from the second group very quickly. Exemplifying the profit of those who carried the project through is Mylam's sale of one-quarter interest in the mills in 1651 for 370*li*.

Statistics drawn from the land records tell the story. In 1639, 64 per cent of the identifiable families of the town owned agricultural property beyond the peninsula (itself a significant decrease from the near 100 per cent of a few years earlier); 18 per cent owned minimal property (no more than a house lot and garden on Shawmut); and 18 per cent owned no recorded property at all. By 1649, however, the number of identifiable Boston families owning agricultural land beyond the Neck (29 per cent) equaled the number of those owning no recorded property, while 42 per cent of the town's families owned no more than a house and garden on the peninsula.

Similarly, the gap between church and town which had opened during the first decade widened during the second, for those attracted to Boston had in mind the material opportunities awaiting them, not thoughts of heaven and hell. At least one-third of Boston's families were not represented in the First Church, and more than one-half of the town's total male population. Of the families who did join during the second decade, twenty-seven were already members of churches in other towns of the commonwealth, at least one member of each family admitted on the basis of a recommendation from an outlying church. Forty-six families attended First Church and brought their children to Cotton or Wilson for baptism, but retained their membership in a church elsewhere. While some newcomers joined the church for the first time in Boston, others, probably a majority of the new arrivals, remained apart.

The newcomers tended to remain legally apart from the town, too, temporarily breaking down the concept of town citizenship even as it was being developed. From the early 1630's there were some in Boston who had no legal position whatsoever—the "strangers" or "sojourners." As the focal point of New England, the town attracted a variety of temporary residents—those who paused on business or while looking about for a place to settle permanently; those satisfying a curiosity about the new commonwealth, for example, tourist John Josselyn in the late 1630's. Some were sojourners in the town only until they could obtain inhabitantship: William Mawer, considered "a strainger" in September 1636, granted land at Mount Wollaston in February 1638, and after the

secession of Braintree referred to as "late of this Towne";[72] carpenter John Friend, who dwelt in the town as a sojourner for a
while, then applied for and was received as an inhabitant. Only a
few during the first decade lived as strangers on what can be considered a near-permanent basis, renting at times, or buying property. Thomas Lechford was an early example. A lawyer, he
arrived in the town in June 1638 and rented a "chamber" for five
pounds a year; there he lived as a sojourner with his wife and maid
until September 1640, when he bought a house and garden from
tailor Henry Gray.[73] When he departed for England in mid-
1641, leaving behind house, wife, and personal property worth 6*li*
13*s* 10*d*, he was still legally a stranger to Boston.

Whether merely pausing in the town, or living as a near-
permanent sojourner, or sojourning as a prelude to inhabitantship,
the stranger was subjected to the screening of the town, for it
attempted to judge his character as it judged the character of the
inhabitant. Town ordinances of 1635 and 1636 required the
permission of the selectmen for the sale of property to strangers
and for their entertainment by a townsman for more than fourteen
days. The following year, "to keepe out such whose Lives were
publickely prophane and scandalous as those whose judgements
were Corrupt," the magistrates assumed a parallel right to screen
the sojourner, a law of the General Court providing that "no towne
or person shall receive any stranger" nor "alow any lot or habitation to any" nor "intertaine any such above three weekes" without the express approval of two assistants. The law was political
in nature and was aimed at the Hutchinsonians, Winthrop recording the expectation that "many of their opinion" were about to
descend upon the commonwealth from England. But it violated
no English tradition, and it filled a need by giving the leadership
a legal control by which it might curb indiscriminate entry into
the towns, church membership and freemanship having proved
weak controls as so many shunned the church and freeman status.
Hence the statute remained on the books after the crisis was over,
in 1638 "renewed and confirmed to bee for continuance from
year to year." Both it and the town regulations were only spo-

72. "Boston Records," 12, 51.
73. *Lechford Notebook,* 234.

radically enforced in the second decade, however, although regularly invoked during periodic attempts to bring about compliance. In 1651, for example, the commonwealth admitted that its order had "longe since expired"; nonetheless it "agayne" revived it.[74]

Although intended as a control over the entrance of the stranger, the town and commonwealth laws—in the absence of enforcement—only succeeded in legalizing his position within the community. He could lawfully reside in the town, own property, establish himself in trade or business. His enjoyment of "the same justice and law, that is generall for the plantation... without partialitie or delay" was subsequently guaranteed him.[75] He could not, in law, hold office. He could not vote, for even the 1647 statute was limited to selected "inhabitants" of requisite age and comportment; but he could attend "any publique Court, Councel, or Towne meeting" and "by speech or writeing" could "move any lawfull, seasonable, and materiall question, or present any necessary motion, complaint, petition, Bill or information, whereof that meeting hath proper cognizance."[76] Permitting the stranger to attend meetings effectively nullified denial of the franchise, for given the mode of holding public meetings and the number of those who were neither freemen nor inhabitants, it is impossible to conceive of the sojourner's being barred from casting a yea or nay to the question or candidate proposed.

Only the material advantages belonging to inhabitants were actually denied the stranger. He was not granted land by the town, nor did he have the right of commonage or of mowing town land. However, he could from the beginning buy or rent all of these appurtenances. Moreover, the material advantages of inhabitantship steadily diminished, largely as a result of the growth of the town. The right to mow disappeared in the mid-1630's, the town grant of land to all intents and purposes in 1642. In 1646 commonage was restricted to the then inhabitants, who could rent (though not sell) their right to graze milk cows on

74. Edward Rawson to John Winthrop, Feb. 7, 1638/39, *Winthrop Papers*, IV, 97; *Colony Records*, I, 196, 228, II, 245; *Winthrop's Journal*, I, 219.
75. "Body of Liberties," 33.
76. *Ibid.*, 35.

the common to any and sundry on a year-to-year basis. This act effectively splintered Winthrop's united society once again, for to the distinction between freemen and non-freemen, church members and non-members, was now added that between proprietors and non-proprietors.

Given the fact that the legal inhabitant had so little of value denied the non-inhabitant, it is not surprising that few newcomers of the 1640's sought more than the status of sojourner. Indeed, one intent on personal profit would avoid inhabitantship just as church members did freemanship, inasmuch as it offered little and could conceivably demand a great deal if one were called upon to hold public office or serve on town committees. The sojourner's reluctance to become an inhabitant is reflected in the declining figures for admitted inhabitants—from 17 in 1642, to 2 in 1643, and 1 in 1644. In all, from 1642 to 1650 only 20 men were moved to assume inhabitantship out of the hundreds who poured into the town. Twice that number from among the newcomers—ignoring inhabitantship—established a legal affiliation with the town through church membership and freemanship. The rest remained in legal anonymity. They entered almost at will, seeking the permission of the authorities only during those times when the acts requiring it were being enforced; they found lodgings, a place of business; they participated in the public meetings of the town to the extent of their interest. John Dand, merchant's clerk, is an example, arriving in the town in 1645 and remaining as a sojourner until moving to Dover in the early 1650's. Only here and there does one glimpse such a resident— renting or occasionally buying property, standing trial (Dand was prosecuted in 1646 as a signer of the Child petition), attesting legal documents (as Dand did in 1648, 1649, and 1650), appearing in occasional letters. Roger Hannadown of Weymouth, a shipwright attracted to the town in 1642, is another example. Presumably he and his wife Sarah rented a house, for all that is known of them is that she bore a child in Boston, presenting it to the First Church for baptism by virtue of her Weymouth membership, and that they returned to Weymouth in 1648.

Boston—bustling, vibrant, energetic, prosperous—was a town

of quick profits and occasionally even quicker losses as its people traded, speculated, gambled in their own town, along the coast north and south, and on the sea lanes of the Atlantic. Valentine Hill was representative of those who gained in the new economy. He had arrived in the mid-1630's with at least some money, for he received a grant of sixty acres at Pullen Point in 1637. But his fortune was made in the second decade. He traded in wheat and, through his connections in London, acted as agent for London merchants in the fish trade, gathering cargoes along the coast from Cape Ann northward for delivery to London vessels; he retailed and wholesaled English imports, lent money, and speculated in town lots, buying and selling at least twelve during the decade; he headed the group developing Town Dock and had a financial interest in the Mill Creek project; he was involved in the Indian trade, being one of four Boston merchants given special privileges in 1641; he was a member of a Bay group which unsuccessfully attempted to break the Dutch and Swedish monopoly of the Delaware River trade. Edward Gibbons, on the other hand, was one who lost. A one-time companion of the roistering Thomas Morton of Merrymount, he pyramided land holdings in the mid-1630's, turned easily to trade at the beginning of the decade, and by the mid-1640's had amassed a fortune of over 2,500*li*—most of which he lost in attempting to break into the fur trade of French Acadia.

On a lower scale, too, there were gainers and losers. Jeremy Houchin arrived from Dorchester in 1644 to operate a tannery for a brief period before turning to trade in a small way; at the end of the decade he began investing in Mill Creek property and ultimately completed the wharfing of its entrance. John Mylam arrived in Boston in 1635 or earlier and received fourteen acres of land at Muddy River from the town; he was, therefore, one of the poorer sort. But in the 1640's he built a small fortune as a cooper, Mill Creek proprietor, and speculator in town plots. At mid-decade he had a half-dozen servants and one-eighth shares in the ships *Zebulon*, *John*, and *Supply*; his trading activities abroad were sufficient to warrant his investing (with merchants William Tyng, Robert Keayne, and Thomas Fowle) in an inde-

pendent naval expedition against the "Turkish" pirates plaguing
the shipping lanes around the Canaries. James Everill, a leather
worker who arrived in 1634 and obtained land on the peninsula
and at Braintree, was another who prospered. Enriched by his
tannery operations in the 1640's, he began trading on a small
scale and, in 1649, when Hill and his associates surrendered the
Dock to the town, he took over the greater part of the property
himself, undertaking to pay an annual quitrent to the town. Among
the losers were three 1647 investors, Clement Campion, John
Shaw, and Thomas Joy, who by then had moved to Hingham.
After dispatching a cargo to the West Indies, the partners at home
received word from Campion, the partner aboard ship, that "all
things have gone very contrary." "Wee had a very leake ship"
and "have beene forced to pump every glasse," "our beere leakt
out[,] our bread mouldy[,] our fish rotten" on arrival.[77] Still
another loser was Isaac Grosse, a husbandman in the 1630's, a
brewer in the 1640's. His investment of small amounts in the
ship *Rainbow* in 1645 and *Hope* in 1648 were apparently his un-
doing, and he turned to selling his beer illegally to seamen stopping in the town. At his death in 1649, his son pleaded his
father's "debts in other mens hands" in seeking permission to open
a lawful pub.[78]

Geography had begun the process of turning the straggling village on Shawmut—no different in its origins from the other towns
—into what it had become; the leadership in selecting and maintaining it as the political center and the shipmasters in choosing it
as their port of call had forwarded the process; the merchants in
the aftermath of depression had completed it. By the end of the
second decade the town was a community of merchants and tradesmen, seamen and artisans. Only along the periphery—on the
North Shore from Winnisimmet to Pullen Point, on the islands
of the harbor, and southward at Muddy River—did it retain
vestiges of its agricultural beginnings. Shawmut itself was
devoted to trade and commerce. Recognizing the nature of their
town, the Bostonians were immensely proud of it. "It hath

77. "Aspinwall Notarial Records," 86.
78. Petition of Edmund Grosse to the General Court, Oct. 29, 1649, Mass.
Archives.

pleased God so to dispose that o[u]r Towne chiefly consists of
Trade," they wrote in a petition of 1648, "a mart to the Countrie
through the resort of Artificers of all sorts, and the accesse of
shipping."[79]   They cited God as their well-wisher, but it was
Mammon who smiled on their endeavors.

79. Petition of the town of Boston to the General Court, *ca. Oct.* 1648, Mass.
Archives.

VIII

THE WELL ORDERING OF
THE TOWN

O[u]R TOWN" the men of Boston wrote when petitioning the
General Court in 1648. The phrase, with its overtones of
proprietorship and pride, was significant. Local government had
evolved from the church congregation and been sanctioned by
commonwealth recognition; throughout the period it was a tan-
gled skein, its threads firmly knotted with those of the commonwealth. Yet to the average Bostonian the church was more and
more concerned with its own members and the affairs of the soul,
less and less equatable with the full town, while the commonwealth was increasingly remote, a political troposphere to be approached only occasionally. The local community alone, by virtue of the general town meeting and the participation of all elements of the population, actually belonged to the townsman.
And through its everyday activities in the affairs of his life, it
had an importance which neither church nor commonwealth had.[1]

To the townsman, town government—the political establishment of town meeting and selectmen—was an arbiter regularizing

1. There is an enormous literature dealing with the functions of the New
England town (and to a lesser extent, Boston specifically), from Carl Bridenbaugh's general consideration of Boston in his *Cities in the Wilderness: The First
Century of Urban Life in America, 1625-1742* (N. Y., 1938), through such
works as Robert W. Kelso, *The History of Public Poor Relief in Massachusetts,
1620-1920* (Boston and N. Y., 1922), to even more specialized studies such as
Robert Francis Seybolt's *The Public Schools of Colonial Boston, 1635-1775*
(Cambridge, Mass., 1935), and Edward H. Savage's *A Chronological History of
the Boston Watch and Police, from 1631 to 1865 ...* (Boston, 1865). There is
a tendency, however, to consider the town as little more than an agency of commonwealth government, to bypass any considerations of the town as the most
immediate and important entity to its inhabitants, and to neglect any discussion
of its independent institutional growth.

his relations with his fellows in the community. He looked to it to see that "noe annoying things eyther by fish, Wood or stone, or other such like things, be left or layd about the sea shore" to his detriment. He expected it to lay out streets and paths for his convenience, and maintain them even against himself if need be. And the town complied. When the townsmen developed a penchant for digging their cellar entrances out into thoroughfares to the hazard of passers-by, or when they used the public highways as mines for clay to daub on their chimneys, the town guarded society's interest with cease and desist orders and fines; when a saw pit was dug in the middle of the marketplace the town ordered it filled in and the scrap timber littering the street removed. In the interest of the townsmen the town licensed new construction in the village, hoping to avoid "disorderly building to the inconvenience of streets and laynes," and to enforce "the more comely and Commodious ordering of them." And when the natural springs of Shawmut would no longer suffice for the population, the town licensed the digging of wells and building of conduits.[2]

In the first decade, when Boston was but an agricultural community and its people were concerned largely with the land, the town's arbitral role was reflected most often in land regulations. The common cultivation of the town's fields, with the community organized as the congregation making decisions about when and what to plant, did not persist beyond the first year or so, for individual ownership followed quickly and the Bostonians cultivated their own garden lots on Shawmut and great allotments abroad. But the community—organized as the town—did decide who should get the land, how much should be granted, and upon what basis grants should be made, page after page of the town records during the first decade being devoted to such matters. Moreover, the holders of land in the various fields of the peninsula fenced their plots in common, as did those receiving allotments in the common fields at Muddy River and the Mount. (Fencing of great allotments elsewhere and around house lots, however, was considered the task of the individual property owner.) To

2. The town's activities as sketched below can be followed in "Boston Records," *passim*; the quotations here are from pp. 11, 12.

the town fell the task of determining the individual's responsibility toward the common fences, and the earliest Boston records show the community requiring that "every man shall make his [portion of the] fences sufficient for all his planting ground on the neck" by a set day and appointing committees to inspect the work. Subsequently, every man who had "any new all[otment of planting] ground upon the necke" was to be shown how much of the common fence he was to maintain, fence responsibility to be in proportion to acreage. "Viewers of fences" were regularly appointed for each field through the 1630's, enforcing the orders and requiring repairs of the prescribed "duble rayle and payle." Heavy fines were levied for non-compliance, as in 1638 when the town demanded 3s 4d "for every rodd" in disrepair. In the second decade the Muddy River common fence was still being kept up by cooperative effort under the direction of town-appointed fence viewers. But on the peninsula large portions of the fields had come to be fenced separately, the town ordering that proprietors maintain "all fences that lie in division betweene on[e] and other" equally. Where common fences were retained the obligation to labor on them was apparently replaced by a money payment, 1s per acre being collected in 1641 from holders of land in Sentry Hill field "towards the mayntaining of the fence thereof."[3]

The town regulated the pasturing of livestock on Shawmut, too, balancing the diverse requirements of cattle and corn, cows and "dry cattle." In the first years, livestock had grazed freely on the peninsula, watched casually by the boys of the town. But indiscriminate grazing was early prohibited. As crops (even when protected by fences) fell prey to unruly cattle and as beef cattle competed with milk cows for the limited grass, the town turned to a system whereby all cattle except milk cows were exiled from early spring to fall. In 1634 the town's stock was assembled in a single herd, driven to Muddy River, and placed in charge of a "cowskeeper" paid by the town. In 1635 Pullen Point was used, the herd being free to graze during the day and confined in a "payled yard" at night; a house was built for the herder at town expense, and the inhabitants paid 5s a head for the privilege of

3. "Boston Records," 3, 5, 13, 33, 61, 90.

incorporating their stock with the common herd from the middle of April to the first of November, "the latter end of harvest." Presumably the cattle, on returning to the town, were wintered partly on the stubble in the fields, partly on hay gathered from the marshes. With the distribution of the great allotments beyond the Neck, provisions for a common herd ended. But the exiling of the cattle continued. In 1638, for example, the town ordered that inasmuch "as our Comon pasturing is but scant upon the necke and cowe keepings for the inhabitants is of necessity," all but milk cows were to be "had away" to their owners' allotments on the mainland by the last of April; in 1639 all were to be gone by May 10; in 1641 "all dry cattle" were to be driven "of the necke, and not be suffered to abide there" by June 5.[4]

Draft animals kept on Shawmut, including oxen, horses, an occasional steer, together with riding horses, goats, swine, and sheep, were similarly curbed by the town. Like "great cattle," stock maintained on the mainland allotments was the responsibility of the owner, who was liable for any damage done to the property of others. On occasion owners were ordered to move their livestock abroad for the planting season; more generally, after the first years, regulations merely limited the number. When permitted on the peninsula, the animals were restricted to their owners' yards and allowed to wander only under the eye of a keeper, usually a young boy of the family. Swine were a special problem and were required to be ringed and yoked at all times, the ring to allow easier control, the yoke to prevent them from squirming through the fences into gardens; special officers or hogreeves were appointed to enforce compliance. Despite all the restrictions strays were an unceasing problem, many a townsman waking in the morning to find an errant sow rooting up his corn and peas. By the mid-1630's the town erected a pound or fold and appointed a foldkeeper to take up "every trespassinge beaste or horse ... Calfe, goat or hogg"; individuals, too, were authorized to seize and pen a stray animal. Those "taken up" by either the keeper or others were advertised on the fold gate, and owners claiming their animals were required to pay fines, indemnities, and the cost of seizing and confining the stray. When no owner came,

4. *Ibid.*, 2, 3-4, 5, 33, 61.

as happened on occasion, the animal was sold and the proceeds used to compensate the keeper and any person claiming damages. The fines seemed to have had little effect, however; strays remained a problem, and for a brief period the town sent them to one of the islands in the harbor so that the owners would have the additional cost and effort of a day's trip to reclaim them. Ultimately goats so plagued the town that they were banished from the peninsula, the town mentioning "the great Damages done" by them to "gardens, orchards, and cornefields; the great grievances that often ariseth among the Inhabitants by reason of them, the many orders made about them, and yet altogether ineffectual."[5]

Milk cows, indispensable to the community and needing daily care, could not be driven from the Neck. Hence, with the end of indiscriminate grazing, they were put in the care of a town-appointed herder—Richard Fairbanks from 1635 to 1638, followed in turn by William Hudson, John Ruggle, Thomas Joanes, and Alexander Beck. Ruggle's schedule was stipulated in the order appointing him. Each morning from spring to fall, an hour after sun-up, he collected the herd in the village, driving it onto the common or down the Neck to the cow pasture just beyond Town Gate; at six in the evening he started back, slowly traversing the winding streets, the number of his charges dwindling as cows dropped out at their proper barns. His pay was a bushel of Indian corn per head, payable by the owner.[6] The shortage of pasture brought a limitation on the size of the herd as early as 1636, when the town stipulated that no family could maintain more than two cows on the peninsula. The same act limited the number of goats to five per family and barred families having goats from keeping cows and vice versa. The limitation of two cows per family was continued in the second decade until 1647, when peninsula grazing rights (commonage) were limited to the then-inhabitants and the herd was fixed at seventy cows.[7]

As the townsmen turned to trade and commerce in the second decade, the town's arbitral role changed, shifting as the occupa-

5. *Ibid.*, 17, 67.
6. *Ibid.*, 69. Cows kept on the farms were not included, nor was their number restricted.
7. *Ibid.*, 5, 88.

tions of the townsmen shifted. The era of allotments passed, and fence and livestock regulations took up less and less of the town's time. More important considerations were wharfing rights and rates, the town's inns and pubs, the apprenticing of errant and idle youths, the maintenance of "a passag boatt" between the harborside and "wher the ships rid," and the "noyesome smells" coming out of Robert Nash's slaughterhouse "to the offence of the Towne."[8] And while the community still maintained a cowherd, a pound keeper, and a hogreeve to control livestock, more vital were those tasks undertaken by various officers charged with enforcing the morality of the marketplace—the "sealers of leather," whose job it was to curtail "the sevrall deceites and abuses which . . . have bene and are comonly practised by the tanners, curriers, and workers of leather"; the "gagers of casks," who measured all containers used for "liquor, fish, or other commodities to bee put to sale" to see that they were of the required "London assize"; the various sealers and viewers of fish, lumber, pipestaves; the measurers of wheat; and the clerks of the market.

Such officers, authorized—often required—by the general government, operated under commonwealth laws establishing minimum standards and even prices for various goods. The size of a loaf of bread, for example, was proportioned to the cost of wheat; when wheat was 3s per bushel, the penny white loaf was supposed to weigh 11¼ ounces, wheaten bread 17¼ ounces, household bread 23 ounces. In order to facilitate the enforcement of the measures by the clerks of the market, the law also directed that "every baker shall have a distinct marke for his bread." Similar regulations were imposed on other trades. "Nor shall any person or persons using or occupying the mysterie or facultie of currying," one read, "currie any kinde of leather, except it be well and throughly tanned; nor shall currie any hyde being not throughly dryed after his wet season; in which wet season he shall not use any stale, urin, or any other deceitfull or subtil mixture, thing, way or means to corrupt or hurt the same."[9] To the Bostonian these laws, protecting him far more than they com-

8. *Ibid.*, 89, 97.
9. *Colony Records*, II, 181; Farrand, ed., *Laws and Liberties of Massachusetts*, 33.

manded of him, were as much a part of his town as were the local
ordinances regulating swine and goats. The regulatory officials
were town officers, his neighbors, elected or appointed within the
framework of the community.

In addition to arbitrating between the individual and society,
the town was equally a vehicle for community action; indeed, at
times the two functions merged, the establishment of the town
herd, for example, being both a communal effort and a means
to keep one man's cattle from another man's corn. Within the
confines of the community the townsmen came together to undertake public works, as in 1635, when Boston set out to complete
the fortifications on Fort Hill begun earlier by the commonwealth.
"The whole towne" was called out to "bestowe fourteene dayes
worke, by equall proportion" under the direction of Lion Gardi-
ner, and a committee was elected by the town meeting to "sett
downe how many dayes worke would be equall for each man to
doe, and what money such should contribute beside their work as
were of greater abilities, and had fewer servants, that there with
provision of tooles and other necessaryes might be made, and
some recompence given to such of the poorer sort as should be
found to be overburdened with their fourteene dayes worke." In
1641 the town gathered to undertake street maintenance, "the
Richer sort" being required to supply "three dayes' worke of one
man," the "men of middle estate, two dayes," the "poorer sort,
one day."[10] The richer sort and those of middle estate undoubtedly sent their servants to do the work, but as before the
poorer inhabitants went themselves.

The commonwealth government called upon the people for
public projects as well. But it worked through the towns rather
than directly, increasing orientation toward the local as against
the general community. At times the commonwealth called on
them for labor, as in 1633 when the towns were ordered to send
their men (magistrates and ministers excepted) to work two days
on the Castle Island fortifications in mid-harbor, or in 1641 when
the Bostonians were divided into six work companies to labor on
a road from Winnisimmet to Lynn at the behest of the commonwealth. More generally the commonwealth government mobil-

10. "Boston Records," 8, 62-63.

ized the society for public purposes through taxation, determining its needs from time to time during the year and assessing each town proportionately. Initially the Court of Assistants set the proportions on the basis of size, but by 1634 in principle and by 1636 in practice the task was being done by a committee of the Court according to its estimate of "the true valewe of every towne," including real and personal property.[11] The accompanying chart shows the assessments as they affected Boston during the years to 1642.[12]

Commonwealth Levies: 1633-42

Year	Total levied by the Commonwealth		Levied upon Boston			Boston's % of the total
	li	*s*	*li*	*s*	*d*	
1633	542		70			12.9
1634	600		80			13.3
1635	700	6	95	8		13.5
1636	1,700		250			14.7
1637	2,300		338			14.7
1638	2,100		311	0	9	14.8
1639	1,000		194	10	1	19.4
1640	1,200		179			14.9
1641	—		—			—
1642	1,000		150			15.0

For its part, Boston raised its proportion of the levy by assessing individual residents on the basis of their estate wherever located, at first including even property they owned in other towns

11. *Colony Records*, I, 175.

12. Commonwealth levies were not generally assessed on an annual basis during the early years, but as the need arose. Thus, in 1637, the General Court required at different times 300*li*, 600*li*, 400*li*, 1,000*li*. The figures are given here as annual figures only for convenience, the chart combining actual assessments recorded in *Colony Records*, and (with regard to certain Boston figures) estimates on the basis of the nearest known proportion between Boston and the commonwealth total. No basis for estimation of either commonwealth levy or Boston's proportion exists for 1641. The figures should not be considered as embodying the whole of commonwealth revenue, for other monies were forthcoming from import duties (that on wine particularly), fines, gifts, and the like, while special tasks were undertaken by the commonwealth by drafting the labor of the townsmen—in actuality a form of taxation. The high levels of 1636, 1637, 1638, are, of course, attributable to the expenses of the Pequot War.

or in England. Town assessments were made by a committee—in
1634 by John Coggshall, William Colborne, Samuel Cole, William
Brenton, Thomas Grubb, and constable William Cheesbrough—
or by the full body of the selectmen, the constables doing the
actual collecting and forwarding receipts to the commonwealth
treasurer. How equitable or truly progressive the system was is
open to doubt, for the evaluation of property (particularly that
beyond the town or in England) could be only rough and all were
expected to contribute something, probably a great deal in the
early years and during the Indian war of 1636-38, when the levies
averaged out to 1*li* per Boston family per year, the range lying
between 10*s* and 7*li*. However, the individual levy dipped sharply as the town and tax basis grew, the average payment per family dropping to approximately 8*s* by 1642, the range falling between 2*s* and 4*li*.[13]

The machinery for assessment and collection of commonwealth taxes became more and more formidable as the period
advanced, culminating in a General Court law of 1646, repassed
in 1647. In July of every year the commonwealth treasurer was
to dispatch warrants to the town constables directing them to call
together the inhabitants to elect one of the freemen as tax commissioner for the ensuing twelve months. By August the commissioner, together with the selectmen, was to have drawn up a
list of all males sixteen years old and upward, together with a true
estimate of the personal and real property of each. (By this time
the principle of taxing the property of an individual in the town in
which it lay and excluding property in England had been established.) As a guide for evaluating personal property and to insure
consistency throughout the commonwealth, the central government occasionally established set values. In 1646, among other
items, it valued "cowes of four year ould and upward, 5*li*;
heifers and steers betwixt 3 and 4 year ould, 4*li*; heifers and steers

13. The subject of taxation and the amount paid by each family has been
approached by a comparison of commonwealth law as recorded in *Colony Records*,
actual town practices as shown principally in "Boston Records," and, in the absence of tax rolls, the application of law, practice, and the ascertainable amount of
the commonwealth levies upon the town, to a modern assessment of the worth of
the identifiable town residents, the results being partially verified by comparison
with the very occasional statements by individuals about the payment of a given
amount in taxes.

between 2 and 3 year ould, fifty shillings; and between 1 and 2 year ould 30s." Similarly the selectmen and commissioner were to estimate the "returnes and gaines" of such artisans, tradesmen, and laborers who, having little real property, were nevertheless "to help beare the publike charge" in proportion to their incomes. The compilation completed, the list was to be carried by the commissioner to a meeting of the commissioners of all towns of the county to be reviewed and corrected, then transmitted to the commonwealth treasurer, who was to send warrants to the constables to collect taxes according to a schedule fixed by the Court. Thus in 1646 the constables were to collect a 20d poll tax (2s 6d or 30d in 1647), in addition to a sum dependent upon ability to pay: 1d per pound sterling assessed value on all real and personal property; a flat 3s 4d from every "laborer, artificer, and handicrafts man" with little property and a minimal income of 18d per day during the summer period of peak employment; and 1d per pound income from "all others . . . as smiths of all sorts, butchers, bakers, cooks, victuallers, etc." with substantial earnings but little property. Magistrates were exempted from poll taxes and were allowed 500li deduction on the assessed value of their estates; in 1648 they were entirely exempted from taxes. Also exempted were those "disabled by sickness, lamenes, or other infirmity." Children and servants who took no wages had their poll taxes paid by parents or masters.[14]

To some extent at least the new laws were an attempt to tap the riches of Boston, for under the older system of evaluating a town through a committee of the General Court Boston's proportion of the commonwealth rates reflected neither its size nor its worth. As late as 1645, for example, the town paid slightly less than one-sixth (16.2 per cent) of the total commonwealth levy, 200li of 1,233li 10s. Yet the new system was only partially implemented during the decade. The selectmen made use of the formal authority given them to assess the property and incomes of the townsmen, but not until 1651 was a tax commissioner regularly elected to join with them in the task. And until well into the third decade the selectmen themselves rated the inhabitants (though using the commonwealth schedules) and directed the col-

14. Colony Records, II, 173-75, 212-15, 239-40.

lection of levies by the constables, sending the receipts to the commonwealth treasurer.[15]   That the Bostonians consistently undervalued their town can be deduced from the fact that payments to the commonwealth in proportion to the total remained about the same as in 1645 and actually decreased in amount in some years—144*li* in 1646, 199*li* 18*s* in 1647, 167*li* 1*s* 6*d* in 1650.[16] Within the town average payments per family—8*s* 6*d* in 1650—were only slightly higher than in 1642. The range was no longer as great, however, lying between 6*s* and 2*li*. Average income is difficult to estimate because of the paucity of figures and the necessity of including as income the home consumption of home-grown or fabricated items. But it is clear that while in 1642 a laborer paid in commonwealth taxes slightly over one day's summer wages (1*s* 6*d*), in 1649 he paid about three and one-half days'; on the other hand, a man of substantial but not immense means who paid three or four days' income in 1642, paid but one day's income in 1649.[17] The tax structure in effect had come to favor "the Richer sort," although that fact did not dissuade the leading townsmen from protesting "the great and waighty charge" which they, "though not without complaints," were obliged to pay.[18]

15. The repetition of the act in 1646 and 1647 implies that it was not effected the first year, while in 1647 the provision requiring review of the lists by the county commissioners meeting as a body and the issuance of warrants by the treasurer was suspended to enable the towns to collect levies faster; in 1648 the Suffolk commissioners apparently met, but Dorchester, Hull, Braintree, and Hingham were fined for not sending their representatives, while there is no indication that Boston elected one. Indicative that the town was still collecting taxes on its own is the fact that in 1648 Boston was reviewing the constables' accounts for the rate; that in 1649 the General Court ruled that it was not "in the liberty of *any toune* or person to pay peage to the country rate" (*Colony Records*, III, 167, italics mine); that in the 1650's a Robert Pateshall, "having five pounds levied upon his estate by the townsmen of Boston towards the country rate" appealed for a rebate on the grounds that he was not subject to the levy (*ibid.*, 277); and that as late as 1654-55, while auditing its accounts, Boston included commonwealth rates as credits (i.e., indicating that the town had collected them) and debits (i.e., indicating that it had paid them to the treasurer). See "Copy from the Book of Accounts for the Town of Boston [1654-55]," Early Files of the Courts and Misc. Papers, Office of the Clerk of the Supreme Judicial Court, Suffolk Co., Boston. Thus, even after electing a tax commissioner for the first time—in 1651—Boston retained control of the gathering of commonwealth levies.

16. *Colony Records*, II, 112, 124; "Boston Records," 90, 92; "Aspinwall Notarial Records," 369.

17. See n. 13 above.

18. Petition of the freemen and inhabitants of the town of Boston to the General Court, Sept. 1, 1653, Mass. Archives. The town may also have served

The town, following the example of the commonwealth, increasingly mobilized its resources through taxation. From very early it relied upon occasional voluntary levies, as in 1634 when it gathered 30*li* to purchase Blackston's property. But by 1638, because many men took advantage of the informality of the town levies and their lack of legal status to "withdraw their helpe in such voluntary contributions," the General Court declared that all residents (including sojourners but excluding the casual transient) were liable for all town rates "proportionable to their ability" and empowered town officers to seek legal redress in the event of non-payment.[19] Under this act Boston began levying regular town rates in 1642, collecting in 1646 133*li* 12*s* for the town's use.[20] By the end of the second decade the tax rolls prepared for the commonwealth were being used in rating the population, the constables collecting town and commonwealth rates together. The town rates more than doubled the taxes of the individual Boston family when added to the commonwealth levies. By then, too, a substantial amount was being collected for the support of the church, the compensation paid to Cotton and Wilson alone amounting to approximately 150*li* a year by the end of the second decade.[21] And while the First Church clung to the principle of voluntary contributions, collecting its tithe in the form of small weekly donations from members and non-members alike and spe-

to collect the "college corn" during the 1640's, although it is doubtful. A voluntary levy initiated by President Dunster of Harvard and the Commissioners of the United Colonies, the college corn was recommended to the towns by the General Court in Nov. 1644. Harvard records indicate that Boston's families contributed 84*li* 18*s* 7½*d* during the years 1645-53, but there is no indication of how the funds were collected. Margery Somers Foster, "*Out of Smalle Beginings* ...": *An Economic History of Harvard College in the Puritan Period* (Cambridge, Mass., 1962), 90. In the absence of any town order one must assume that contributions were made directly to the College treasurer or someone delegated by him, and not through the town. Only in the third decade, when the General Court ordered the appointment in every town of an agent to collect gifts for the College, did Boston officially respond, the town electing John Coggan, John Newgate, and Samuel Cole to receive funds for the "mayntenance of the president and fellowes or pore Scollers of Hervert College." "Boston Records," 116.

19. *Colony Records*, I, 241.
20. "Boston Records," 65ff, 88.
21. *Good News from New-England*, in Mass. Hist. Soc., *Collections*, 4th Ser., 1 (1852), 212. Pastor Wilson received as estimated 60*li* a year in cash and produce, Cotton, 90*li*—a figure matched only by one other minister in the Bay commonwealth.

cial contributions to meet extraordinary expenses, there was always in the background the law requiring the payment of church levies.

The reliance on taxation as a means of gathering the strength of the town gradually displaced the actual calling together of the townsmen to labor on public projects. From the early 1640's on, when the commonwealth required the town to act, it did so either by subcontracting the work or dispatching laborers to do the job. Within the town, streets and paths came to be built and maintained not by the townsmen personally, but by hired men paid through special levies such as that of 1649 when 33*li* 1*s* was raised "to be expended on the Hygh wayes," or through allocation of other town funds or assets. Thus in 1644 two shopkeepers were authorized to hire laborers "to mend the highway at the head of the Cove neere their Shops, and charge it to the Townes account"; a new street being desired by the same two shopkeepers, they were empowered to build it "by what [financial] helpe of the neighbours they can attaine," the town's treasury to pay half the cost. In 1649 a group of townsmen contracted to build a new road by their property in return for the abatement of highway rates to the extent of 8*li* 16*s*. The same year, Peter Oliver contracted with the town to maintain a certain road "sufficient for Carte and horse" for seven years at 15*li* a year. In addition to tax abatements and direct payments, land was sometimes used as compensation for building and maintaining streets, James Johnson, at the end of the decade, contracting to "make and maintaine forever a sufficient hyh way for foot and Cart" in return for a sixteen-foot strip between his house lot and garden.[22]

All town projects came to be undertaken in a similar manner. Thus Henry Messinger's rates were abated by 6*s* in 1645 as compensation for his work in mending the schoolmaster's fence; Nathaniel Woodward, Sr., was paid 5*s* "for laying a water channell of Timber in one of the Cause wayes towards Rocksbury" in 1644. The work of fortification, begun with cooperative labor in the 1630's, was carried on through taxation in the 1640's. In 1644, the Fort Hill works having fallen into decay, the town met and agreed that restoration was vital, voting unanimously "to supply all necessary labours and charges" which the task might entail and

22. "Boston Records," 82, 94, 96, 99.

appointing a committee to direct the work and make "an equal Rate." New fortifications were begun at Merry's Point as well, though they had not progressed far when, in 1646, the inhabitants of the North End agreed to do the work on the condition that they "be freed from all rats and assessments" for other town fortifications until the rest of the town "have disbursed and layd out in equall proporcion of their estats with ours." The Bostonians took the lead among the harbor towns in the maintenance of the Castle Island fort after the commonwealth abandoned the works there, appointing a committee in 1644 "to Treat" with the neighboring towns and ultimately agreeing to undertake repairs, supply part of a permanent garrison, and pay 52*li* of a 280*li* annual charge. Roxbury, Dorchester, Cambridge, and Charlestown were to contribute 78*li*, the commonwealth, after much entreaty, agreeing to contribute the remainder. Boston's share was met by special rates—60*li* collected in 1646, 75*li* 11*s* 10*d* in 1647—though occasionally the town fell behind in its commitment, as in 1645, when it was fined by the General Court 20*li* for its dereliction, and in 1646, when a general town meeting agreed to send the constables to the Court "to answer the defect in not payinge that which is behind on the Garrison's wages."[23]

The town was a vehicle for community action in still other ways. No formal fire protection existed in the first two decades; it emerged in the 1650's in the form of town ordinances requiring the community to maintain buckets and ladders "outsyd of the meeting house" and the individual householder to have a ladder "that shall rech to the ridge of the house" and "a pole of about 12 foot long, with a good large swob at the end of it, to rech the rofe of his house to quench fire."[24] The danger of fire was ever present given wood construction and thatched roofs, and the whole town turned out when the cry of "fire" went up.

Within the community, too, the men of Boston armed themselves and trained for war; for while commonwealth law established the general framework of the militia, the organizational structure was basically town oriented. All adult males, including

23. *Ibid.*, 77, 80, 87, 89; *Winthrop's Journal*, II, 155, 158-60; *Colony Records*, II, 56.
24. "Boston Records," 114.

servants but excluding certain officeholders, were members of the Boston company or, after 1639, of the Artillery Company, an elite group of prominent townsmen from the various harbor communities organized independently of the general militia structure in emulation of London's famed Artillery Company and largely self-regulated.[25] The command structure of the militia stretched from the town company upward to the regiment—organized in 1636 when Boston's company under Captain John Underhill was joined with those of Roxbury, Dorchester, Weymouth, and Hingham as the South Regiment, commanded by "colonel" John Winthrop—and to the various agencies of commonwealth defense.[26] But the average militiaman's gaze did not extend farther than the company. Periodically the Bostonians trudged out to the Common to drill with matchlock and pike under the watchful eyes of their officers and the approving smiles of their wives and children. Into a company treasury, they paid fines for non-attendance, tardiness, or failure to have or maintain the requisite weapons, the money to be expended for company drums, banners, and other impedimenta. After 1637 they had the right to nominate their own officers from among the town's freemen, the General Court almost without exception appointing their choices. Their town government was itself involved in the militia organization, being required to maintain a watch house for the militiamen, to build facilities for the production of saltpeter, and to maintain a store of powder and extra weapons, the meetinghouse serving as the town "armory."[27]

The Bostonians were not always good soldiers. On the training field they wounded each other (a Watertown incident in which a servant inadvertently brought a loaded piece onto the field, fired it, and wounded himself and three others was not unique); they stumbled over each other (Captain Underhill, "to try how they would behave," sounded an alarm and "discovered the weakness of our people, who, like men amazed, knew not how to behave

25. In the third decade the town would be divided geographically into four foot companies; a company of horse would be organized for Suffolk County on a multi-town basis.
26. *Colony Records*, I, 186-87.
27. *Ibid.*, 344.

themselves");[28] they argued (in 1634, Ensign Richard Morris quarreled with the captain and resigned in a huff, while during the Hutchinsonian affair the church quarrel led the Boston men to refuse for a while to serve in an Indian expedition to which John Wilson was attached as chaplain). They missed training days and failed to keep up either their weapons or their discipline. But they guarded the town, maintaining posts on Beacon Hill and at Town Gate with militiamen from other towns. They kept watch and ward on the village streets. And when the test came, they allowed themselves to be drafted to serve with Underhill and Israel Stoughton against the Pequot Indians in far-off Connecticut.

The town served not only as an arbiter and a vehicle for common action, but as the prime agency of what can be termed, even in that day, "social welfare." The social conscience noted in Winthrop, the traditional role of the English parish in regard to its poor, the precedent of the English poor laws, all obliged the community to care for its indigent and sick, while the minor roles played by church and commonwealth left a vacuum which only the town could fill.

In theory, the church's deacons and "Widowes"—"Antient women of sixty yeares of age, well reported of for good workes"—were charged with the care of "the poore brethren, whether of their own body [i.e., of the church] or strangers."[29] And to a certain extent at least, money and commodities were paid into the church's coffers and distributed to those in need, or left as legacies to be administered by the church in the interest of the poor of the community. But as the church turned inward and as church and town became distinct entities, the social conscience of the church tended to be confined to its own members, and even then it was not as conscientious as it might have been. Indeed, the ministerial preoccupation with God tended to overcome mere charitable impulses. Calamities fell upon the individual by the will of God and as punishment for sin; hence one did not alleviate suffering but pointed out the justice of it and the ways to make amends, as Thomas Hooker did during the height of the depression in 1640:

28. *Winthrop's Journal*, I, 91-92.
29. Cotton, *Doctrine of the Church*, 4; idem, *Way of the Churches of Christ in New-England*, 39.

The fall in values, the indebtedness of so many and their inability to pay, the whole tragedy was to him the result of "our synfull departure from the right and righteous wayes of God." "The Churches and the commonwealth, by joynt consent and serious consideration must make a privy search what have been the courses, and synfull Cariages, which have brought in, and increased this epidemicall evill: Pride and idlenesse, excesse in apparell, building, diet." As for immediate relief, he could only advise that "the debtors . . . freely and fully tender themselves and all they have unto the hands and be at the mercy and devotion of the creditors: . . . It is too much that men have rashly, and unjustly taken more than they were able to repay and satisfie; Ergo they must not add falsness and dissimulation when they come to pay: and so not only breake their estates; but their consciences finally."[30]

Hooker's sentiments, impractical as they were, were not uncommon,[31] and it remained for the secular authorities to seek ways to alleviate the general economic plight and succor the individual through stay laws and similar legislation. In the 1640's, moreover, widows seem to have existed only in theory, Cotton writing that "wee finde it somewhat rare to finde a woman of so great an age . . . and withall, to be so hearty, and healthy, and strong, as to be fit to undertake such a service."[32] The deacons were businessmen in their own right, and had the care of church property and the maintenance of the ministry to worry about. And the general membership—whose concern might have evoked action by the church—undoubtedly found the long hours "spent in the publique Ordinances" detrimental to what Thomas Lechford called the "necessary duties of the Sabbath," the "visitation of the sick, and poore."[33]

There were few to care for in proportion to the total population, for except during the depression, opportunity for subsistence, if not wealth, was ready to hand. Yet there were cases. Thomas Scotto fell into debt in the mid-1640's, and the town gave him

30. Hooker to Thomas Shepard, Nov. 2, 1640, Hutchinson Papers, Mass. Archives.
31. On the contrary, the energetic work of the Reverend Hugh Peter in espousing practical solutions to the economic problem was uncommon.
32. Cotton, *Way of the Churches of Christ in New-England*, 39.
33. Lechford, *Plain Dealing*, 129.

public employment; in exchange for his house (valued at 55*li*), it assumed his debts and granted him a plot of marshland. In 1644 the proceeds of land sold at Braintree (10*li*) were paid to Henry Flint "on consideration of his late greate losse through the hand of Gods Providence by fire." The same year John Berry, a servant left ill and uncared for in the town, was lodged with Charity White, the town paying Mistress White 26*s* for his thirteen-week stay; Elder Thomas Oliver, a physician by profession, was ordered paid 7*li* for seven months spent in curing him, a sum ultimately increased to 9*li* by accrued interest as a result of the town's delay in paying. Presumably Berry, like another of Elder Oliver's charity patients, Daniel Mansfield, was sold as an indentured servant to reimburse the town. Somewhat earlier, the rates of "John Smith, Gent." were remitted "upon consideration of the great losses that of late have befallen him in Ireland."[34]

By the early years of the third decade the cost of social welfare averaged as much as 50*li* a year, the accounts of one year indicating direct payments of 26*li* 15*s* 6*d* and the rebate of taxes amounting to a total of 26*li* 6*s* 3*d*.[35] Rising welfare costs throughout the commonwealth led to arguments between towns over which should assume the responsibility for an unfortunate individual, and the general government had of necessity to intervene, directing that any two magistrates should have the power "to determine all [such] differences" and "to dispose of all unsetled persons into such townes as they shall judge to bee most fitt for the maintenance of such persons and families and the most ease of the countrey." Only where neither the town nor church was "able to releive their pore," the Court subsequently ruled, was it "fit they should be helped out of the publike treasury" of the commonwealth.[36] In Boston, rising costs resulted in the town's attempting to exclude the potentially troublesome by scrutinizing the financial resources of those applying for inhabitantship or admission as sojourners and on occasion, demanding that an established resident put up bond for the applicant, as Theodore Atkinson did to the extent of 20*li* "to

34. "Boston Records," 71, 80, 83, 86, 87, 89; *Assistants' Records*, II, 127, 128.

35. "Copy from the Book of Accounts for the Town of Boston [1654-55]," Office of the Clerk of the Supreme Judicial Court, Suffolk Co., Boston.

36. *Colony Records*, I, 264, II, 199.

secur the Town harmless from all Charge that shall com" by virtue of the admittance of one James Pitney "or any of his famyly."[37] However, the problem of the indigent—sick and well—continued to plague the community and to be a charge on the town.

It was through the town, too, that the men of Boston acted when, anxious for the formal education of their children, they set out to establish a school. Philemon Pormont was "intreated" by a town meeting in 1635 "to become scholemaster, for the teaching and nourtering of children with us." Pormont taught for no more than a year, for in 1636 Daniel Maud was engaged as master, receiving from "the richer inhabitants" over 40*li* to build his house and gather educational materials and from the town a grant of land and a small annual stipend. When Maud left in 1643 to go as teacher to the Dover church, John Woodbridge, an indentured servant, carried on until a permanent teacher could be engaged, his master, Deacon Eliot, receiving 8*li* for his services for a year. Robert Woodmancy followed, at a salary of 50*li* per annum in 1645.[38]

Attendance at the school was both free and voluntary, but only a minority of Boston's boys and few if any of its girls chorused their lessons at Mr. Maud's or Mr. Woodmancy's, learning their letters and ciphers and moving on to Latin and Greek. Formal education was not generally considered fit for women; they were to learn their letters and "huswiferie" in the home.[39] Most boys worked of necessity and obtained what education they could through the family or as apprentices. Edward Johnson commented in regard to Harvard College that "although they were not among a people who counted ignorance the mother of devotion, yet were the greater part of the people wholly devoted to the plow." "How to have both go on together, as yet they know not"; hence "it was thought meet [that] learning should plead for it self, and ... plod out a way to live." John Hull's education was as much as most Boston boys could expect: Ten years

37. "Boston Records," 111.
38. *Ibid.*, 5, 17, 82, 99, 160.
39. The will of John Cogswell of Ipswich, dated Dec. 13, 1652, Mass. Archives, is exceptional in providing for the formal education of a daughter: "And my daughter, Elisabeth, I desire that she may be bred at schoole, untill she is fourteen years old, and then to goe to service and earne her living."

old when he arrived with his father in 1635, he had "a little keeping at school," seven years helping his father as a farmboy, and finally was apprenticed to his brother, a goldsmith.[40] However, the embryo of mandatory public education under local auspices existed. In 1642 the town assumed responsibility for its children when the General Court, "taking into consideration the great neglect of many parents and masters in training up their children in learning, and labor, and other imployments which may be proffitable to the common wealth," directed the towns "to take account from time to time of all parents and masters ... concerning their calling and implyment of their children, especially of their ability to read and understand the principles of religion and the capitall lawes of this country" and where necessary apprentice to another family "the children of such as they shall [find] not to be able and fitt to imploy and bring them up."[41]

Master Maud's schoolhouse was also his home; his minimal compensation was augmented by his own labor in his half-acre garden and about his livestock. As a result, in the first years the cost to the town for education was negligible. But by Woodmancy's time a formal schoolhouse was deemed necessary and was built through a special levy of 40*li* laid on the town's "drawers of wine." A town-owned house—that purchased in 1645 from Thomas Scotto for 55*li*—was placed at the master's disposal. Education, including the upkeep of the schoolhouse and the master's dwelling, and Woodmancy's 50*li* salary, constituted a far from negligible expense; indeed, by the mid-1640's it had become, apart from the maintenance of Castle Island, the largest single item among the town's regular expenditures. This cost was covered in part by town levies, Woodmancy's salary being paid from the rates in 1649. But so vital was "teachinge the schollers" that the town sought ways to build a permanent endowment, allocating various rents due it as a perpetual revenue for the school. In

---

40. *Johnson's Wonder-Working Providence*, 200; "The Diaries of John Hull ...," American Antiquarian Society, *Archaelogia Americana*, 3 (1857), 142. In regard to his sons, the Cogswell will is typical: "If any one of them be capable of being good Scholler then I would have him brought up to it; And the other to be bound Prentice at ten yeares old to a Godly honest man where he may be well brought up, and know how to order husbandry affairs."
41. *Colony Records*, II, 6-7.

1644 revenue from Deer Island was set aside, rents from John
Oliver and James Penn (7li in 1645, 1646, 1647) and Edward
Bendall (14li in 1648, 1649, and thereafter for an anticipated
twenty-one years) to be paid "for the scooles use." By 1649 the
income from five hundred acres of Braintree land, Spectacle
Island, Long Island, Town Dock, a parcel bequeathed to the town
by Christopher Stanley specifically for the school, and a miscellaneous array of lots and marsh plots—in addition to Deer Island
—had been allocated for the school, a total of 36li 11s 4d. The
rents were frequently in arrears (so often in fact that in ensuing
years the town would gradually give up its attempt to collect
them on most of the land), but in the early 1650's actual payments to the school from the rents during one year totaled 34li 5s
9d.[42]

The organs of town government, through which the community acted and by which the individual's relations with the community and his neighbors were established, were those which had
evolved in the mid-1630's: town meeting and selectmen. Yet
there were changes over the years. Inevitably, change resulted
from a growing, ever more complex population, from a materialism which evoked individual effort at the expense of the community, and from the necessity of restraining individualism in the
community's interest.[43]

The authority of the town rested upon English tradition, the
course of events in the first years, and the General Court statute
of 1635. But power accrued to it. Within the community itself,
new functions evolved out of old or out of new situations, the town's
involvement in wharfage rights, for example. On the commonwealth level the scope of law and governmental activity steadily expanded and the central government, overburdened by the mass of
its own regulations, regularly delegated more and more authority to
the town. Thus the responsibility for both wage and price regulation fell to local authorities late in the first decade, although Boston

42. Robert Child to Samuel Hartlib, Dec. 24, 1645, Col. Soc. Mass., *Publications*, 38 (1959), 53; "Boston Records," 65, 82, 86, 92, 93, 94, 95, 97, 99,
109; "Copy from the Book of Accounts for the Town of Boston [1654-55],"
Office of the Clerk of the Supreme Judicial Court, Suffolk Co., Boston.
43. The changes can be followed in "Boston Records"; *Colony Records*, I and
II; and *Assistants' Records*, II.

did little in this regard in the 1640's. In 1639 the town assumed the task of nominating "fit" men to operate its ordinaries and sell wine, the actual license to be obtained from the commonwealth; before this the commonwealth had both selected and authorized the purveyors of alcohol. By 1647 the selectmen were licensing pubs in the town, authorizing the sale of beer and establishing its price, without reference to the central government. Similarly, the town's concern for fortifications and its involvement in the affairs of the marketplace through sealers and viewers of a variety of products were extensions of its activity. The town frequently acted in anticipation of the commonwealth, and the law merely ratified what the town was already doing. For example, long before the General Court recommended wage and price regulation to the towns, Boston had attempted on its own but without success to establish ceilings on "cattell comodities, victualls and labourers and Workmen's Wages," while the Boston school was established over a decade before the "ould deluder, Satan" act, which empowered and ordered the towns to erect schools.[44]

The regular extension of the functions of the town—its ever-increasing role in the everyday affairs of the townsmen—brought an end to the predominance which the selectmen had established during the first decade. The townsmen, whose lives were touched on every side by the activities of town government, were not content merely to select a governing body and retire from the scene. Following the reassertion of the authority of the town meeting in 1642 (on the issue of land distribution), the general meeting met more often as a local legislature. The town as a whole agreed to assume the burden of Castle Island in 1643, to set down commonage regulations in 1646, and to accept the reversion of Town Dock from the Hill proprietors in 1649, in each case leaving the administration of the general decision to the selectmen.[45]

Town elections became more formalized, too. In the first decade, deputies to the General Court had been elected on the

44. "Boston Records," 5; *Colony Records,* II, 203.
45. "Body of Liberties," 74, stipulated that the selectmen act "according to Instructions given them in writeing" by the town, but there is no indication of the Boston meeting undertaking written instructions until 1651 when a committee was appointed "to Draw up the power to be given to the Select men, which is first to be presented to the Towne and Consented too." "Boston Records," 103.

eve of the Court's meetings. Town selectmen had been elected
irregularly, although the tendency had been to hold elections
every six months. Among other officers, only the constables' term
was regularly set (at one year), the rest being elected when the
need arose and directed to serve "untill another be Chosen." At
the turn of the decade began the annual election of deputies to
serve in all sessions of the General Court during the year, and in
1646 a general town meeting agreed to convene annually on the
second of March to elect the deputies, selectmen, and other officers
for the year. Paper ballots were used in the election of deputies
according to a 1635 requirement of the General Court; presumably by the 1640's ballots were used in the election of all
town officers, the electoral procedure following that of the commonwealth.

Other features of town government were fixed by agreement
or usage. The same general town meeting which regularized
annual elections fixed the number of selectmen at seven; the size
of the board had ranged from twelve to seven prior to 1638, nine
being elected from 1639 through 1645. The word "selectman"
itself began to come into usage as the second decade progressed,
replacing the previous "men for prudential affairs," "townsmen,"
or the "nine" or "ten men." The selectmen's meetings became
more regular. During the first decade they met in one of the
members' homes, but by 1641 they were holding meetings around
the table of an inn, the constable being ordered that year to pay
Robert Turner 2*li* 18*s* "for diet for the Townsmen."[46] In 1649
they were attempting to build a townhouse in which they, the
general town meeting, and the various courts centered in Boston
could meet, a project completed only in the third decade with the
aid of a bequest from merchant Robert Keayne.[47]

The number of town officers grew as the size and character of
the town changed. In the 1630's the townsmen had elected the
selectmen, two constables, two surveyors to lay out paths and
streets "as need shall require," and the deputies or, as they were
first called, the "committees" to the General Court who repre-

46. "Boston Records," 53, 63.
47. *Ibid.*, 94.

sented the town's interests in the central government.[48] The few simple tasks of an agricultural village were overseen by elected or appointed *ad hoc* officers and committees—allotters, fence viewers, water bailies, a committee to see that the cattle were put away from Shawmut, another to direct the work on Fort Hill. And what can be considered town employees included the herder, hogreeve, pound keeper, drummer, and schoolmaster.

In the second decade, however, two constables were not enough. The town had grown, and so too had the office. Beginning as simply the right arm of the magistrates, the constables had become jacks-of-all-trades charged with a variety of commonwealth and town functions. They were officers of the courts, serving warrants and writs, summoning jurors, inflicting punishments when the executioner was absent, collecting fines. They were officers of the selectmen, doing their bidding in every conceivable area. Thus at one meeting of the selectmen in 1642 the constables were ordered to take care of the building of a saltpeter house in the prison yard, to give "speedy warning" to Walter Merry to clear the highway by his house of the obstruction he had built upon it, and to have the cemetery fenced in "with all convenient speed."[49] They were peace officers maintaining (from the second decade onward) a "constables watch" in the town—armed men drawn from the militia tramping Boston's streets by night.[50] They set in motion "*Pursutes* or *Hue-and-cries* after Murtherers, Man-slayers, Peace-breakers, Theevs, Robbers, Burglarers and other Capital offenders," apprehended "without *Warrant*, such as are overtaken with drink, swearing, Sabboth-breaking, lying, vagrant persons, night-walkers, or any other that shall offend in any of these," and presented malefactors to the courts for punishment.[51]

48. *Ibid.*, 7.

49. *Ibid.*, 70.

50. In the 1630's the Boston watch was commanded by Captain John Under-hill, the law stipulating that the watch was under the direction of the constables only in those towns where no militia captain dwelt. During Indian troubles of the mid-1630's, the watch everywhere was an offshoot of the militia. In 1640 the watch "in times of peace" was committed to the charge of the constables throughout the commonwealth, although the constables were to be guided as to where and when to set the watch by general legislation. In 1652 the select-men of Boston were empowered "to give order to the constables" about setting the Boston watch. *Colony Records*, I, 293, III, 265.

51. *Colony Records*, II, 150-51; Farrand, ed., *Laws and Liberties of Massachusetts*, 13.

They were part of the legislative process, charged with publishing
new laws by posting them on the meetinghouse door and preserving copies bought from the commonwealth secretary and open
to any townsman's perusal.   Electoral officers, they summoned
the townsmen and freemen to elections.   They were fiscal officers,
collecting both town and commonwealth rates and on occasion
disbursing town and commonwealth funds.   Onerous and expensive—for the constables were regularly fined for failing in one or
more of their multifarious tasks—the office by the end of the
period was sometimes refused, men choosing to pay the fine for
refusal in preference to accepting the burdens of office.   It is no
wonder that the number of constables was increased to four and
by the third decade, to six, four on Shawmut, and one each at
Muddy River and Rumney Marsh.

Similarly, the number of surveyors of highways was increased
from two to four by the end of the second decade.   And where
before they had both laid out and maintained the streets, they
came to confine themselves to maintenance; when a new street
was to be laid out, special officers were appointed to do the work.

Not only did the number of officers grow but wholly new
offices were created, some filled by election, some by appointment.
A town recorder made his appearance, charged with keeping the
minutes of the town and of the selectmen, records having previously been kept informally by one of the selectmen.   In 1641
the office of clerk of the writs was established to issue summonses
and attachments pertaining to civil proceedings, formerly within
the province of the magistrates; subsequently the clerk was
charged with recording the births and deaths of the community.
Schoolmaster Maud was appointed to the office by the General
Court in 1641, William Aspinwall in 1643.   But when Aspinwall
left in 1651 the town itself was allowed to choose his successor.
The surveyor-of-arms appeared, charged with caring for the
town's weapons, powder, and equipment under the direction of
the selectmen and the commonwealth surveyor-general.   There
were the various sealers and viewers of market activities, regular
rather than the earlier *ad hoc* officers who patrolled the streets
and waterfront to see that refuse and garbage did not accumulate to the public's displeasure, and additional town employees—a

bellringer who tolled the Bostonians to bed and to awakening, a cemetery keeper. A treasurer was named, at first merely to collect monies due to the town from the sale or rent of land, but subsequently to keep all town accounts in order, a next to impossible task.

Fiscal confusion abounded. It was unavoidable, for from the days of the depression specie was scarce, and commonwealth and town levies could be met in kind according to fixed schedules. Thus in 1649 the constables had to accept for taxes wheat at 5*s* a bushel, barley at 6*s* 6*d*, rye and peas at 4*s*, and corn at 3*s*. Fines and rents were payable in kind as well. The difficulties of the collecting officers were great; the variability of commodity prices frequently resulted in the acceptance of goods at one price level and their sale at another, while the cost of transportation and storage, faulty measurement, and spoilage had somehow to be absorbed. Such difficulties were less important in Boston, the political and commercial capital, where "mony Billes" and "shop comodyties" were more common than elsewhere and where merchants could so easily put produce collected as taxes into the stream of trade and commerce.[52] (Pity poor Constable Morton of Weymouth, who collected his rates in wood products, only to find them too difficult to transport, then in cattle which he drove to Boston, where he hoped to pay his commonwealth levies with them or to exchange them for wheat or grain which the commonwealth treasurer would accept. After spending several days "thereabout" he drove them home again, for it was a bad market and "none would be received.")[53] Those collecting Boston's funds had always to balance their accounts with a notation similar to one from the third decade: "To loss in corn in price and measure and charges 4*li*."[54]

No single officer in Boston had complete fiscal responsibility, a fact compounding the confusion. The constables were collectively responsible for the collection of general levies and fines, yet they

52. Draft order of the General Court for the raising of 150*li* for the support of the garrison at Castle Island, 1645, MS Photostats, Box 3, Mass. Hist. Soc. Library.

53. Petition of Nicholas Morton, late Constable of Weymouth, to the General Court, Nov. 22, 1655, Mass. Archives.

54. "Copy from the Book of Accounts for the Town of Boston [1654-55]," Office of the Clerk of the Supreme Judicial Court, Suffolk Co., Boston.

proceeded as individuals. Invariably merchants, they incorporated what they collected in kind with their own goods, exporting them on their own individual accounts. Their collections being merely credits upon which the town could draw to meet expenses or pay the town's portion of the commonwealth levy, the constables were disbursing officers as well. And while the town's orders-to-pay were directed to them collectively, they paid individually, occasionally in cash but more usually in goods, bills-of-exchange drawn upon a particular constable, or upon someone indebted to the constable, or upon his English agent. The constables' account delivered to their successors was an amalgamation of their four separate accounts, while cash on hand was in the form of credit instruments certifying the indebtedness of the old constables to the new. Account-keeping was further confused by the selectmen's practice of abating town rates for services rendered or in consideration of need, the constables being ordered not to collect such rates.

The treasurer for his part was charged with collecting revenues accruing from town land and disbursing what he received. Yet little money actually passed through his hands. Rents allotted to the maintenance of the school, for example, were frequently paid in produce directly to the schoolmaster, Edward Bendall paying his Deer Island rent to the master "in provisions and clothing."[55] Various town services were paid for by the inhabitants through fees paid directly to town officers or employees such as the herdsmen, or as fines, the officers normally keeping as compensation a portion of those levied.[56] In any balance sheet of the town's credits and debits such direct payments can be accounted as part of the revenue and expenditures of the community. Similarly, special assessments were frequently paid directly to those officers concerned. Thus special levies for highways were collected and expended by the surveyors; levies for maintenance costs of common fences around given fields were paid to elected fence committees, which hired laborers to do the work. The town treasurer, in keeping his "Book of

55. "Boston Records," 92.
56. Treasurer and constables (and deacons of the church) were considered reimbursed for their efforts by the profits they might make through the use of public (or church) funds while in their hands. Officials such as the selectmen and deputies served without compensation as a public obligation.

Accounts," could not possibly gather all the diverse strands of this complex financing together, though in a single extant page covering 1654-55 it is apparent that he made a valiant attempt. Upon the basis of this account, of the known expenditures and collections of the town during the last few years of the second decade, and of an estimate of what passed directly from townsmen to town officers and employees, one can hypothesize a town account for the last year of the 1640's to indicate the extensiveness and complexity of the town's operation.[57]

For all of its importance in the life of its people, however, for all its growth and assumption of authority, the town was never completely disentangled from the commonwealth. The connections between the two were manifold. The functions of the constables, the marketplace officers, the clerk of the writs, and the militia were avowedly half-commonwealth, half-town. Town government itself frequently served as an agent of the central government, its actions often commanded by it and its derelictions fined. The relationship between the town and commonwealth was still—as it had been in the first years—a variation of that between the English county and the local parish, although the commonwealth was stronger vis-à-vis the town than was the county in its relations with the parish, inasmuch as there was no superior element of government to supersede commonwealth authority or to which one could appeal, the link to England being but tenuous and undefined. Hence, while it was the town's responsibility to care for its own indigent, it was the commonwealth's responsibility to insure that the town did not shirk, or if it did that the individual

57. The Book of Accounts was presumably kept throughout the 1640's, for there are a number of mentions of it; only one page has been located, however, the "Copy from the Book of Accounts for the Town of Boston [1654-55]" in the files of the Clerk of the Supreme Judicial Court, Suffolk Co., Boston. The "Hypothetical Balance Sheet for Boston at the Turn of the Second Decade" is based upon this page, a computation of the actual expenses and income of the town indicated in "Boston Records" for the year 1649 (augmented by indications in the various commonwealth records), and estimates of the expenses and income for 1649 made on the basis of known figures for the years 1645-54. That it is a hypothetical balance sheet is stressed. It is presented here to indicate only in a very general way the sums collected and expended by the town and the proportionate expenses for various services (for example, the proportion of highway expenses to school expenses). The greater number of individual items listed under "expenses" are drawn from the 1654-55 account and are included to show the types of expenditures current in 1649 rather than the actual amounts.

HYPOTHETICAL BALANCE SHEET FOR BOSTON AT THE TURN OF THE SECOND DECADE

Expenses

Expenses	li	s	d	li	s	d
To the commonwealth (levy)				167	1	0
To the commonwealth (fine imposed on town)				10	0	0
To the maintenance of the Castle				75	5	0
To diet for deputies to the Gen. Ct.				7	3	0
To diet for the selectmen				8	3	6
To the school:						
Salary to Mr. Woodmancy	50	0	0			
Arrears in salary	3	18	9			
To Goodman Gridley for the well	5	19	6			
To work at the schoolhouse		8	6			
To mending the school window		12	0			
To repair of the schoolmaster's fence	3	2	0	63	18	3
To welfare:						
To G. Rust for keeping G. Palmer	25	12	9			
To A. Beck for G. Edwards	1	0	6			
Disbursements for G. Edwards		2	5			
To T. Oliver for medical services	9	0	0			
To abatement of rates	19	8	0	55	3	8
To highways:						
Expended by the surveyors of highways	33	1	0			
To Peter Oliver for maintenance	7	0	0			
To Bro. Rawlines for land for highway	1	0	0			
To work at Rumney Marsh and Muddy River	7	18	8			
To abatement of rates for highway work	9	8	3	58	7	11
To repair of the common fences				8	8	3
To repair of town property:						
To I. Cullimore for the stocks	1	6	0			
To G. Matson for the beacon and material	8	7	0			
To mending Roxbury Gate, and iron work		18	11	10	11	11
To a new bell for the bellman				1	1	0
To the purchase of town powder				1	5	0
To firing the guns on election day				1	15	0
To town employees:						
Bellringer	4	10	0			
Cowherder	7	0	0			
Cemetery keeper	2	10	0			
Pound keeper	3	10	5			
Hogreeve	2	5	0			
To Misc. Officials (viewers, sealers, etc.)	25	0	0	44	15	5
To Misc. debts owed by the town				6	11	6
To loss in corn in price and measure and charge				4	0	2
Total expenses				521	18	2
Balance on hand with treasurer				6	4	0
Balance on hand with constables				32	3	10
Arrears in payments to town				24	5	0
Total				584	11	0

Income

Income	li	s	d	li	s	d
Levies:						
For the commonwealth	167	1	0			
For the town	194	17	8			
For the highways	33	1	0			
For the maintenance of the Castle	75	0	0			
For the common fences	8	0	0	477	19	8
Sale of land:						
At Braintree	10	0	0			
Misc.	3	0	0	13	0	0
Fines and forfeitures				12	10	0
Rents:						
James Everill, Town Dock	6	16	10			
Thomas Painter, Fox Hill	2	0	0			
Benjamin Ward, marsh	3	0	0			
Edward Bendall, Deer Island	14	13	4			
William Phillips, Stanley bequest						
Moses Paine, 500 acr., Braintree	2	1	0			
Spectacle Island	1	10	0			
Long Island	5	8	0			
Misc.	3	3	2	38	11	4
Payments on arrears owed to the town				5	10	0
Fees and fines paid directly to town employees and officers				37	0	0
Total				584	11	0

himself did not suffer for it. Similarly, while the townsmen yoked and ringed their hogs in obedience to local regulations and under the supervision of town officers, there lay behind the town a whole body of commonwealth statutes ordering them to do the very same thing, and a commonwealth officialdom prepared to punish both townsmen and town officers if the hogs remained unringed and unyoked.

From the commonwealth government, moreover, the Bostonians individually and collectively sought favors or redress of grievances. Together they appealed through their deputies or by petition to the General Court for favors for the town, asking for an augmenting of town land, a second annual fair, the status of a borough. They solicited its aid in resolving boundary disputes with other towns or conflicts over which of two towns was responsible for a bridge between communities. They appealed to it against high taxes, against the exemption of the magistrates from the rates. The women of the town, led by Ann Cotton, Elizabeth Winthrop, Mary Coggan, Margery Colborne, Lydia Oliver, and Elinor Shrimpton, petitioned on behalf of midwife Alice Tilly, accused of the "miscarrying of many wimen and children under hir hand." (The women had a logical argument, for while they wrote "in childlike boldness" as befitting their sex, they could point out that "whereas the Honord Magistrates and many men more can speake but hearesay; wee and many more of us can speake by experience.")[58]

The merchants and artisans of the town solicited the commonwealth most often. They asked for favorable trade regulations or the right to establish themselves as self-regulating companies with commercial monopolies in various areas. Thus "diverse of the merchants of Boston" successfully petitioned to be established as "a free company of adventurers" to enjoy a monopoly of the trade of the Delaware River for twenty-one years.[59] (This particular venture was singularly unsuccessful inasmuch as the Dutch and Swedes were already established on the river.) The vintners of Boston and Charlestown together petitioned for and

58. Boston's petitions are spread through Mass. Archives; those of the women on the subject of Mistress Tilly are to be found in vol. IX.
59. *Winthrop's Journal*, II, 164; *Colony Records*, II, 60.

received a monopoly of the retailing of wine for a period of five years, while various artisan groups—shipwrights, coopers, shoemakers—received from the commonwealth the right to regulate their own trades.   Bostonians sometimes circumvented the town by petitions, soliciting tavern licenses, for example, long after the commonwealth had left the selection of taverners to local government.

To the average Bostonian the most obvious symbols of the commonwealth were the magistrates, the members of the Court of Assistants, including the governor and deputy governor, resident in the town and sitting as justices of the peace, a role they had assumed during the first year—Winthrop throughout the period, Bellingham and John Winthrop, Jr., intermittently from the mid-1630's, Coddington from 1633 to 1637, Henry Vane and Atherton Haugh briefly in 1635 and 1636, William Hibbens from 1643 through 1649.   But even these obvious symbols of commonwealth authority were themselves familiar figures to the Bostonians—neighbors and acquaintances, if not quite friends.   Before them the townsmen appeared to pledge their oaths of fidelity. All adult males, including servants but excluding transients resident in the town for less than six months, were required after 1634 under pain of punishment and even banishment to swear "by the greate and dreadfull name of the ever lyveing God" to be "true and faithfull" to the commonwealth, giving it "assistance and support" with both their "person and estate," and submitting "to the wholesome lawes made and established by the same."[60] The town's young couples, after announcing their intention at three separate town meetings or Thursday lectures, sought out a magistrate to join them in marriage, a civil rather than religious ceremony.   Before the magistrates town officers in the first decade took their oaths of office after being elected by the town.   The consent of at least one magistrate was necessary for certain town actions, the apprenticing of an idle townsman, for example, although in Boston the invariable presence of a magistrate among the

60. *Colony Records*, I, 354.   In 1634 all males over twenty were required to take either the freeman's oath or inhabitant's oath of fidelity (the only difference being a reference to voting in the former).   In 1635 the oaths were required of all over sixteen.

selectmen meant that no special application to higher authority was necessary.[61]

The Bostonians sought justice in commonwealth courts, and to them the magistrates were the primary guardians of the law. The magistrate's home was a criminal court, where he acted upon direct knowledge of the offense or upon presentment by town officials or constables. Minor offenders went no further along the road to punishment. Thus in July 1639 Richard Hanon, Edward Simonds, and William Firnwell, "taken loytering and sleeping abrod in tyme of exercise upon the Lords day," were fined 3s apiece by Governor Winthrop, while Nicholas Davison "for swearing submitted to a fine of 20s."[62] The assembled magistrates alone determined guilt or innocence in lesser cases during the first decade, but the more serious offenders were committed to prison or bail pending an appearance before a higher tribunal —the full Court of Assistants prior to 1638—there to be indicted by a grand jury and tried before a petty jury should the crime be of such a nature as to entail capital punishment.

The magistrates constituted informal civil courts, too. Lay and church leaders initially frowned upon "going to law," the church inveighing against it and attempting to resolve disputes among members by itself, the laymen trying to arbitrate disputes in a friendly way rather than resolving them by resort to impersonal law. Employment of lawyers was discouraged. Even though Winthrop was one, he had complained in England of the "multitude of Atturnies" who "take out processe against their neighbors upon very slight occasions," and he was echoed in John Cotton's description of "unconscionable Advocates" who "bolster out a bad case by quirks of wit, and tricks and quillets of Law" and "use their tongues as weapons of unrightousnesse . . . to plead

61. Farrand, ed., *Laws and Liberties of Massachusetts*, 37-38, and *passim*.
62. "John Winthrop's Memoranda on Court Cases [1639]," *Winthrop Papers*, IV, 128-29. Boston always had resident magistrates, but elsewhere—in towns without such—elected "commissioners" constituted small cause courts, presumably for civil suits alone. In such towns, criminal offenses were heard by the nearest magistrate according to an act of 1647 (*Colony Records*, II, 192-93) and by the county court before then. The Boston magistrates were presumably limited to levying fines of 40s or less, though during the first years they were allowed to inflict corporal punishment while sitting as pairs. Appeals were allowed to the Great Quarter Court and County Court.

in corrupt Causes."[63]   Nevertheless the Bostonians, even in the 1630's, sued each other.   Church members at times took their complaints to the elders, but to an ever-increasing extent a would-be litigant appeared before a magistrate seeking advice and counsel, the magistrate undertaking "either [to] divert the suit, if the cause be unjust, or direct it in a right course, if it be good." Arbitration would be attempted, and this failing, the case would come to court, possibly before the same magistrate to whom the initial appeal had been made (a justifiable cause of complaint, for the magistrate had already heard and determined the justice of the suit).   Adjudication was swift once the law was appealed to.   Matters were "presently heard, and ended the same court," and the collection of costs and damages was put in the hands of the constables or the commonwealth marshal, although the Bostonians began displaying a penchant for the law toward the end of the decade, one observer noting that "some causes come to be heard again, and new suits grow upon the old."   For the most part the contenders spoke for themselves during the first decade, stumbling and hesitating, unable "to open the cause fully and clearly," though occasionally (if the sum involved was large enough to warrant hearing it before the Court of Assistants) a magistrate might act as advocate, arguing the cause in the interest of justice without "fee or reward for his paines."[64]

The prejudice against lawyers did not last.   It gave way before need, for a people grasping for the rich opportunities of the New World unavoidably trespassed upon each other.   Thus those skilled in law became necessities—Lechford at the turn of the decade, George Story representing Goody Sherman in her suit against Robert Keayne for the value of one sow, John Chidley representing the plaintiff in a suit against John Coggan for 253*li* 15*s* 2*d* and costs in 1647, and Henry Rashley.   Judicial procedures were refined, and the English legal tradition, somewhat ignored in the first years, was reinstated.   The number of courts multiplied under the pressure of civil disputes and criminal in-

63. Winthrop, "Common Grevances," *Winthrop Papers,* I, 309; John Cotton, *An Exposition upon the Thirteenth Chapter of the Revelation* (London, 1655), 163.

64. *Winthrop's Journal,* II, 37; Lechford, *Plain Dealing,* 69; "Body of Liberties," 39.

dictments. In 1638 a "particulare Courte" consisting of three or more magistrates residing "in or near" Boston—the governor or deputy governor always to be one—was set up to assume jurisdiction in civil cases involving up to 40*li* (a limitation subsequently abolished) and in criminal cases where the accused was not in jeopardy of life, limb, or banishment. In the early 1640's, with the emergence of counties, the "particular" court would become the "Boston" or "County" or "Quarter Court" serving Suffolk and until 1648, Middlesex; the Court of Assistants took the name of Great Quarter Court.[65] To the Quarter Court were given all the appurtenances of the Court of Assistants: a grand jury "to inform the Court of any misdemeanours that they shall know or hear to be committed by any person or persons whatsoever within this jurisdiction"; petty juries to establish the facts, with the right to summon and pay witnesses; the use of the commonwealth marshal and his deputies in levying executions and distraints; the power to appoint arbitrators to resolve conflicts and hence avoid an extensive and expensive court fight.[66] To the new court, too, were assigned duties formerly belonging to either the Court of Assistants or individual magistrates. Thus, town officers were normally installed in their places by the Quarter Court; for the Bostonians it became a probate court; and to its clerk the townsmen came to apply for the filing of deeds and con-

65. *Colony Records,* I, 276. Description of the emergence of the county courts has frequently been confused. In Mar. 1636 the General Court established local courts, consisting of resident magistrates and associates appointed from the local gentry, at Ipswich, Salem, Newtown (Cambridge), and Boston, the courts to have jurisdiction over civil cases in which damages did not exceed 10*li* and criminal cases exclusive of those involving life, loss of a member, or banishment. The courts at Cambridge and Boston lapsed almost immediately, associates being appointed in Boston only in 1636 and in Cambridge in 1636 and 1637. Probably there was little need for them with the Court of Assistants sitting close by at either Cambridge or Boston and with the First Church attempting to arbitrate all disputes between members. The Boston court was revived as the "particular court" in 1638 when the Court of Assistants found itself overburdened. The Ipswich and Salem courts continued to function until combined as one court alternating between the towns in 1641. At that time, too, a similar court was established for the region beyond the Merrimac. These three courts—at Boston, Salem-Ipswich, and Salisbury-Hampton—became the county courts of Suffolk-Middlesex, Essex, and Norfolk respectively. The Cambridge court was not revived until 1648 when it became the Middlesex County Court. Occasional records of Boston's particular court are to be found in *Assistants' Records,* II, for example, 91, 92, 95.

66. Farrand, ed., *Laws and Liberties of Massachusetts,* 32.

veyances as property passed from hand to hand. In 1638 a special court "for the more speedy dispatch of all causes, which shall concerne strangers, who cannot stay to attend the ordinary courts of justice" was established in Boston, signifying recognition of the town's position as a commercial capital frequented by merchants and shipmen.[67] However, the "strangers' court" was only the particular court in another guise.

The "particular" or "quarter" court was intermediate between the single magistrate and the Court of Assistants. The magistrates still functioned in effect as police courts and in civil matters as "small cause" courts, their civil jurisdiction being formally defined in 1638, when, "for avoyding of the countryes charge by bringing small causes to the Court of Assistants," they were empowered to "heare and determine by [their] discretion all causes whearin the debt or trespas, or damage, etc., doth not exceede 20s."[68] (By 1647 the sum had been raised to 40s.) The magistrates' court was Boston's coroner's court as well. In 1640 Winthrop called together a jury to determine the cause of death of servant William Richards, found hanging in one of his master's outbuildings, and the jury found that "he murdered himself and was guilty of his owne deathe."[69]

On the higher level, the Court of Assistants, at least in theory, held forth only as a superior court trying major civil actions and capital crimes. The General Court, too, had come to exercise judicial functions by the second decade, when it could assume at will jurisdiction in any case and did so in regard to state crimes, as in the trial of the Child petitioners in the mid-1640's. Similarly, it could hear any case, civil or criminal, previously tried before a lower court, the "Body of Liberties" providing that "everie man shall have libertie to complaine [by petition] to the Generall Court of any Injustice done him in any Court of Assistants or other."[70]

Jurisdictional lines were vague, particularly between the Quarter Court and the Court of Assistants, and the Bostonian accused

67. *Colony Records*, I, 264.
68. *Ibid.*, 239.
69. "Inquest on the Body of William Richards [Sept. 15, 1640]," *Winthrop Papers*, IV, 285-86.
70. "Body of Liberties," 41.

by magistrate, constable, town official, or grand jury might find himself before any court, the prevailing rule being the quick dispensation of justice and the trial of any case before whichever court met first. Civil jurisdictions were similarly vague, despite the law, for the Bostonian brought his cause before whichever court he thought might afford more certain and quick redress. Thus while theory directed that civil cases under 20*s* were to be determined before a magistrate, subject to appeal before each higher court in turn, the Bostonian went his own way. Goody Sherman's suit against merchant Keayne exemplifies both the readiness to sue and the disregard for procedure which was rampant. Heard originally by the elders of the First Church as a matter of church discipline, the cause was resolved in Keayne's favor "upon hearing all Allegations, and the most materiall wittnesses on booth parts." Subsequently, the case was heard by the Quarter Court—the "small cause court" being ignored—where the jury again found for Keayne. But Goody Sherman and her advocate would not rest. "Declyning the Court of Assistants to which [an appeal] properlye belonged," she took her complaint to the General Court by petition; again she lost, but in the General Court the case became a *cause célèbre* which ultimately led to the permanent division of the Court into its two houses.[71]

Throughout the 1640's attempts were made to clarify legal procedures and relieve the higher courts of petty matters. Petitions for rehearings by the General Court were limited by restricting their submission to the first days of any given session and later by instituting a 10*s* filing fee. In 1642 the General Court, taking cognizance of the "great charge by the Courts attendance upon suites commenced or renewed by either appeales, petitions, etc.," ordered that where either plaintiff or defendant was found to have proceeded without just cause of action, the court might impose not only costs but a fine. By the end of the second decade the Court of Assistants was refusing to take cognizance of any case triable in any county court except on appeal, and the county courts were ordered to refrain from acting in any case under 40*s* which was not first heard in the magistrates' court. Barratry was

71. "John Winthrop's Summary of the Case Between Richard Sherman and Robert Keayne [July 15, 1642]," *Winthrop Papers*, IV, 349-50.

severely prosecuted, and fines were levied upon plaintiffs who failed to prosecute their cases (the Bostonians at times seem to have used the nuisance suit to accent their tiffs or scare their debtors), all in an effort to clear the court dockets.[72]   But it was to little avail. The restrictions and regulations could not override the penchant for going to law, and the courts remained as crowded as ever, seven Boston men complaining in 1648 of "Courts of Judicature so cumbred with Litigious (and many times frivolous) Suites at Law, especially Actions of Slaunder . . . that the publicks safety and peace is disturbed."[73]

As the third decade opened still another court was erected, a special court especially designed to cope with Boston, the preface to the act reading: "Whereas it doth appeare unto this Courte that suites at law are growne more frequent of late in this jurisdiction than formerly, and especially in the towne of Boston, by reason of the great concourse of people and increase of trade there, whereby County Courtes are much prolonged, and forasmuch as many crimes are also committed in the said towne, both by night and by day, both by straungers and other inhabitants."[74]   The new court, consisting of seven Boston freemen selected by the town and installed by the Great Quarter Court, was to have jurisdiction over all civil actions up to 10*li* damages arising on Shawmut or Noddles Island and all criminal acts formerly within the cognizance of any magistrate.

The law enforced by the courts or invoked for redress of personal injury was commonwealth law.   Like the system of courts, like town government itself, it was constantly developing. In the mid-1630's it was but a conglomerate of statutes and *ad hoc* rulings of the magistrates made on the basis of English tradition, natural equity, and the word of God.   Ultimately, and largely at the insistence of the generality which would not leave it to the magistrates' discretion, a more precise and orderly law, one drawn from the same sources but established by statute and enunciated

72. *Colony Records*, II, 3, 261-62, 279.
73. Petition of Valentine Hill, John Mylam, Richard Parker, William Aspinwall, Michael Powell, Isaac Walker, Henry Webb, and others to the General Court, *ca.* 1648, Mass. Archives.
74. *Colony Records*, III, 244.

in printed codes, made its appearance. Ultimately, too, the law came to run the gamut of human activities. Crimes were defined —murder, rape, treason to the commonwealth, burglary, forgery, theft, the holding of false gods, blasphemy, Sabbath breaking— and punishments prescribed; standards of personal morality and industry were established and deviations made subject to penalties; the morality of the marketplace was defined.

Yet in its all-inclusiveness, the law of Massachusetts was not unique; indeed, in large measure it was drawn from English precedent. In the English villages of the time "the most intimate family relationships" were laid bare at the behest of the churchwarden or constable; "men were held responsible for their wives' misdeeds and were expected to see that their children behaved circumspectly. No one was allowed to waste his estate by card playing or riotous living, no feasts or banquets were to be given after nine o'clock in the night, and no person might behave in such a manner as to cause inconvenience to the community." In English society as a whole "industry" was theoretically ranked "next to godliness and loyalty," and all three were commanded as obligations to God and the state.[75]

So it was in Massachusetts and so the law came to stipulate, the process beginning in the first year when the Assistants found it necessary to regulate wages and punish market frauds and drunkenness. The elaboration of the law, its intrusion into every cranny of private life, the very pervasiveness of government— none of these was part of Winthrop's ideal, though portions of the ideal were echoed in a law more equitable in many respects than that of England. A perfect society in which men would do their duty to each other out of their godliness would have had no need for law; only man's innate depravity, as the theologians would say, his concern for self, required that society circumscribe him with "thou shalts" and "thou shalt nots."

"Our town," the men of Boston had written. All about him the individual inhabitant could see and hear society at its most vital tasks of commanding and enjoining: the constable's watch

75. Trotter, *Seventeenth Century Life in the Country Parish*, 178; Bindoff, *Tudor England*, 293.

clanking through the night, the magistrate intoning sentence, the selectmen curtly ordering John Mylam to remove his new building from the public way, the town meeting wrangling over an amendment to the swine laws, the clerk of the market hefting loaves of bread. Boston was not a town of men moved by God, as Winthrop would have had it, but it was the Bostonians' town and to them it represented order and stability.

IX

THE CITY BY THE WATER

To an observer at the turn of the second decade Boston presaged "some sumptuous City" of the future. It was "the Center Towne and Metropolis of this Wildernesse worke," a "City-like Towne" "crowded on the Sea-bankes and wharfed out with great industry and cost." Its major buildings were "beautifull and large, some fairely set forth with Brick, Tile, Stone and Slate," its streets lined with "good shopps well furnished with all kind of Merchandize," noisy, busy, "full of Girles and Boys sporting up and downe, with a continued concourse of people." Not even the great were immune from the activity of the streets, and tradition tells the tale of the Reverend Mr. Cotton, grown a little deaf with age, plodding along the way, thinking of his next sermon. A street boy twitched his cloak and called in his deaf ear, "Cotton, thou art an old fool!" But the minister heard and responded in kind: "I know it, I know it," he chirped. "The Lord make both thee and me wiser."[1]

Walking along those streets—still unnamed and known only by such phrases as "the road to the Fort," "the way to Centry Hill," "the way from Cove to Cove," "the high street"—one could make sense of the old nursery rhymes. There, facing on the Dock, was the home and shop of John Shaw, butcher, whose tallow also made fine candles; here on the high street just north of the market square, Thomas Hawkins, baker, lived and worked; Thomas Oliver, an elder of the First Church, was also a doctor;

1. *Johnson's Wonder-Working Providence,* 70-71; Samuel Maverick, "A Briefe Discription of New England and the Severall Townes therein...," Mass. Hist. Soc., *Proceedings,* 2d Ser., 1 (1885), 238; Thomas Wentworth Higginson, "Address at the Centennial Commemoration of the Society," Mass. Hist. Soc., *Proceedings,* 2d Ser., 6 (1891), 281.

Richard Bellingham and John Winthrop had been lawyers in old England. Many a merchant chief (even an occasional Indian chief) could be seen, and although Daniel Fairfield was not a thief, his abuse of "the tender body" of nine-year-old Dorcas Humphrey—in expiation of which he walked Boston's ways with "an hempen roape about his neck" for almost ten years—was even more heinous a crime.[2] Everywhere, in the ship and boat yards of the North End, around the Dock and Market, one saw a busy people: merchants and seamen; artisans, apprentices and servants; farmers with their country wares to sell; Scottish and Irish laborers; ministers and magistrates; Solomon Francho, a Spanish Jew drawn to the town in the course of trade; "Mincarry, the blackmore."[3]

It was not Winthrop's Boston now. Indeed, early in the spring of 1649 the old Governor had surrendered his soul to the mercy of the God he loved so well. The Bostonians, the commonwealth in general, had mourned him, then gone about their business. But even while he lived, the town—Massachusetts Bay itself—had slipped away from him.

He had thought of men as capable of perfection with God's help, of being able to walk the thin line of moderation, of being able to subordinate themselves to the demands of the community and the commandments of God. Yet they could not. From the beginning some men had sought earthly pleasures in gaming, debauchery, drink, and could only be held to decency by the law sternly enforced. With the turn to commerce, the number of dissolute increased; "many and great miscariages are committed by saylors," the General Court declared in 1650, while four years earlier Winthrop had written of an epidemic of "lues venerea" spreading through the town from a Boston man "gone cooper in a ship." By the mid-1650's one Dermin Mahoone would be operating a brothel in the town.[4]

2. Fairfield was convicted in 1642 of what can be termed "statutory rape." *Colony Records*, II, 12-13, 61, III, 273.

3. *Assistants' Records*, II, 118.

4. *Colony Records*, III, 184; *Winthrop's Journal*, II, 268; "Boston Records," 141. Pity the poor jailer who, in 1654, petitioned the General Court for additional compensation for receiving "into his custody Danniel Gum accused for adultery, a person so filthily corrupted with the french disease haivinge fourteene sores running on him: whom he was forced in person day and night to attend . . .

But this side of Boston's society can be overemphasized. Less colorful but more important was the fact that men were generally failing in their duty to the community, seeking their own aggrandizement in the rich opportunities afforded by the land, commerce, crafts, and speculations, to the detriment of the community. Although men showed this predilection throughout the commonwealth,[5] the Bostonians particularly fell prey to ungodly materialism and ostentation. The civil government responded with sumptuary and prudential laws commanding men to follow God's dictates toward their fellow men, though economic reasons for the laws played their part, too. Laws regulating the wearing of lace, for example, were economic in the sense of cutting down imports from England, and godly in being aimed at the sin of ostentation.

Worldliness was not confined to the unregenerate, and the church too struck out against immorality and the excessive worship of Mammon. Cases of First Church discipline increased rapidly, from one during the years through 1635, to nine from 1636 through 1639, and twenty-four through 1640-49. The charges varied: Simon Bird excommunicated "for . . . uncleane Dallyances with his maid servant"; Nicholas Charlett excommunicated "for breaking open another mans Chest with intent to steale out of it"; John Webb admonished for absenting himself from church on "a Day of Humiliation" and spending "part of the day in feasting and sporting at Quoytes abroad, and that in the Company of such whereof some of them were Scandalous." But most frequently they were associated with the marketplace. At the turn of the first decade the church dealt with Robert Keayne for "extortion" following his trial before the General Court. "Being convented, he was charged with many particulars; in some, for taking above six-pence in the shilling profit; in some above eight-pence; and, in some small things, above two for one." The Court fined him 200*li*, alleviating 100*li* of the sum, while the

---

to the endangeringe of his life." Petition of George Munnings, Keeper, to the Court, Oct. 20, 1654, Mass. Archives.

5. Sumner Chilton Powell, *Puritan Village: The Formation of a New England Town* (Middletown, Conn., 1963), *passim* and particularly chap. 8 indicates that the same ardent quest for personal aggrandizement was going on in a small, interior, agricultural village (Sudbury).

First Church admonished him for his errors, Cotton taking the opportunity to define "just price": "A man may not sell above the current price, i.e., such a price as is usual in the time and place, and as another (who knows the worth of the commodity) would give for it, if he had the occasion to use it."[6]   And there were others disciplined by the church: Richard Waite cast out for "having purloyned out of buckskyn lether brought unto him, so much thereof as would make 3. mens gloves"; Arthur Clark "cast out . . . for scandalously stealing many gallons of wine out of a pipe of wine, and corrupting the rest by filling it up with beare"; George Clifford "Admonished for presumptuously undertaking unto Mr. Woory a Member of the Church of Charls Towne more then he was able to performe, and for dealing unfaithfully and falsely in what he was betrusted with"; Thomas Marshall excommunicated for his lies and "much unfaithfullnesse in his Dealing" as a tailor.[7]

The church, Winthrop, society in general, were ambiguous in their attitudes toward wealth, thereby opening the door to rampant individualism.   The subordination of the individual to the interest of the community was propounded from the pulpit and echoed in law.   But clearly riches in and of themselves were not antisocial or sinful, for material success (or its lack) was God-ordained.   Aboard the *Arbella* Winthrop had been at pains to justify riches while giving them a godly function.   In analyzing Robert Keayne's sin, Cotton had explained God's part in ordaining wealth and poverty: "When a man loseth in his commodity for want of skill, etc., he must look at it as his own fault or cross, and therefore must not lay it upon another."   "Where a man loseth by casualty of sea, or etc., it is a loss cast upon himself by providence . . . ; but where there is a scarcity of the commodity, there men may raise their price; for now it is a hand of God upon the commodity, and not the person."[8]   Wealth, moreover, was the reward of diligence in one's calling, and diligence was com-

6. First Church Records under dates of Dec. 15, 1639, July 5, 1646; *Winthrop's Journal*, I, 315ff.

7. First Church Records under dates of Nov. 26, 1639, Jan. 13, 1638/39, June 24, 1644, Oct. 27, 1644, Feb. 7, 1645/46. Keayne himself was only "notoriously above others observed and complained of" for extortion.

8. *Winthrop's Journal*, I, 317-18.

manded by God, while the individual's economic success (particularly in trade) bettered society and so was good. Sin lay only in the means to wealth and, once gained, in its use, or in the inordinate quest for material prosperity to the exclusion of all else. Hence Winthrop could warn against embracing "this present world" and prosecuting "our carnall intencions, seekeing great things for our selves and our posterity," but acknowledge that "that which is lawfull for a private person to do, in the way of his calling, the magistrate (if he judge it also expedient, or not hurtfull to the Commonwealth) ought to furder or not to hinder him in it."[9]

However, the careful balance between the energetic following of one's calling and the pursuit of wealth for its own sake and by any means was difficult to maintain.[10] Who could tell the waves thus far and no farther? Who could tell men to seek material success out of proper motivation and shun it when they were driven by improper motives? Robert Keayne, a kind and God-fearing man, would eventually be torn apart by the ambiguity, finding an imperfect solution in drink and a long apologia.[11] Others were not so bothered, for in them acquisitiveness was easily rationalized by ambiguous morality, or morality was neglected entirely in their business affairs. "Indeed it was a very sad thing to see how little of a public spirit appeared in the country, but self-love too much," Winthrop wrote in describing the depression of the early 1640's. And a decade later, Edward Johnson would comment: "An over-eager desire after the world hath so seized on the spirits of many . . . as if the Lord had no farther work for his people to do, but every bird to feather his own nest."[12]

Adding to the difficulty of vigorously pursuing one's calling

9. Winthrop, "Modell of Christian Charity," 1630, and Winthrop to Richard Saltonstall and others, ca. July 21, 1643, in *Winthrop Papers*, II, 294, IV, 407.

10. The difference, in Max Weber's terms, between the Protestant ethic and the spirit of capitalism, Winthrop representing the former in all its purity, his Boston the latter.

11. "The Last Will and Testament of me, Robert Keayne . . . [1653]," in City of Boston, *Report of the Record Commissioners*, X (Boston, 1886), 1-53; "Testimony of Johana Joy and Joseph Armitage Concerning the Drunkennesses of Mr. Keayne [June 2, 1652]," MS Photostats, Box 5, Mass. Hist. Soc. Lib.; Bernard Bailyn, "The *Apologia* of Robert Keayne," *Wm. and Mary Qtly.*, 3d Ser., 7 (1950), 568-87.

12. *Winthrop's Journal*, II, 92; *Johnson's Wonder-Working Providence*, 260.

without overstepping the limits was the status accorded wealth in
the community. The better sort among the inhabitants of Boston
—the men of more than average means—constituted a gentry and
dominated the town economically, socially, and politically in the
1640's as they had in the 1630's, the Bostonians looking to such
men naturally as those most apt for the conduct of public business,
paying deference to them on the streets, in public councils, in the
church. Winthrop easily approved of this deference, for here was
the hierarchical structure of society so familiar in England and
hence so acceptable. But in the first decade the gentry had consisted of men who carried property and status with them from
England; in the second, new men were emerging from the com-
monality to take up positions within the gentry by virtue of their
accomplishments in the New World, receiving status as a reward
for diligence in their individual businesses.[13] Such men demon-
strated ways to wealth and a social mobility which the Governor
had not envisioned.

This new breed of gentry springing up in the town was
exemplified by the selectmen gravely considering the town's
business at the end of the second decade, the constables, and,
to a lesser extent, those Bostonians holding high office in the commonwealth. The elected lesser officers—surveyors of highway
and sealers of leather—represented a level of material achieve-
ment only a step below.[14] A few of the officers (listed in the
accompanying chart of "Officers In and Of the Town: 1649")
were holdovers from the 1630's, notably Richard Bellingham,
William Colborne, and Jacob Eliot. The rest were new either to
Boston or to positions of power in the town. They had been men
of middle or lower rank in England, ordinary men with little
hope of achieving wealth and status, and had risen with Boston.
And unlike the leaders of the first decade whose wealth was in
land, they owed their positions for the most part to activity in
commerce. Some owned farms worked by tenants and servants,

13. A phenomenon concisely described by Robert F. Berkhofer, Jr., "Space,
Time, Culture and the New Frontier," *Agricultural History*, 38 (1964), 26-27.
14. The analysis of Boston's gentry and the specific examples given on the
chart and below are based upon the compilation of data about identifiable
Bostonians described in "A Note on Sources and Methods." The officers for 1649
are listed in "Boston Records," 94-95.

Officers In and Of the Town: 1649

Name	Office	Date and Place of Arrival in Mass. if not Boston	Date in Bos.	Early Status	1636 Cont.	Occupat. 1640's	Bos. Church	Free-man	Perm. Res.?	Family in Bos.?	Sources of Wealth
Richard Bellingham	Magistrate	—	1634	Gent.	7 li	Gent. Farmer	'34	Chart.	Yes	Yes	Ext. farm land, Bos. prop., lmtd. trade
William Hibbens	Magistrate	—	1639	Gent.	—	Leatherwork	'39	'40	Yes	Yes	Farm land, leatherworks in Boston
William Aspinwall	Suffolk Cty. Recorder	—	1630	Gent.	8s	Gent. Farmer	'30/1	'32	Yes	Yes	Farm, local investments
Robert Keayne	Deputy	—	1635	Mercht.	1 li	Shopkeeper	'36	'36	Yes	Yes	Farm land, land spec., shop, lmtd. trade
James Penn	Deputy, Selectman, Town Recorder & Treasurer, Clerk-of-Market	—	1630	"beadle"	6s 8d	Innkeeper & professional off. holder	'30/1	'30	Yes	Yes	Officeholding, inn, local investments, brewhouse (sold '46)
William Colborne	Selectman	—	1630	Gent.	8s	Gent. Farmer	'30/1	'31	Yes	Yes	Farm, limited and local trade
Jacob Eliot	Selectman	—	1631	Gent.	6s 8d	?	'31	'32	Yes	Yes	Lmtd. farm, trade, investments
Anthony Stoddard	Selectman	—	1639	Linen Draper	—	Shopkeeper	'39	'40	Yes	Yes	Farmland, shop, ship invest., lmtd. trade
Jeremy Houchin	Selectman, Clerk-of-Market	Dorchester, late 1630's	1640	Tanner	No	Merchant	'44	'40	Yes	Yes	Tannery (sold '46), ext. trade, ship victualing
James Everill	Selectman	—	1634	"poorer sort"	No	Leatherwork	'34	'34	Yes	Yes	Leatherworks, farm, Boston lots, local investments
Thomas Marshall	Selectman	Dorchester, '36	1633	ferryman	No	Shoemaker	'34	'35	Yes	Yes	Shop, farm
Thomas Clark, Sr.	Constable	Dorchester, '36	1646	Gent.	—	Merchant	'47	'39	Yes	Yes	Warehouse, town lots, local trade
Thomas Clark, Jr.	Constable	—	1644?	Minor?	No	Merchant	**	No	Yes	Yes	Extensive trade
Theodore Atkinson	Constable	Dorchester, '35	1634	Servant?	—	Merchant	'34	'42	Yes	Yes	Ext. trade, ship invest., town lots
Barnabas Fawer	Constable	—	1646?	?	—	Merchant	'46	No	Yes	Yes	Extensive trade
Isaac Walker	Constable***	—	1646?			Merchant	'46	'46	Yes	Yes	Ext. trade, land spec., wharves
Edward Bendall	Horse Registrar, Customs Collect.	—	1630	Farmer?	****	Entrepreneur	'30/1	'34	Yes	Yes	Farm, town lots, docks, warehouses, lighterage to ships, ext. local trade
Christopher Gipson	Surveyor of High.	Dorchester, '30	1646	Servant?	No	Soapboiler	*****	No	Yes	Yes	Soapworks
Walter Merry	Surveyor of High.	—	1632?	Servant?	No	Shipwright	'34	'34	Yes	Yes	Boatyard, town lots
John Button	Surveyor of High.	—	1632	Miller	****	Entrepreneur	'33	'34	Yes	Yes	Town lots, farm land, local investments
William Blanton	Surveyor of High.	Weymouth, '39?	1638	Carpenter	—	Carpenter	'42	'43	Yes	Yes	Carpentry
Richard Webb	Sealer of Leather	—	1644?	?	—	Shoemaker	'44	No	Yes	Yes	Shop
Robert Turner	Sealer of Leather	—	1635	Servant?	No	Shoemaker	'43	No	Yes	Yes	Shop

*Except for Hutchinsonian exile, 1637–42
**Retained Dorchester membership, although children baptized in right of father in Boston Church, 1644, 1647, 1648
***Replacing Thomas Clark, Sr. early in year
****Contributed less than 6s
*****A founder of Boston's Second Church, 1650

and some even held waste land for speculation. But all of them owned and speculated in town lots and houses, shops, warehouses, and wharves; or operated shops, leatherworks, or inns; or carried on trade.

If wealth brought status, status could lead to wealth. The indentured servant felt the pinch of his position, for in a society in which work was plentiful, laborers comparatively few, and wages consequently high, the free laborer enjoyed ample opportunity. The servant, dissatisfied with his lot and difficult to control, was anxious to rise in status.[15] Among the generality in Boston, participation in government had a decided value in satisfying material ambitions. It was natural to the times that men in power did favor other men in power—five selectmen selling town land to a sixth, the selectmen granting to one of their number an easement of building regulations and appointing another selectman to oversee the work.[16] But more was involved than such direct profit—the rudiments of democracy. For given the material opportunities afforded by the town and the power of the government over these opportunities—the town's activities in regulating land distribution and usage, laying out streets and sketching incipient building codes, licensing inns and wharves—governmental agencies were all-important to the Bostonian. He not only actively participated in government, but constantly strove to extend his area of participation. Thus in the first decade the division of the land and its regulation by the town promoted political activity. In the second, a tanner or butcher, subject to regulation concerning the smells and dirt of his establishment, his very right to carry on his trade in the town, would be sure to participate in the election of selectmen who in a moment could endanger his profitable activities—even forward his own candidacy should he have sufficient stature within the community to make it seem not impertinent. Similarly, those subject to the inspection of the various sealers and viewers and clerks of the market operating under

15. Lawrence W. Towner, " 'A Fondness for Freedom': Servant Protest in Puritan Society," *Wm. and Mary Qtly.*, 3d Ser., 19 (1962), 201-19.

16. "Boston Records," 82; Excerpts from the town records of Mar. 13, 1648/49 and Feb. 26, 1654/55, Early Files of Courts and Misc. Papers, Office of the Clerk of the Supreme Judicial Court, Suffolk Co., Boston.

commonwealth law would be quick to make known their choice for these officers, and for the deputies to the General Court and the Assistants inasmuch as these were the lawmakers of the commonwealth. For their part, Boston's officers tended to be responsible to those who in effect were their constituents, for while they were drawn from the town's gentry they were as a group too near in origin to the generality to pretend superiority, at least for the moment. To Winthrop, however, who had envisioned a relatively static society in which the laborer would be as content to labor as the mouth was to mince the food of the body, in which rulers and ruled constituted two separate entities and proper liberty was defined in terms of "subjection to authority," the dissatisfaction of servants, the ambitions of the generality, the political activity, were still another disappointment.[17]

The pervasive individualism rooted in economics—acquisitive men seeking to slake their ambition in the fertile soil and commerce of the New World—was but part of a greater failure of Winthrop's ideal, a fragmentation of society where he would have had perfect unity. The idea of a single community was gone, shattered by the circumstances of the first year, and two-dozen odd towns had sprung up. The most immediate loyalty was that being given by the inhabitants to their particular towns, and among the towns there was bitter partisanship, most notably between those of Essex County and Boston, the former jealous of the prosperity of the latter. The merchants and tradesmen of the northern towns—Ipswich, Salem, Newbury—bitterly resented the fact that "Boston, being the chiefest place of resort of Shipping, carries away all the Trade,"[18] that tariffs on imported wines or on goods from Connecticut River (for indeed the various jurisdictions of New England were competitive and jealous, too, and engaged in local trade wars) were collectible in Boston.

For their part, the country artisans—those of Concord, Dedham, Saugus, and the rest—resented the domination of Boston's artisans. When the shoemakers of Boston organized as a company and sought a monopoly over shoes sold in the Boston market, for example, the shoemakers of the countryside objected: Do not allow

17. *Winthrop's Journal*, II, 239.
18. *Johnson's Wonder-Working Providence*, 96.

"our Brethren of Boston" to "have power put into their hands to hinder a free trade," they wrote to the General Court. "Keeping out Country shoomakers from Coming into the Market ... wilbe a greate dammage unto the Country ... for it wil weaken the hands of the Country shoomakers from using their trade, or occasion them to Remove to boston which wilbe hurtfull to Other townes." Facetiously they asked that if the request of the Bostonians were to be granted, they too should be allowed "Libertye and Priviledge that wee may have power to search their shooes as well as they have power to search ours."[19] The partisanship was felt on many levels throughout the 1640's: in a movement early in the decade to remove the capital from Boston, the Essex men in particular recognizing Boston's political position as one source of its prosperity; in a continuing attempt to elevate the authority of the counties to Boston's disadvantage; in the competition of Essex and harbor merchants for General Court favors; in politics where the Essex leaders allied with the country towns to form a concerted bloc in the House of Deputies in opposition to the towns immediately around Boston.[20]

Within Boston itself there was fragmentation. Geography dictated a basic division between Shawmut, increasingly devoted to commerce and handicrafts, and the agricultural periphery, the peninsula dominating at the expense of the countryside. The division was felt in the church in the early 1640's, when the

19. Gowen Anderson, Robert Williams, John Frany and others to the General Court, 1648, Mass. Archives.

20. The effect of what can be termed the "Essex clique" in the politics of early Massachusetts, although touched on by Lawrence Shaw Mayo in his *John Endecott: A Biography* (Cambridge, Mass., 1936), has not been fully explored. One hint lies in an analysis of the officers and committeemen (serving on major and minor committees) of the House of Deputies as found in *Colony Records,* III, which indicates the predominance of Essex men during the years of the most bitter conflicts of the 1640's. Thus in 1644 and 1645, deputies from Essex held 3 offices, 22 major committee posts, 13 minor posts; those from Norfolk, 1 office, 6 major posts, 7 minor posts; those from Middlesex, 2 offices, 13 major committee posts, 20 minor posts; from Suffolk, 2 offices, 16 major posts, 24 minor posts. Salem and Ipswich together, during these years, monopolized the speakership and held 10 major committee posts and 5 minor. Boston and Charlestown, on the other hand, held no offices, 2 major posts, and 10 minor posts. In contrast, Suffolk dominated the Court of Assistants. In the light of such an analysis one might easily interpret the "democratic" and "liberal" acts of the Deputies in their battles with the Assistants as nothing more than symptomatic of the economic competition between Suffolk and Essex, Boston and Salem-Ipswich.

residents along the North Shore asked that Peter Oliver be sent as a lay reader "to Instructe theare servants and to be a helpe to them because they cannot many times come heather [to church] nor sometimes to Lynn." The request precipitated a sharp exchange in the church, part theological, but part practical. The Bostonians remembered that Braintree had broken away to the detriment of the town's financial position, and that the first act of separation had been the dispatching of the Reverend Mr. Wheelwright to minister to those who could not come to the peninsula. Now they raised the question: Was this not merely the first step to still another secession? Cotton answered their objections. "If any say this is the way [in time] to make a villidg and soe to raise a church theare which may be a hindrance to this church I argue to multiply churches is a greate blessinge of God and we are to rejoyce in it and to helpe." He had his way and what Thomas Lechford referred to as one of several "Chappels of ease" (though the church insisted that they were not at all similar to the sinful chapels of England inasmuch as communion and baptism were available only through the Boston church) was established at Rumney Marsh. But the laymen on Shawmut were uneasy and watched carefully for any signs of secession.[21]

Even on the peninsula there was division. Interests were becoming definable, those of similar economic outlook banding together to advance their own well-being. Thus the vintners solicited and received a promise from the General Court that no additional vintners would be licensed during a given period. Shipbuilders, coopers, merchants, shoemakers, leatherworkers—each craft became a separate force in the community, sometimes organized in guild-like societies following the spirit and occasionally the letter of English models, frequently competing with each other. In 1648 the coopers complained against the fishermen and the merchants dealing in fish: "It is the order in England," they wrote, that "no fisherman was to pake his fish for the marcht: they pakt them at sea to save them, but when they come to be pakt for the Marcht or for a market, ther were coopers sworne for that service: and non but accounted merchantable but such as they pak; and

21. Manuscript Journal of Robert Keayne, 1639-42, Mass. Hist. Soc. Lib., under date of Apr. 23, 1640; Lechford, *Plain Dealing*, 40-41.

her[e] both marchants and seamen compley much of abus in this kind amongst us."[22]

And the jarring of interests was felt within the church. When a new meetinghouse was to be built, the site became a matter of controversy. "Some were for the green ... others, viz., the tradesmen, especially, who dwelt about the market place, desired it might stand still near the market, lest in time it should divert the chief trade from thence." Ultimately Cotton "cleared it up to them," arguing "that the removing it to the green would be a damage to such as dwelt by the market ... but it would be no damage to the rest to have it by the market." "For peace sake" those of contrary opinion "yielded to the rest by keeping silence while it passed."[23]

Divergent interests characterized the gentry, too. The town officers of 1649 with Buttolphs, Coles, Davises, Franklins, Gibbonses, Leveretts, Mylams, Hills, Newgates, Savages, Tyngs, and Ushers comprised only a portion of Boston's gentry, one which was firmly committed to the town and commonwealth. They were moral men, although their morality was sometimes compromised by business; permanent residents all; sons, though not always dutiful sons, of the church and in some cases non-freemen by choice. They were devoted to commerce or to their crafts, but basically within the town—in their shops and speculations, in projects such as the Mill Creek or Town Dock, in shipbuilding, outfitting, and provisioning—or a short distance away, in trading ventures to Nova Scotia or the Delaware. Their ventures into the Atlantic commercial world were frequent, yet more often than not on a small scale and largely on their own account during these years. If, like Valentine Hill or the Tyng brothers, they were linked to English merchant houses in large-scale overseas trade, their involvement was offset by their extensive investments in local concerns.[24]

But there were others who were oriented less to the town and more to the broader community of the Atlantic. Some were early residents of the town who turned to commerce and made quick

22. Orders made by the Company of the Coopers, 1648, Mass. Archives.
23. *Winthrop's Journal*, I, 318-19.
24. See n. 14 above.

and easy connections with merchants elsewhere—men like Samuel Maverick, a pre-1630 settler in the Bay; Robert Harding, who arrived aboard the Winthrop fleet and, in 1645, transferred his commercial operations from Boston to London; Edward Hutchinson, Jr., who remained in the commonwealth to serve his London uncle when most of the family left; Thomas Fowle, Henry Shrimpton, Henry Webb, John Manning, all of whom arrived at the crest of the emigration of the late 1630's; Robert Scott, a servant of John Sanford's in 1630 who became Harding's Bay agent when Harding left for England. Others were drawn to the town from elsewhere in Massachusetts after Boston turned so energetically to commerce: Michael Powell, who arrived at Dedham in 1639 and moved to Boston in 1647; David Selleck, a Dorchester settler of 1639 who transferred to Boston in the early 1640's; David Yale, who traveled with his stepfather Theophilus Eaton to New Haven in 1638 and returned in 1641 to settle for a decade in Boston. Still others were newcomers to the commonwealth: Jacob Sheafe, coming in 1643 to marry Henry Webb's daughter; Robert Nanney, who operated a Barbados estate from a Boston base after 1645; Thomas Lake and Thomas Breedon arriving at the end of the decade. Some, but not all, were church members; some few were freemen; and some were inhabitants. Some owned property in the town, but others apparently operated from rented quarters. They were alike, however, in that their eyes were on the Atlantic trading routes. There their profits were made, not in the town. They shunned investment in local enterprises in favor of their connections with the broader community. They avoided local office as expensive in time and money. Fowle, for example, served only one six-month term as selectman during the decade, while Henry Webb served but a year as surveyor of highways. They placed the interests of their commerce above all else.

This second group, although it avoided office, was not mute in the councils of the town and commonwealth. Its members looked upon the restrictions on newcomers, the laws requiring that strangers register with the proper authorities, as curtailing free movement into and through the Bay to the detriment of trade.

In the same light they saw the tendency to use the law to insure
the purity of the church—the law against Anabaptists of 1644,
for example, and indeed the whole moral emphasis of the law.
Hence they worked for change. In 1645 they pressed for the
annulment or at least suspension of the Anabaptist law; they
fought the "strangers' laws" on both town and commonwealth
levels. And when Robert Child appeared at mid-decade—a man
whose intellectual activity, if not his economic activity, was a part
of the larger world, but who in all likelihood intended merely
the embarrassment of the commonwealth in the interest of English Presbyterianism—it was from among this part of the gentry
that he received his strongest support. Fowle, Maverick, and
Yale were among the six signers of his 1646 petition to the General Court soliciting an enlarged church membership and greater
participation in government. And together with Child they were,
as a result, heavily fined for defaming the government, slander-
ing the churches, and, in 1647, conspiring against Massachusetts
Bay by attempting to prosecute an appeal to England.[25]

In the long run the influence of the Atlantic was to pre-
dominate in the town. Others with an Atlantic orientation would
come, while those laying down firm foundations in Boston investments would be driven beyond the narrow confines of the
community in search of the Atlantic's profits. Already the future
could be sensed as the sons of the first leaders turned their gaze
seaward: Winthrop's sons, Stephen and Samuel, taking to the
Atlantic; John Winthrop, Jr., displaying his entrepreneurial
ability on both sides of the ocean; Edward Bendall's son Free-
grace, at fourteen, beginning a life of Atlantic trade. But in the
1640's the Atlantic-oriented merchants could do little. In town
and commonwealth their efforts to effect changes were defeated,
in part by the church but in part, too, by those whose commit-
ments were equally to commerce but whose vision was still limited
to Boston and the Bay area. To Samuel Danforth it was a contest of "White Coates" (the Atlantic oriented) who would set
"all opinion free" and "Blew-coates" (the town oriented) who had

25. George L. Kittredge, "Dr. Robert Child the Remonstrant," Col. Soc.
Mass., *Publications*, 21 (1920), 1-146. The various petitions concerning the
Anabaptist law and the Childites are to be found in Mass. Archives.

to withstand the assault else "Hobgoblins will be insolent."[26] For the moment blue-coats won, with a consequent hardening of political distinctions within the town.

The laws formally divided the community between inhabitants (in the sense of permanent residents legally accepted into the town) and sojourners, between freemen and non-freemen, and the legal distinctions were clear. Sojourners were in the community upon the sufferance of the authorities, and while they could legally appear at a public meeting and participate to the extent of speaking on the issues and even presenting business, they could not vote. Inhabitants who were not freemen could vote in town affairs, but were excluded from holding or voting for certain offices. Only the freemen had complete freedom of political action. In the 1640's these distinctions had tended to blur, but the contest between blue-coats and white-coats revived them. The town-oriented blue-coats were largely inhabitants and freemen while the Atlantic-oriented white-coats were more often than not mere sojourners in the town; consequently the competition between the two settled into one of freemen and inhabitants versus sojourners, the former emerging as a conscious group anxious to preserve its position within the town and commonwealth against the pretensions of the latter, who while levying demands, avoided responsibility. The various restrictions on entertaining strangers or selling property to them were revived, the town regulations being restated and enforced as the inhabitants asserted their right to regulate those seeking admittance to the town.

Thus in 1651 a general town meeting agreed that "noe inhabitant shall Let any house, Housing or Land within the Neck of Boston to any Forriner without the Consent of the Select men"; a year later the selectmen stipulated that "the formar Order made about None for to receive any into theyr house as inmaates or to let any house or any parte of any house or ground Unto any forrener without the aprobation of the Select men shall stand in force." Town meetings for election tended to be called "upon publique notes from house to house," a method by which only the qualified townsmen were summoned. At the same time, and

26. Samuel Danforth, *An Almanack* . . . (Cambridge, Mass., 1647), under date of May.

partly as a result, the number of newcomers seeking formal inhabitantship and the right to vote in town meetings rose. In the
early 1650's the freemen solicited a double vote from the General Court to counteract frequent voting by non-freemen, though
their petition brought no results; later in the decade they attempted to meet apart from the regular town meeting for the
election of town deputies and other offices for freemen only,
having "judged [it] convenient that the Freemen should meete
distinctly as to what concerns them."[27]

Fragmentation disturbed the roots of society. The family
had been disrupted by the move from old to New England, by
the abandonment of familiar places and relationships, by the
physical separation of families as some members departed and
others chose to remain. Now it was disrupted again. The opportunities of the New World attracted fathers away from familiar
occupations, and sons from the occupations and even towns of
their fathers. Winthrop's own sons, for example, were scattered
by the end of the second decade from Rumney Marsh to Antigua
in the West Indies, from New London in Connecticut to old
London; on a lesser level, the son of a Saugus farmer or Marble-
head fishermen thought nothing of seeking life's rewards as a
Boston carpenter or laborer. The general confusion was apparent
in the failure of the servant to accept a dutiful association within
the family of his master (as ideally he should) and in the laws commanding filial obedience and those charging the town with responsibility for the "training up" of children "in learning and
labor" when the parents were found deficient.[28] And while the
church attempted to bolster the family by insisting upon the
duties of the church member within it and his responsibility for the
morality of the whole, the church was in part accountable for the
weaknesses it sought to remedy.

For in this fragmented community, the church itself was a
divisive factor affecting even the family. Thomas Lechford
commented that "sometimes the Master is admitted" to member-

27. "Boston Records," 103, 109, 122, 149; Dan[iel] Gookin, Rich[ard]
Russell, Thomas Savage, Francis Norton, and Roger Clap to the General Court,
ca. 1655, MS Photostats, Box 7, Mass. Hist. Soc. Lib.
28. Colony Records, II, 6.

ship "and not the servant, *and e contra*; the husband is received, and not the wife; ... the child and not the parent."[29]   It separated the population as a whole into communicants gathered in the congregation and subject to the discipline of the church and the unregenerates excluded from the churches' sacraments and subject to the discipline of the secular authorities alone.   The non-member might or might not attend church services as required by law, and the church admitted in the abstract that hypocrites might conceivably be within and invisible saints without; yet the practical division of the populace was not tempered.   The exclusion of men and women from communion, of families from the baptismal font, of a whole segment of the population from the government of an institution second only to the town in its importance in the lives of the people, drove a wedge into the community.   If the church had merely separated the good from the bad, the moral from the immoral, the division would not have been painful.   But all without were not "reprobates" in the modern sense of the word—vicious, wicked, corrupt.   The non-members, increasingly the children of communicants who would not or could not cross Cotton's high stiles, could well have a morality equal to or greater than that of the members.

The disparity between town and church was reflected in the increasingly tenuous institutional connection between the two, the link at the end of two decades being far weaker than the close connection of the early years when the townspeople assembled as the church to discuss land policy and a town meeting forbade the townsmen's going to law without first presenting the conflict to the elders and leading laymen.   In the aftermath of the Hutchinsonian outbreak, the church lost its most direct voice in town affairs when the ruling elders, Thomas Oliver and Thomas Leverett, who had sat among the selectmen from the beginning, were left out of office after the election of December 1639.   The church came to accept the fact that civil authorities were, in their public duties, above church discipline.   It abandoned its claim "that all criminal matters concerning Church members, should first [be] heard by the church" and that "in causes betweene

29. Lechford, *Plain Dealing*, 29.

brethren ... the matter should be first told the Church, before they goe to the civill Magistrate," contenting itself with parallel jurisdiction. The errant or contentious saint was now dealt with by church and state independently.[30] By default, inability, or by virtue of its preoccupation with its inner purity, the church tended to leave to the civil authorities vital community functions. Pastor and teacher pleaded for morality from the pulpit and catechized the children of the church in Sabbath classes; yet education was basically a civil affair, and morality was defined in law and enforced in the courts. And while the church evinced a concern for the physical welfare of its members through the deacons and widows, ultimate responsibility for the care of the indigent and sick was left to the town and commonwealth.

The gradual definition of spheres which was taking place both in fact and in theory—for Cotton's writings are replete with efforts to distinguish carefully the means by which the relationships of church and state to each other and to the society could be regulated—was not an easy task, nor was it completed during the period. The church required "sweet and wholesom laws" from the magistrates for the furtherance and protection of its truths, while the civil government continued to call upon the elders for advice and to expect the church to play a social role. Neither was the definition of spheres undertaken without dissent and acrimonious debate, the elders in particular becoming anxious guardians of their prerogatives within their particular congregations and within the society as a whole. Thus in 1643 the overly earnest intervention of an elder in a matter before the Assistants drove one magistrate to exasperation: "Do you think to come with your eldership here to carry matters?" At another time, when the elders of Essex went beyond the bounds that Winthrop considered proper in espousing the cause of their towns against Boston—for when town argued with town, the elders tended to identify with their communities, aggravating the difference rather than resolving it—the Governor lashed out. They "had done no good offices in this matter, through their misapprensions both of the intentions of the magistrates, and also of the matters them-

30. "Boston Records," *passim; Winthrop's Journal,* I, 256, II, 15, 40; Lechford, *Plain Dealing,* 34-35.

selves, being affairs of state, which did not belong to their calling."[31]

On the other hand, when the General Court, "taking into
consideration the great disorder general through the country in
costliness of apparel, and following new fashions," asked the ministers to intervene "by urging [reform] upon the consciences of
their people," the churches failed to act. Winthrop wrote that
it was because "divers of the elders' wives, etc., were in some
measure partners in this general disorder." Perhaps he was
thinking of Sarah Cotton, wife of Teacher John, to whom years
later her son would write of God "weaning you from creature
comforts, and teaching you, to be above them . . . ; how many
times, alas! how many times . . . your flesh and your heart hath
failed you." But more likely the failure grew out of the opposition of the elders to the interference of the magistrates in church
affairs. "The Magistrate [must] kisse the Churches feet," minister Thomas Shepard jotted in his journal, and "meddle not
beyond his bounds." Subsequently Winthrop noted that "there
were so many lectures now in the country" that "many poor persons" were resorting "to two or three in the weeke." The General Court acted from the same motives that it did when passing
laws against idleness—to prevent "the great neglect of their
affairs, and the damage of the public"—when it asked the elders
to meet "to consider about the length and frequency of church
assemblies." But while the elders extolled the law against idleness as a law against sin, they denounced the magistrates' request
"as if it would cast a blemish upon [them], which would remain
to posterity, that they should need to be regulated by the civil
magistrate, and also raise an ill savor of the people's coldness,
that would complain of much preaching." Still later the civil
authorities were to doubt the wisdom of "divers days of humiliation" which had the same detrimental effect upon the commonwealth, "but they would not contend with the elders about it,
but left the churches to their liberty."[32]

31. *Winthrop's Journal*, II, 117, 190.
32. *Ibid.*, I, 279, 325-27, II, 91; "The Autobiography of Thomas Shepard,"
Col. Soc. Mass., *Publications*, 27 (1932), 397; John Cotton, Jr., to Sarah Cotton,
Dec. 27, 1670, "Mather Papers," Mass. Hist. Soc., *Collections*, 4th Ser., 8 (1868),
226.

Within the church itself there was fragmentation. In Boston the idea of one church, one town—an idea reflected in Cotton's draft law code of the mid-1630's—failed when geography led some of those of Rumney Marsh to the Lynn or Charlestown churches, and some of Muddy River to Roxbury; in 1650 it would be completely abandoned when the size of the congregation necessitated a division and the second church was formed on the North End. Interests in the town were reflected by the congregation in the discussion of the site for a new meetinghouse, in the debate over the chapel at Rumney Marsh, or in the basic conflict between the interest of the community and the individualism evoked by material opportunity. One example of the last is the church's dealing with merchant Keayne, when Cotton set forth his definition of "just price." In the second decade strong pressure arose for a solution to the related questions of church membership and baptism, pressure against the exclusion of those —particularly the baptized children of the church—who did not meet the hardened standard established for membership, and the consequent exclusion from baptism of their children. The question cut across the arbitrary line distinguishing members and non-members, for while it was debated outside the church, those within were not united "in one mind, and one judgement, and one speech, in one truth," despite the imposition of ministerial authority in defining truth.[33] Indeed, the ministerial authority asserted in theory by Cotton and others was denied in practice on this and other questions, creating schism between communicants and presbyters.

Concerned for the purity of God's truth, the elders of New England were hardening against what they considered error. The hardening had begun in the aftermath of the Hutchinsonian struggle and was quickened by the prevalence of error in England, wracked in the 1640's by civil war and ecclesiastical dispute, and the spread of error to the New World. In a sense at least, the presbyters or church officers were becoming little more than one of the many interests within the town and commonwealth, stronger than most because the word of God was on their

33. Cotton, *Doctrine of the Church*, 5.

side and because, to the civil authorities, the church represented a desirable order and morality in society.[34]   But the presbyters were little different in pressing for legislative sanction for their truths to use against the erroneous both within and without the church than the shoemakers or coopers when they pressed for economic advantages.   In part it was the elders, for example, who defeated the attempt in 1645 to alleviate the laws against Anabaptists and those forbidding the entertaining of sojourners without permission of the magistrates when "divers merchants and others" petitioned the commonwealth for changes.   The magistrates were "well inclined" to favor the petition, but "many of the elders, hearing of it, went first to the deputies and after to the magistrates, and ... entreated that the law might continue." A counter petition was solicited in the towns, seventy-eight freemen asking that "there may not be a dore open for ... Dangerous errors to infect and spread in the Countrey as some doe Desire." The Court hesitated in 1645, refusing to take action; the next year it declared that the laws would remain in force.[35]

The same year (1646) a whole series of ecclesiastical laws was passed by the General Court: "Against Blasphemy of the Name of God," against "damnable heresies, tending to the subversion of the Christian faith, and destruction of the soules of men," requiring (again) church attendance by all "seeing that the word [of God] is of generall and common behoofe to all sorts of people, as being the ordinary meanes to subdue the harts of hearers not onely to the faith, and obedience to the Lord Jesus, but also to civill obedience, and allegiance unto magistracy, and to just and honest conversation toward all men."   The practices of the New England church, and the ministerial position within the churches, were made the law of the land, despite the profes-

34. For example, *Winthrop's Journal*, I, 326, where the Governor, in commenting upon a dispute between the magistrates and ministers, notes that the magistrates gave in, "for the elders had great power in the people's hearts, which was needful to be upheld, lest the people should break their bonds through abuse of liberty ... ; and indeed the people themselves, generally, through the churches, were of that understanding and moderation, as they could easily be guided in their way by any rule from scripture or sound reason."

35. *Ibid.*, 259-60; Petition to the General Court "of divers of Dorchestr, Roxberry," for the continuance of the laws against Anabaptists, *ca.* May 1646, Mass. Archives; *Colony Records*, II, 149.

sion that "no humane power be Lord over the faith and consciences of men." "It is ordred and decreed by this Corte, that
if any person whethr in churchfellowship or out of it, shall go
about to destroy or disturbe the ordr of the churches established
in this country, by open renouncing their church estate, or their
minister, or othr ordinaces dispensed in them," they shall be fined;
"forasmuch as the open contempt of Gods word and messengrs
therof is the desolating sinn of civill states and churches, and
that the preaching of the word by those whom God doth send is
the cheife ordinary meanes ordained of God for the converting,
edifiing, and saving the soules of the elect ... and the ministry
of the word is set up by God in his churches, for those holy ends,"
it is ordered that if any "shall contemptuously behave himselfe toward the word preached, or the messengrs thereof ... eithr by
interrupting him in his preaching, or by charging him falsely with
any error which he hath not taught ... or ... cast upon his true
doctrine or himselfe any reproach, to the dishhonor of the Lord
Jesus, who hath sent him," he shall be punished.[36]   And when
synodical authority was resorted to in order to resolve dissension
among the various churches—in effect to declare the New England Way which was being fossilized in law—the presbyters sought
the sanction and protection of the secular state, a bill being presented in May 1646 "by some of the elders for a synod to be held
at the end of the summer."   The synod was ultimately to produce the Cambridge *Platform of Church Discipline*, embodying
a formal statement of church polity, and this too received the
sanction of the state, the General Court attesting in 1651 "that
for the substance thereof it is that wee have practised and doe
beleeve."[37]

The *Platform* was the culmination of the drive toward ministerial domination both within the particular churches and, by
virtue of the synodical authority, among the churches, establishing
as credo that which had previously been presented as ministerial
theory.[38]   As such it precipitated strong opposition, for it ran in

36. *Colony Records*, II, 176-79.
37. *Winthrop's Journal*, II, 274; *Colony Records*, IV, Pt. I, 58.
38. For all the casuistry by which it was asserted that the synod had no
binding power—Cotton, for example, in [John Cotton], *The Result of a Synod
at Cambridge in New-England, Anno. 1646* ... (London, 1654), *passim*—Ed-

the face of reality: the emerging individualism, the urge to participate in public affairs, and a particularism as strong within the church as in the town. As Captain Edward Johnson wrote, there were too many "inured with the broad beatten path of liberty" who feared "to be confined in the straight and narrow path of truth" as enunciated by a synod. Thomas Hooker, writing to Thomas Shepard from far-off Connecticut, noted: "I wish . . . that the binding power of Synods be not pressed too much"; "in that business [you] will find hott and hard work, or else my prospective much fayles."[39] Moreover, the resort to civil authorities for sanction smacked of the Erastianism of Archbishop Laud, and though some like Samuel Danforth rejoiced that elders and magistrates—Moses and Aaron—were about to proclaim

one God, one Faith profest
To be New-Englands interest[40]

others did not.

In the Boston church particularly the call for the synod raised angry dispute.[41] Opponents within the congregation—between thirty and forty men, Winthrop wrote, although he might well have understated the number in opposition since he favored the synod—lashed out against the interjection of "civil authority" in church business and the fact that it was "some of the elders" who had surreptitiously sought Court sanction for the synod. To them the synod "was appointed by the elders, to the intent to make ecclesiastical laws to bind the churches, and to have the sanction of civil authority put upon them, whereby men should be forced under penalty to submit to them." There were too many of "the opposite party" to be silenced by admonition; hence Cotton, Wilson, the ruling elders, and pre-eminent laymen such as Winthrop argued through two Sabbath meetings. It was not for the mem-

ward Johnson let slip a truism in his *Wonder-Working Providence*, 240. In speaking of the Child petitioners, he commented: "not that they cared for a Presbyterian Church, for had they so done, they might have found out one in the country before they petitioned."

39. *Johnson's Wonder-Working Providence*, 243; T[homas] Hooker to [Thomas Shepard], n.d. but after Sept. 17, 1646, Hutchinson Papers, Mass. Archives.
40. Danforth, *Almanack* (1647), under date of June.
41. The following narrative is drawn from *Winthrop's Journal*, II, 278ff.

bers to inquire "what or who gave the court occasion to call the synod," they declared, whether it was the elders or the magistrates; all that they should concern themselves with was whether the council would be helpful "in any matters which concerned religion and conscience" and if it would be, it was their "duty to yield." To question the intent of the elders or the Court to establish a binding ecclesiastical code was "against the rule of charity," for given the language of the order—the statement that the Court would give the results of the synod "such allowance as is meet"— it should not be inferred "that they will put any such sanction or stamp of authority upon them, as should be unmeet." But their arguments availed them nothing. At the close of the second meeting the ministers declared that they felt obliged to attend the synod, "not as sent by the church," which was refusing its consent, "but as specially called by the order of court."

The formal approbation of the largest church in the commonwealth was necessary, however, and when the synod met on September 1, presumably with Cotton and Wilson in attendance, it immediately dispatched letters to the Bostonians "inviting" their approval "and pressing them also by arguments." The letters arrived on a Wednesday and were delivered to the ruling elders, who attempted a bit of political sleight of hand by calling a sudden meeting of the church to consider a reply, but enough of the opposition managed to attend to block any action. The next day was Cotton's regular lecture day and the whole of the assembled ministers trooped down from Cambridge to attend. Undoubtedly Cotton felt his own arguments had been spent and so he turned the pulpit over to the Reverend John Norton of Ipswich. Norton's text was "of Moses and Aaron meeting in the mount and kissing each other"; his lesson was "the nature and power of the synod, as only consultative, decisive, and declarative" and "the power of the civil magistrate in calling such assemblies"; his conclusion was "the duty of the churches in yielding obedience" and "the great offence and scandal which would be given in refusing."

But Norton's efforts could not move the hard core in opposition, and the following Sabbath the elders resorted to still another piece of political manipulation. An innocuous motion was presented to the congregation and the members were asked to signify their approval or disapproval by a show of hands: "Whether the church would hold communion with the other churches?" It was a generally accepted proposition which even the most adamant against the synod could approve, but the opposition refrained from voting "because they knew not what would be inferred upon it." The motion was declared carried, and a second proposition presented: "Whether they would exercise this communion in sending messengers to the synod, and if not, then . . . whether the church would then go" as a body. Instantly the opposition was in an uproar, objecting to "this way of doing a church act by the major part, which had not been our practise in former times." But the change of procedure—from "silent consent" by which a single negative voice could block an action, at least temporarily, to a more easily controlled majority rule—was validated by the pastor and teacher, using the word of God as justification: "In some cases (as the choice of officers, etc.) it is needful to have every man's consent but in other cases, as admission of a member, etc., it was sufficient, if the major part assented." Moreover, the church could not stand mute on the question; "the order of the court, and the letters of the synod" required some sort of reply and inasmuch as "the minor part" could not answer for the church "the major part (of necessity) must."

The ground was slipping away from the opponents to the synod, and they knew it. In desperation they moved that the elders' alternative be adopted: The church itself should go rather than send its elders and messengers. But this would not do, the ministers replied. "It would not be convenient or of good report, to go in a singular way"; "it would savor of disorder and tumult"; "it might produce an impossibility, for . . . if all (or but the major part of our church) should go thither, it were almost impossible any business could proceed." Given, therefore, the acceptable first premise—that communion with other churches was warranted— and the impossibility of all going, the solution could only be that representatives be dispatched, and, by majority vote, "the elders and three of the brethren" were authorized to go in the name of the church.

The messengers were not needed that year. The assembly, having waited for a resolution of the Boston dispute and the appearance of messengers from Connecticut River, broke up because of the lateness of the season. In June 1647 it met again, Cotton, to allay any lingering reluctance, having meanwhile prepared a justification of the synodical authority and the rights of civil authorities in such matters.[42] But there was little chance to do more than listen to the Reverend Ezekiel Rogers of Rowley harshly condemn "the practise of private members making speeches in the church assemblies to the disturbance and hindrance of the ordinances" before an epidemic forced adjournment.[43] In August 1648 the assembly met for its third and last session. Cotton, Richard Mather of Dorchester, and Ralph Partridge of Duxbury (Plymouth) had been charged with preparing drafts for a "model of church government" and both Partridge and Mather presented platforms for consideration, Mather's probably written in conjunction with Cotton.[44] The assembly quickly chose Mather's draft as a basis and after deliberation and amendment adopted it unanimously, closing their work with a hymn, "the song of Moses and the Lamb":

> Great and marvellous *are* thy works,
>   Lord God Almighty;
> Just and true *are* thy ways,
>   thou King of Saints.[45]

The *Platform* was subsequently printed[46] and in October 1649 presented to the General Court, which recommended it "to the judicious and pious consideration of the severall churches within

---

42. His *Result of a Synod at Cambridge in New-England*. The published pamphlet merely states that it was "drawn up by some of the Members of the Assembly" but there is good evidence to support Cotton's authorship.

43. *Winthrop's Journal*, II, 324.

44. Mather, *Magnalia Christi Americana*, II, 211; the drafts are in the manuscript collection of the American Antiquarian Society Library, Worcester, Mass.

45. Mather, *Magnalia Christi Americana*, II, 211; Rev. 15:3.

46. As *A Platform of Church Discipline Gathered out of the Word of God: Agreed upon by the Elders: and Messengers of the Churches Assembled in the Synod at Cambridge in New England To Be Presented to the Churches and Generall Court for Their Consideration and Acceptance* . . . (Cambridge, 1649).

this jurisdiction," thus precipitating another battle which lasted until 1651.[47]

Again Boston was a center of contention, though no record of the discussions has survived, and there was undoubtedly confusion and delay as a result of the splitting of the church and the formation of the Second Church on the North End. In 1651 Cotton was delegated by the General Court to receive the objections to the *Platform* and pass them on to another assemblage of elders. To judge from a list of "Exceptions against some things in the Synod at Cambr." found among the Cotton papers, the objections ran through a wide range: The approval of the Westminster Confession which the synod had "engrafted" onto the first page of the *Platform* to alleviate difficulties with the English churches was rejected; those parts of the *Platform* which endowed the church officers with "Power of Office" to the exclusion of the congregation itself and the teacher and pastor with sole authority to preach, which established "that man may not speake without the Elders leave, nor continue speaking when they require silence," which required the consent of the elders to church actions, which laid down a basis for tithes to maintain the ministry—all were denied. Denied, too, was the power of a synod over a particular church and the section of the *Platform* "in which they say, the Synod is an Ordinance of God."[48] Undoubtedly this last was the major point at issue, having precipitated a long discourse by Cotton the year before—a set of "Propositions Concerning of Consociation and Communion of Churches, tendred to the Elders and Brethren of the Church for their Consideration and acceptance according to God"—in which he had argued that "as there is a Brotherhood of members in the same Church, so there is a Brotherhood of Churches, being all Fellow members of Christ Jesus, and so bound to have a mutual Care one of another."[49] Dutifully collected, the objections were as dutifully considered

47. *Colony Records*, II, 285; Walker, ed., *Creeds and Platforms of Congregationalism*, 186.

48. The "Exceptions" (in the Cotton Papers) are unsigned and undated, but *ca.* June 1651.

49. Printed by Increase Mather, presumably from a manuscript in Cotton's hand, in *First Principles of New-England*, 28-33. The argument seems to have been prepared for delivery at the ordination of Jonathan Mitchell as pastor at Cambridge but reflects the controversy in Boston.

by the assembled elders and an answer "retourned" which "cleared
and remooved" all doubts as to the *Platform* expressing the true
word of God for the General Court.[50]   The declaration that the
Platform was "agreeable" to the word "and the principles of the
Congregational Way" followed, though Boston's two deputies—
Thomas Clark and John Leverett—together with twelve other
deputies (of a total of forty) voted against adoption.[51] As printed
in London in 1653, the revised platform was to all intents and
purposes that of 1649, no changes having been made in response
to the objections so assiduously compiled.

The foisting of the *Platform* upon the protesting members of
the First Church—and upon others, for the First Church was not
alone in its opposition—resolved nothing.   The ministerial and
synodical authority had been proclaimed anew and authoritatively,
but it was a hollow victory.   Dissension persisted and neither
ministers nor synods (even with the sword of the civil authorities
wielded in their behalf and frequently at their behest) would be
able to still it.

Even as the synod was meeting, the Childites were seeking to
embarrass church and government with their petitions and appeals
to England; Baptists, Quakers, and Seekers were beginning to
plague the commonwealth with criticism and new ideas.   In years
to come the number of such "opinionists" would increase, and
some would suffer death on Boston's gallows.   Arguments were
breaking out within the church, and not infrequently the civil
government was being called upon by the elders to assert their
authority.   The gap between town and church was growing, ag-
gravated by the continuing exclusion from membership of the
merely baptized and the exclusion from baptism of their children,
and year by year pressure for change was growing stronger.

The synod of 1646-48 had in part been gathered to search for
godly truth "about baptisme, and persons to be received thereto,"
the order convening the assembly having noted that "the aprhen-
cions of many persons in the country are knoune not a litle to

50. *Colony Records*, IV, Pt. I, 57.   The answers to the objections, in the
handwriting of Richard Mather, are in the possession of the American Antiquarian
Society Library.

51. [Scotto], *Narrative of the Planting of the Massachusetts Colony*, in Mass.
Hist. Soc., *Collections*, 4th Ser., 4 (1858), 304; *Colony Records*, III, 240.

differ" on the matter. Most churches in the commonwealth, the Court stated, "doe [baptize] only such children whose neerest parents are one or both of them setled members in full communion," others "doe baptise the children if the grandfather or grandmother be such members though the immediate parents be not"—Boston's First Church, for example.[52] Still other churches, and "many persons living in the country, who have binn members of the congregations in England, but are not found fitt to be receaved at the Lords table here" "doe much encline . . . as thinking more liberty and latitude in this point ought to be yeelded then hath hetherto binn donne."[53] When the synod met, there were some ministers who were ready to acknowledge the unpleasant New England reality—that the churches were losing the children and, by virtue of the gap between members and non-members, their identity with the whole of the community. God's holy truth might seem to limit the sacraments, baptism and holy communion, to the visible saints, but to these ministers such truth was not practical. They introduced a provision that would acknowledge those "borne in the ch[urch]" who were not "culpable of such scandalls in Conversation as do justly deserve ch[urch] Censures" to be half-way members "though yet they be not found fitt for the Lords Supper."[54] As such they would be subject to the covenant at least in part and entitled to the baptism of their children. In essence there would be a division of the seals of the church into one of lesser and one of greater degree, preserving the purity of the churches by limiting the greater (communion) to the proven and tested saints while expanding the basis of the church within the population by opening the lesser (baptism) to the children of the half-way members. To other ministers, however, the provision was unacceptable, one declaring that *"he would oppose it with all his might,"* that in effect he would insist on truth regardless of its consequences.[55]

52. The only instances of such baptism in First Church Records are the baptisms in 1634, 1635, and 1639 of the children of Samuel Dudley and Mary Winthrop in the right of grandfather John Winthrop.

53. *Colony Records,* III, 71.

54. Mather, *First Principles of New-England,* 6; Richard Mather's manuscript draft of the platform, American Antiquarian Society Library.

55. John Allin, *Animadversions upon the Antisynodalia Americana . . .* (Cambridge, Mass., 1664), 5.

The assembled elders could unite in proclaiming ministerial and synodical authority, but they could not unite on a point of doctrine, once again indicative of the fact that orthodoxy in New England applied only to polity and not to deeper questions. Half-way membership was not pressed, for the ministers urging the reform, like Cotton in the 1630's, subordinated their desires to the semblance of ministerial unity. The *Platform* as adopted excluded from the Lord's Supper those "baptized in their infancy, or minority" who had not "come to their tryall and examination, and manifest[ed] their faith and repentance by an open profession therof," but it was mute on the baptism of the children of the baptized non-member, neither allowing nor disallowing it, leaving the matter to the resolution of the individual churches. The *Platform* did, however, attempt to resolve the problem which had provoked the proposal, extending the churches' sway over the baptized non-members by declaring that "if not regenerated" they were nevertheless "in a more hopefull way of attayning regenerating grace" and were therefore "under Church-watch, and . . . subject to the reprehensions, admonitions, and censures therof, for their healing and amendment."[56]

Yet it was not enough merely to claim a moral jurisdiction over the half-way member and allow him nothing in return, and before two decades had elapsed synodical sanction would have to be given to the half-way covenant defeated in 1648. By then the failure of synodical authority, the triumph of congregationalism with all its localism and individualism, would be apparent. Some churches, including Boston's First Church, would cling to the absolute purity of the saints by continuing to limit baptism, but others would accept the newly authorized practice; the First Church itself would divide on the issue, some members departing to form the Third or South Church.

To the ministers, the continuing dissension was agonizing. There was but one truth; God provided no alternatives. The ministry was ordained by God to search out and assert that truth, and once pointed out it was irresistible to the godly. But there was no single truth in New England, and even the saints held

56. *Platform of Church Discipline,* 18.

their own against the ministers. In their failure, the ministers changed. Some were saddened. Cotton, for example, his battles almost over—he was to die in December 1652—bemoaned "Popular and familiar Disputes" when a "Reverend and dear brother" solicited his intervention in a theological argument; "such scholasticall Questions as you propound to me are too subtile for my old Head to Dispute on." Others were driven to bitterness and even cruelty, the gentle, poetical John Wilson, an ardent proponent of order and authority within the church since the days of his harassment by the Hutchinsonians, striking one of the defendants during the trial of the Quakers in 1651, cursing him, "saying, the Curse of God or Jeusus goe with thee," and on his deathbed citing as "those sins amongst us, which provoked the displeasure of God" the rising up of the people *against their Ministers . . . when indeed they do but Rule for Christ,*" and "*the making light of, and not subjecting to the Authority of* Synods, *with which the Churches cannot long subsist.*" Some were coming to accept their role as mere purveyors of religion to a secular society, anxious for preferment, squabbling over fees. And a few were to strive manfully to recover what was coming to be looked upon as a golden age, giving vent to a vast jeremiad, lamenting their own time and extolling for the edification of their hearers the presumed virtues of the first years.[57]

In these lamentations years some of the laymen of New England would join, for the materialism and fragmentation was evident to many. They prayed to God to save them from themselves:

> O Lord, take pity on thy people poor,
> Let them repent, amend, and sin no more;
> Forgive, dear Father, what is done and past,
> Oh save us still, and not away us cast.

They clung blindly to the stability and order which the churches at least represented, although they did not achieve either completely—men like Thomas Dudley, to whom dissension and disparate beliefs were unbearable, leaving as a legacy to his "dear

57. [John Cotton] to "Reverend and dear brother," n.d. but after 1650, Cotton Papers; Rutman, "God's Bridge Falling Down," *Wm. and Mary Qtly.*, 3d Ser., 19 (1962), 416, 419ff.

wife, children and friends" a warning against "such as do a *tolera-tion* hatch." They pointed to Boston, where trade and commerce ruled, as New England's cancerous sore. "The Lord he speaks in particular to Boston . . . and calls you to a through reformation in your Town, you being set up as a Beacon upon the top of a mountain," an English correspondent wrote to Increase Mather later in the century; "your candlesticks should give light to all the neighbour Towns and Churches round about you: But when they see your famous Town abound with drunkennesse, swearing, excesse in apparrel, etc. what encouragement is there for Towns round about you to follow your example." Even Boston's own Joshua Scotto would shed an old man's tears for declining times: *"It concerneth* New-England *always to remember, that originally they are a* PLANTATION *Religious, not a* PLANTATION *of Trade;* . . . a spot of this vast *Jeshimon* converted into Corn-fields, Orchards, Streets Inhabited, and a place of Merchandise cannot denominate *New-England."*[58]

And what of Winthrop? Faced with a proliferating materialism and individualism, fragmentation and dispute, the necessity of accepting, even abetting, what was happening, of resorting to law and bolstering the church in the hope of tempering man's nature, of acquiescing in banishments and imprisonments to preserve the safety and unity of the commonwealth, did he sense the crumbling ideal which was all about him in Boston? Did he sometime during his last years stroll down to Town Dock at dusk on an evening constitutional and look outward, past the ships in the harbor, toward the Atlantic and the islands and ports around its rim—London, Tenerife, the unnamed rivers flowing into Africa's Bight of Benin, Antigua, and Barbados? Did he gaze across the harbor to Rumney Marsh with its rich farms and pastures? The farms and shipping lanes meant prosperity for Boston, but by virtue of their temptation to men, his own failures as well. Home from his walk, did he sit among the books and

---

58. William Bradford, "A Descriptive and Historical Account of New England in Verse," Mass. Hist. Soc., *Collections,* 1st Ser., 3 (1794), 84; Mather, *Magnalia Christi Americana,* I, 134; John Westgate to Increase Mather, May 8, 1677, "Mather Papers," Mass. Hist. Soc., *Collections,* 4th Ser., 8 (1868), 578; [Scotto], *Narrative of the Planting of the Massachusetts Colony,* in Mass. Hist. Soc., *Collections,* 4th Ser., 4 (1858), 327.

carpenter tools of his study and wonder what his Boston had become, and would become? Did he, like his counterpart in Plymouth, William Bradford, feel somewhat saddened that

> love and fervent zeal do seem to sleep
> Security and the world on men do creep?[59]

Perhaps. At times there is a hint of disappointment in his writings, when he speaks of the wickedness among the settlers, or of too much self-love, or recounts the arguments in town, church, and commonwealth. When one Captain Partridge, a zealous Parliamentarian but a deviant from New England's truth, arrived and was immediately banished, Winthrop wrote: "But sure the rule of hospitality to strangers, and of seeking to pluck out of the fire such as there may be hope of to be reduced out of error and the snare of the devil, do seem to require more moderation and indulgence of human infirmity where there appears not obstinancy against the cleare truth."[60] Yet he never bewailed the whole as others were beginning to do, never wrote of total failure. Indeed, one suspects that he was not fully aware of the extent of the failure, for he was never called upon to surrender all of the ideal all at once, only constantly required to surrender one small part of the whole in the interest of another part. In the end, he was more than likely content. If man had not come up to the optimistic expectations of the "Modell of Christian Charity," it was God's will. Having done his best with what his Lord had given him, Winthrop could turn to his Bible and find "comfort in God, and delight in heavenly things."[61]

59. Bradford, "A Descriptive and Historical Account of New England," Mass. Hist. Soc., *Collections*, 1st Ser., 3 (1794), 83.
60. *Winthrop's Journal*, II, 260-61.
61. "John Winthrop's Experiencia, 1616-18," *Winthrop Papers*, I, 190.

X

EPILOGUE

MUCH HAS BEEN WRITTEN of Puritanism in America, as though somehow it had injected a constant factor into the moving stream of history. But in the beginning, if one is to judge from the vantage point of Boston, there was no Puritan way, no constant to be injected, merely actions, reactions, interactions: Winthrop's ideal "Citty upon a Hill"; the ministerial preoccupation with God's true and holy dictates; the superb confidence in salvation of the Hutchinsonians; the merchant's profit and the little man's grasping at opportunity; the preconceived ideas imported with the settlers and the environment they found. Fragmented and splintered, these jostling forces passed from the Winthrop years to the years immediately after, there to be splintered and fragmented still more, mixed with new forces, and passed on again. If what eventually emerged was uniquely American—and Americans regularly seek to explain their peculiarities—it was only because one found here a continuing juxtaposition of varied elements which could not be duplicated elsewhere, any more than can the shifting patterns of a kaleidoscope to which are constantly being added new pieces of colored glass.

What emerged from the succession of actions and counteractions in early Massachusetts? A peculiar Puritan state? A Bible commonwealth? An oligarchy to be disposed of in the latter half of the century? Historians have written in such terms, but they are meaningless. They neither fit the facts that one finds in Winthrop's Boston nor establish a basis upon which to proceed through American history. One can find, however, certain institutions, practices, and attitudes emerging in the town and exemplifying general tendencies observable in subsequent periods.

Some have long been recognized: the town form of government, congregationalism, a concern for the young, and the beginnings of public education. Others are less obvious.

There is individualism and the pursuit by the individual of his own material well-being. Indeed, it confronts even the casual observer of the Boston scene. And while one is inclined to bemoan the materialism and the individualism which so regularly thwarted the Governor's concern for the community and marked the decline of his ideal, the definition of social good in terms of the well-being of the free individual was to be the way of the future, a new ideal. Of course, the assumptions of the Massachusetts Bay society, as voiced from the pulpit and magistrates' bench, still reflected the idealized community; not for over a hundred years would the individual be so ardently idealized. But the reality of New England was changing faster than its assumptions.

One finds an abiding, pervasive morality in the town. Although the Bostonian was solicitous for his own advancement in the world, and he tended to ignore the arbitrary morality demanded by the ministers, the proper cut of one's hair, for example, when the church lamented the mode of wearing it long, nevertheless the pulpit and the law—the latter through the misguided notion that moral conduct can be precisely legislated—had their effect. Also important in strengthening morality was the very nearness to God of the seventeenth-century man, for whom the divine presence was made more awful by the strenuous preaching of the New England minister. With few exceptions, the Bostonian was ever concerned with his soul. He was, however, defining salvation in terms of the moral and good life and thus establishing at that early date the climate from which emerged Benjamin Franklin's dictates about frugality, industry, and prudence. The easiest way to heaven for the Bostonian of the seventeenth century was essentially the way of Franklin in the eighteenth.

The development of a commercial system in Boston created a market for the commonwealth's surplus agricultural goods and thereby laid down the basis for the prosperity of the town, the Bay, and indeed, for all New England. Commerce also paved

the way in Boston for cosmopolitanism.   By virtue of its trade,
Boston was not an out-of-the-way corner of the Atlantic world;
rather, it was an integral part with ready correspondence with the
rest.   Political and intellectual winds blowing in from the water
would affect the town, giving it an air unique in New England.
This uniqueness was not particularly evident as yet, although
the presence of merchants with an Atlantic orientation was a precursor, as was the attraction of the town to men like Robert Child,
whose mind was already infected with the new learning of western Europe.   Yet it should be no surprise to find that by the end
of the century, Boston would have an imperial outlook, or that
here the Mathers—Increase and Cotton—would hold forth.

One finds a separation of church and state, too, for though the
two were linked throughout the period—the elders of the churches
constituting a pressure group, soliciting protection, advising, ca-
joling, the civil authorities ever responsive to their pressure—the
church and the state were irrevocably drifting apart.   In the early
1650's the separation was symbolized by the removal of town
and commonwealth government from Boston's meetinghouse,
where the General Court and town meetings had previously
gathered, to a newly completed Town House.   The medieval
unity of church and state, their existence as but two facets of the
same society, was disappearing.   The church in Boston in the
1640's consciously embraced only a part of the population; and
with the multiplying of churches after 1650, with their diversity
in matters of doctrine (the First and Third Churches divided on
the issue of the half-way covenant), any single church included
only a fraction of the town.   Moreover, church and state had
varied concerns.   Both played vital roles, being the separate poles
around which the community revolved.   But the concern of the
church—both in the sense of one congregation and in the sense of
the synodical union of churches—was increasingly its own denom-
inational purity, the accenting of God's truth, even though the
elders could not agree upon truth, for its own sake rather than for
the sake of the community.   To an extent the church busied itself
about the doings and misdoings of its communicants, even attempting to extend its sway within the community by compromising

purity and practicality in that movement culminating in the half-way covenant. Reflecting the way of its communicants, its sermons more and more stressed conduct and morality and less and less God's free grace. Yet from the latter 1630's it tended to ignore the broad social role of organized religion insofar as the whole community was concerned. Within the walls of the church, within its ever more formal, more institutional framework, the Bostonians periodically sought communion with God, but life itself was being lived outside.

As the church tended to withdraw from life, the secular authorities of both town and commonwealth assumed a broader and broader social function, in part by virtue of an imported tradition, in part by design. As George Lee Haskins has pointed out,[1] it is in the innovations within the law that the thrust for social reform so evident in Winthrop is ultimately seen. But in part, too, necessity required the assumption of social functions. Within this fragmented society, where long-established relationships were non-existent, where families were disrupted, where the church itself was a divisive element, where materialism and individualism were tending toward social chaos, only the secular authority—the political organization of society—could unite, could define the relationships of one individual to another. It was, in effect, becoming the grand arbiter that it is in theory today, the impartial, amoral arbiter regulating in order to avoid collisions as the members of society followed their individual yet concentric orbits. For their part, the inhabitants were eager to participate in the political structure, to assume some role in the regulation of their affairs, the political organs of society being much too close to everyday life for any individual to be apolitical. In Boston, certainly, this was true, for there the generality was never mute. At the same time there was a willingness on the part of the gentry to bring the populace into public affairs, a ready correspondence between ruler and ruled born of common problems and, increasingly, the lack of any great division between classes. (Status coming to be defined in terms of material well-being in a land of material abundance, class structure inevitably was marked by mobility and a

1. In *Law and Authority in Early Massachusetts*, 211, and *passim*.

lessening of distinctions.) It was not political activity in the modern sense, with parties and campaigns. Nor was it popular government in Jacksonian terms. Far from it, for governors were chosen from the better people as a matter of course. It was, however, responsible government based upon the political awareness of the populace.

One finds, finally, the idea of the covenant, both social and religious. It was in the air of Winthrop's times, the intellectual origin and rationale of the New England Way in both church and state. It too was to be passed on to the future. The vision of man driven from the Garden, his moral sense numbed by an angry God, forced to form societies on a covenant basis, surrendering the liberty of the brute in exchange for the liberty to live an orderly life, is not radically different from John Locke's theory later in the century of man in a state of nature forming governments and delegating limited authority in order to achieve the security of property. Indeed, the Lockean doctrine, when it dropped from England, would land on fertile ground. Nor is there a great distance between the covenant of the First Church—"Wee whose names are hereunder written, being by His most wise, and good Providence brought together into this part of America in the Bay of Masachusetts, and desirious to unite our selves into one Congregation"—and the preamble to the federal Constitution—"We the people of the United States, in Order to form a more perfect Union, establish Justice, insure domestic Tranquility, provide for the common defence, promote the general Welfare, and secure the Blessings of Liberty to ourselves and our Posterity."[2]

Individualism and materialism, a Franklinesque morality, a clear distinction between the sacral and secular affairs of men, the associational nature of society—none of these qualities found in Boston as the second decade gave way to the third were Winthropian; none had had a place in that paean delivered aboard the *Arbella* in the grand moment of beginning. Then Winthrop had spoken of society being united in deed and purpose; of men singly and collectively devoted to God; of a subordination of self in the interest of the community for the greater glory of the deity. It

2. See Richard Niebuhr, "The Idea of the Covenant and American Democracy," *Church History*, 23 (1954), 126-35.

was a medieval dream, and it was not to be. The Governor had sought to bridge the gap between God and man, but the nature of man and the historical process (of which the dream was only a part) had deemed otherwise. In Winthrop's Boston the ideal of the medieval community was transformed into the reality of modern society.

APPENDICES

I

THE INTENTION TO SETTLE A
SINGLE COMMUNITY

No DIRECT EVIDENCE exists of the form of settlement contemplated by the leadership of the Winthrop fleet as they sailed in 1630. The historian must rely, therefore, on the evidence of events during the first year, and this clearly indicates the intention to settle in a single community.

By far the most extensive account of the crucial first year is Thomas Dudley's long letter to Lady Bridget, Countess of Lincoln, of March 12, 1630/31, printed in Alexander Young, comp., *Chronicles of the First Planters of the Colony of Massachusetts Bay, from 1623 to 1636* (Boston, 1846), 303-41. Dudley's story is clear: The Winthrop fleet straggled into Salem harbor in June and July of 1630 and the leaders, finding the area not to their liking, "began to consult of the place of our sitting down" (p. 312)—note the singular *"the place."* There followed two exploratory journeys to Massachusetts Bay during which Governor Winthrop uncovered "a good place upon Mistick" River and a second party "a place" on Charles River, extensive deliberations as to which site to settle upon, a landing at Charlestown half-way between the two sites and the establishment of a temporary camp, finally a dispersal into numerous small groups as a result of disease at Charlestown and a vague rumor of an impending French assault—all of which is described in chap. 2. "We were forced to change counsel and for our present shelter to plant dispersedly," Dudley wrote (p. 313); "this dispersion troubled some of us; but help it we could not, wanting ability to remove to any place fit to build a town upon" (p. 314)—again, note the singular. Subsequently he wrote of the abortive attempt in the spring of 1631 to regroup the settlers in one community, an attempt described in chap. 2.

Dudley's letter is not the only evidence to these occurrences and the intent to be inferred from them. James Kendall Hosmer, ed., [*John*] *Winthrop's Journal "History of New England,"* *1630-1649*, 2 vols. (New York, 1908), I, 50, contains the singular form in describing the search for "a place for our sitting down"; J. Franklin Jameson, ed., [*Edward*] *Johnson's Wonder-Working Providence, 1628-1651* (N. Y., 1910), 74, written twenty years after the event, notes that Watertown was initially settled not out of purpose but "by occasion of Sir Richard Saltingstall, who at his arrivall, having some store of Cattell and servants, they wintered in those parts," the temporary nature of "wintered" being implicit; *Winthrop's Journal*, I, 54, 84, substantiates and adds to Dudley's account of the discussions relative to regrouping in late 1630 and early 1631; Emmanuel Downing, in England, heard of the decision to regroup and wrote Winthrop on April 30, 1631, that he was "glad you have begunn to remove and plant some what higher up the river" (Massachusetts Historical Society, *Winthrop Papers*, 15 vols. [Boston, 1929-47], III, 30).

Dr. Samuel Fuller of Plymouth adds his evidence, although indirectly. The Winthrop fleet per se consisted of eleven vessels and some seven hundred settlers gathered by the leadership and under its direct control. But two other groups of settlers sailed that year, one of eighty men, women, and children from the West Counties aboard the ship *Lyon*, another of 140 dispatched from Dorchester on the *Mary and John* under the auspices of the Reverend John White. Both groups seem to have sailed under some sort of license from the Winthrop leaders (who were the officers of the company). Whether or not they were to settle within the single community is not clear, although it would seem that at least the *Mary and John*'s passengers had not been instructed to do so. The *Lyon* entered Salem harbor and her passengers imperceptibly merged into the main body. The *Mary and John* sailed directly into Massachusetts Bay and her passengers moved to "Mattapan" peninsula (Dorchester). The merger of the Dorchester people with the main group was subsequently contemplated, however, for on June 28 Dr. Fuller wrote to Governor William Bradford at Plymouth that the main party intended to settle as a group and that "they of Matapan purpose to go and plant with them" (Mass. Hist. Soc., *Collections*, 1st Ser., 3 [1794], 74).

Two additional pieces of circumstantial evidence should be taken into account. Prior to the assumption of control of the Massachusetts Bay Company by the Winthrop group, the company had spent a great amount of time working out a land policy for its settlement. The policy finally adopted embraced a single community, in which the settlers would have their homes and small garden lots, surrounded by outlying farms for extensive agriculture, the size of the lots and farms to be dependent upon investment in the company (with the transportation of individuals being accounted an investment) and the status of the person soliciting the land (Nathaniel B. Shurtleff, ed., *Records of the Governor and Company of the Massachusetts Bay in New England*, 5 vols. in 6 [Boston, 1853-54], II, 42-43). As is shown in chap. 3, Winthrop did not reject this scheme. On the contrary, he endorsed at least a part of it in an address to the company late in 1629 (viz., that part by which land would be used as a dividend for investment), and in his notebook he sketched what are obviously town lots of an acre, half-acre, and quarter-acre (*Winthrop Papers*, II, 176, and the plates following p. 276). Speech and sketches clearly suggest that the company plan of 1629, including the central community, was the Winthrop plan of 1630.

It should be noted too that the Winthrop fleet carried but two ministers to New England. Two ministers associated with a single church were not uncommon in England, while the dispatching of two ministers on a hazardous journey to a single settlement in the New World was, indeed, most common. If the intention had been to establish more than one community with the settlers aboard the ships of the Winthrop fleet, more than two ministers would undoubtedly have been engaged. (Subsequent to the dispersal into many communities the shortage of ministers was to be a hardship, prompting the solicitation of additional ministers described in chap. 5.) Two other ministers traveled with the Dorchester settlers of 1630, while two already resided at Salem. The presence of the former would indicate that the Dorchester settlers intended to settle apart; certainly their presence would have made a merger with the main body difficult if the dispersal had not intervened. The presence of the latter perhaps contributed to the decision not to settle the main body at or in the vicinity of Salem.

II

WERE THE EMIGRANTS OF 1630 "NON-SEPARATING CONGREGATIONALISTS"?

FOR OVER TWO DECADES, almost any discussion of the church in Massachusetts, indeed in New England, has begun with the assumption that the emigrants of 1630 arrived fully committed to a non-separating congregational way. The basis of this assumption is, of course, the late Perry Miller's *Orthodoxy in Massachusetts, 1630-1650* (Cambridge, Mass., 1933). The link between the Winthrop migration and the thought so precisely described by Miller is, however, tenuous. In essence, Miller indicated a similarity between the professions of certain English ministers of the William Bradshaw-Paul Baynes-William Ames school before 1630 and the practices and professions in Massachusetts in the late 1630's and 1640's. But he made too much of the solicitation of Ames and others in 1629. Ames, indeed, had been solicited for service in New England, suggesting in reply that he might join the emigrants "upon the news of your safe arrivall, with good hope of prosperitie" (*Winthrop Papers*, II, 180). The celebrated "close" relationship which this implies is more accurately described by John Humphrey in a letter to Winthrop of December 18, 1630, however: "Dr. Ames holds his first affections to you, and the worke, notwithstanding the late neglect of him, in not giving a word eyther to him or of him. I wrote to him excusing all as well as I could, and the good man takes nothing amisse for ought I understand" (*ibid.*, 336). Again, Miller merely presumed that the migration had been preceded by extensive discussions as to church polity. For him, the lack of direct evidence in this regard meant only that the evidence did not exist, not the possibility that little thought had been given to polity. "Most assuredly," he wrote (p. 122), "these men were busy at the time discussing what form the churches of the New World should assume," quoting a 1645 polemic defending the New England Way as it then existed and written by two ministers unassociated with the 1630 venture to indicate as much. He forced the evidence concerning the discussion of church polity in Massachusetts in 1630 into a desired mold, ignored the lay nature of the 1630 leadership and attributed a homogeneity to the leaders which, if we are to judge by their actions in the New World, was nonexistent, and paid scant attention to the actual events of the early 1630's, the years when Massachusetts congregationalism evolved. And throughout, Miller insisted that a ministerial pamphlet or tract of 1645 or 1655 was an adequate mirror of the ideas of 1630—hardly sound historical method!

Miller has, moreover, been severely amended by a number of authors who have pointed out that English non-separating congregationalism was not the precise thought which he described. Edmund S. Morgan, for example, in his *Visible Saints: The History of a Puritan Idea* (N. Y., 1963) can note only a general tendency toward non-separating congregationalism among ministers who, in England, did not concern themselves with its details. If not a consistent synthesis among churchmen, are we to accept it as a consistent synthesis held by the laymen who led in 1630? Even Morgan cannot do that. Hence, while he insists that the Winthrop migrants "belonged to that group of Puritans who ... believed like the Separatists in a congregational organization of the church, but unlike the Separatists ... considered the churches of England, while corrupt, to be still true churches"— i.e., non-separating congregationalists—he is of necessity forced to acknowledge that "the settlers of Massachusetts Bay had not previously worked out the details of Congregational polity" (pp. 54-56, 82-83*n*).

The present author goes one step further. The most that can be said is that basic congregational notions were familiar to some of the leaders of the 1630 migration, but not all, and the main reason for their leaving England was not necessarily to effect congregationalism, but a broad desire to live a godly life. In sum, the equation non-separating congregationalists in England equals congregationalists in New England is much too simple. The origins of the New England Way were more complex, involving not just an English tradition carried as intellectual baggage aboard the Winthrop fleet but New World necessity, the available models at Plymouth and Salem, and, as is indicated in chap. 5, the direct teachings of ministers of the Bradshaw-Baynes-Ames cast *after* 1630, by letters, books, and ultimately in person.

NOTE ON SOURCES AND
METHODS

FUNDAMENTAL TO ANY STUDY centered upon a seventeenth-century New England community are the records of the government, the land, the marketplace, and the church. In the case of Boston, documentary material exists for each of these areas. The historian could wish that it were more complete and less scattered, however. And given the interrelationship between the areas, there is much overlapping; the five-volume *Winthrop Papers* published by the Massachusetts Historical Society (Boston, 1929-47), the Winthrop family's writings in an older series scattered through nine volumes of the Society's *Collections* (from 3d Ser., 10 [1849] through 6th Ser., 5 [1892]), and Winthrop's own history (James Kendall Hosmer, ed., *Winthrop's Journal "History of New England," 1630-1649*, 2 vols. [New York, 1908]), for example, contain vital material relative to all these facets of the society.

Government records—legislative, judicial, executive—include those of the commonwealth, county, and town, foremost among those of the commonwealth being Nathaniel B. Shurtleff, ed., *Records of the Governor and Company of the Massachusetts Bay in New England*, 5 vols. in 6 (Boston, 1853-54), supplemented by missing records printed in William H. Whitmore, *A Bibliographical Sketch of the Laws of the Massachusetts Colony from 1630 to 1686* (Boston, 1890); a "Fragment of the Original Journal of the Massachusetts House of Deputies for the May Session and a Part of the October Session of 1649," Colonial Society of Massachusetts, *Publications*, 5 (1902); and the various codifications of the laws, notably those of 1641 printed by Whitmore (the famous "Body of Liberties") and of 1648, Max Farrand, ed., *The Laws and Liberties of Massachusetts; Reprinted from the Copy of the 1648 Edition in the Henry E. Huntington Library* (Cambridge, Mass., 1929). Only slightly less vital is John Noble and John F. Cronin, eds., *Records of the Court of Assistants of the Colony of the Massachusetts Bay, 1630-1692*, 3 vols. (Boston, 1901-28). The town records are published as "Boston Town Records [1634-1660/61]," in City of Boston, *Report of the Record Commissioners*, II (Boston, 1877), subsequent volumes of this series containing "Boston Births, Baptisms, Marriages, and Deaths, 1630-1699" (vol. IX [Boston, 1883]) and, among the "Miscellaneous Papers" of vols. X and XXIX (Boston, 1886 and 1900), "Lists of Freemen [1630-91]" and "The Last Will and Testament of me, Robert Keayne."

Town, Suffolk County, and commonwealth governments are represented in the manuscripts included in the Massachusetts Archives, State House, Boston, while among the manuscripts filed in the Office of the Clerk of the Supreme Judicial Court for the County of Suffolk are the Charles P. Greenough Collection, containing a few applicable items, and the Early Files of Courts and Miscellaneous Papers, an exceptionally well-preserved run of documents. The rich collection in the possession of the Massachusetts Historical Society Library, Boston, includes many vital items, particularly in the six-volume Miscellaneous Bound Manuscripts, Boxes I through VII of the Manuscript Photostats, the Winslow Papers, 1638-1759, and Endecott Papers. The Chamberlain Collection of the Boston Public Library contains an occasional piece.

Land records include the original grants by town and commonwealth recorded in the pertinent government records; the survey of Boston land holdings undertaken by William Aspinwall and published as "The Book of Possessions" in City of Boston, *Report of the Record Commissioners*, II (Boston, 1877); the continuing record of sales, leases, and the like contained in Edward E. Hale *et al.*, eds., *Note-Book Kept by Thomas Lechford, Esq., Lawyer, in Boston, Massachusetts Bay, from June 27, 1638 to July 29, 1641* (Cambridge, Mass., 1885); "A Volume Relating to the Early History of Boston Containing the Aspinwall Notarial Records from 1644 to 1651," in Registry Department of the City of Boston, *Records Relating to the Early History of Boston*, XXXII (Boston, 1903); and in Suffolk County, Mass., Registry of Deeds, *Suffolk Deeds*, 14 vols. (Boston, 1880-1906). An interesting series of records tracing the history of two North Shore farms is in the possession of the Winthrop Public Library, Winthrop, Mass. Note, too, the material included in Mellen Chamberlain, ed., *A Documentary History of Chelsea including the Boston Precincts of Winnisimmet, Rumney Marsh, and Pullen Point, 1624-1824*, 2 vols. (Boston, 1908). Probate records are indispensable to a consideration of land, but unfortunately the Suffolk County records (unlike Essex County) are unpublished. The extant manuscript records are in the custody of the Suffolk County Register of Probate, Suffolk County Court House, Boston.

Commercial records for the town during these years are relatively scant, and the few available are scattered through the published and manuscript records of government and land, the largest number being found in the *Note-Book Kept by Thomas Lechford* and "Aspinwall Notarial Records" cited above.

The First Church records have only recently (1961) been published as vols. 39-41 of the Col. Soc. Mass., *Publications*. The present author, however, utilized the records from manuscript copies in the Massachusetts Historical Society Library. The records are scant for the years under consideration and must be supplemented by the pertinent material contained in *Winthrop's Journal* and the *Winthrop Papers*; in the manuscript journals of Robert Keayne, 1639-42 in the Massachusetts Historical Society Library, 1643-46 in the Rhode Island Historical Society Library, Providence, and portions of a volume 1638-39 published in the Mass. Hist. Soc., *Proceedings*, 2d Ser., 2 (1889); and by such descriptions as Thomas Lechford's 1642 *Plain Dealing; or, News from New England*, ed. J. Hammond Trumbull (Boston, 1867).

The Boston church did not exist in isolation but was part of the broader stream of New England's (and old England's) religious development. Thus to the records of the church must be added the vast number of pamphlets emanating from New England, and from England about New England. The list of such works is long, John Cotton alone (and because this study centered on Boston his writings were accented) accounting for well over thirty of them in the compilation of Julius H. Tuttle, "Writings of Rev. John Cotton," *Bibliographical Essays: A Tribute to Wilberforce Eames* (Cambridge, Mass., 1924). One cannot, however, as has so often been done, approach this literature with the idea that it is applicable to a general and relatively static scene—a given "New England Way" conceived in old England and brought to fruition in the New World. All the accepted standards of historical criticism must be applied, for each pamphlet was written at a moment in time, for a specific purpose, aimed at a specific audience by a specific person with a specific point of view; its primary value (in this study in any event) has been to show the ministerial reaction to certain pressures emanating from within and without the commonwealth. The documents relating to given incidents in the development of a New England Way must be considered too. Many of these documents were collected by Williston Walker for his *The Creeds and Platforms of Congregationalism* (N. Y., 1893). Those concerning the Hutchinsonian outbreak have been brought together by Charles Francis Adams in *Antinomianism in the Colony of Massachusetts Bay, 1636-1638* (Boston, 1894). Those concerning the Cambridge Platform are scattered, but the most vital are in the possession of the American Antiquarian Society, Worcester, Mass. Useful too is a volume of Ecclesiastical Papers, Boston Public Library.

Finally, the letters and papers of the ministers must be considered. In many ways, because they were not generally meant for the public, they are more revealing than sermons and tracts. John Cotton's papers, in particular, have been of value in the present study, for while most were destroyed at his death, those that have survived are tremendously revealing. The largest single body is preserved as part of the Prince Collection in the Boston Public Library, but isolated items are to be found in the manuscript collections cited elsewhere in this note, and in a variety of contemporary and near-contemporary pamphlets—his "Propositions Concerning of Consociation and Communion of Churches, tendred to the Elders and Brethren of the Church for their Consideration and acceptance according to God" of *circa*

1650, together with a number of letters dealing with baptism, for example, being found in Increase Mather, *The First Principles of New-England Concerning the Subject of Baptisme & Communion of Churches* ... (Cambridge, Mass., 1675).

Supplementing these records are the descriptions and comments of contemporaries and near-contemporaries. The number of such—framed as letters, pamphlets, or histories—is phenomenal and only a few of the most valuable are mentioned here. Some are valuable for their descriptions: William Wood, *New Englands Prospect. A True, Lively, and Experimentall Description of That Part of America, Commonly Called New England* ... (London, 1634); "Report of Edmund Browne," Col. Soc. Mass., *Publications*, 8 (1905); *New Englands First Fruits* ... (London, 1643); Robert Child's descriptive letter to Samuel Hartlib, 1645, in Col. Soc. Mass., *Publications*, 38 (1959); *Good News from New-England: With an Exact Relation of the First Planting That Countrey* ... (London, 1648); John Eliot's "Description of New England in 1650," in Mass. Hist. Soc., *Proceedings*, 2d Ser., 2 (1886); William Bradford's descriptive poetry in Mass. Hist. Soc., *Collections*, 1st Ser., 3 (1794), and *Proceedings*, 1st Ser., 11 (1871); Samuel Maverick, "A Briefe Discription of New England ...," Mass. Hist. Soc., *Proceedings*, 2d Ser., 1 (1885); John Josselyn, *An Account of Two Voyages to New-England* ... (London, 1675), the first voyage being in 1638; and the various works of Joshua Scotto, including his *A Narrative of the Planting of the Massachusetts Colony* ... (Boston, 1694).

Others are more valuable for the events they describe: the letters of Plymouth's Samuel Fuller in 1630 included in "Governor [William] Bradford's Letter Book," Mass. Hist. Soc., *Collections*, 1st Ser., 3 (1794); Israel Stoughton, "A relation concerning some occurrences in New England [1635]," in Mass. Hist. Soc., *Proceedings*, 1st Ser., 5 (1862); John Child, *New-Englands Jonas Cast Up at London: Or, A Relation of the Proceedings of the Court at Boston in New-England Against Divers Honest and Godly Persons* (London, 1647) and Edward Winslow's answer, *New-Englands Salamander, Discovered by an Irreligious and Scornfull Pamphlet, Called New-Englands Jonas* ... (London, 1647); John Clark, *Ill Newes from New-England:*

Or a Narrative of New-Englands Persecution. Wherin Is Declared That while Old England Is Becoming New, New-England Is Becoming Old (London, 1652).

Samuel Danforth's *Almanacks* for 1646, 1647, 1648, and 1649 contain occasional items of interest. "The Diaries of John Hull ..." in American Antiquarian Society, *Archaelogia Americana*, 3 (1857), although principally applicable to the post-1650 period, contain some comments on the earlier years. Much can be gained from J. Franklin Jameson, ed., *[Edward] Johnson's Wonder-Working Providence, 1628-1651* (N. Y., 1910); William Hubbard, *General History of New England*, in Mass. Hist. Soc., *Collections*, 2d Ser., 5-6 (1816); and Cotton Mather, *Magnalia Christi Americana; Or, The Ecclesiastical History of New-England* ..., 2 vols. (Hartford, 1852). Plymouth's historians throw light on an occasional point: William Bradford, *Of Plymouth Plantation: 1620-1647*, ed. Samuel Eliot Morison (N. Y., 1953), and Nathaniel Morton's 1669 *New Englands Memoriall*, ed. Howard J. Hall (N. Y., 1937).

Other commentaries—together with occasional documents— can be found scattered in the many volumes of the *New England Historical and Genealogical Register*; Essex Institute, *Historical Collections*; Bostonian Society, *Publications*; American Antiquarian Society, *Proceedings*; and in various collections of letters and papers such as the "Mather Papers," Mass. Hist. Soc., *Collections*, 4th Ser., 8 (1868), supplemented by the manuscript Mather Papers in the Prince Collection, Boston Public Library (among which are a few Cotton items); "Pincheon Papers," Mass. Hist. Soc., *Collections*, 2d Ser., 8 (1819): also helpful are the letters and papers included in such works as Alexander Young, comp., *Chronicles of the First Planters of the Colony of Massachusetts Bay, from 1623 to 1636* (Boston, 1846); Ebenezer Hazard, comp., *Historical Collections: Consisting of State Papers and Other Authentic Documents*, 2 vols. (Philadelphia, 1792-94); Peter Force, comp., *Tracts and Other Papers Relating Principally to . . . the Colonies in North America . . .* , 4 vols. (Washington, 1836-46); Thomas Hutchinson, *History of the Colony and Province of Massachusetts-Bay*, ed. Lawrence Shaw Mayo, 3 vols. (Cambridge, Mass., 1936)—where, for example, one can find the record of Anne Hutchinson's trial before the General Court—and his *Collection of Original Papers Relative to the History of the Colony of Massachusetts-Bay* (Boston, 1769), the latter supplemented by volumes CCXL, CCXLI, CCXLII of the Massachusetts Archives, "Papers Relating to Massachusetts Assembled by Thomas Hutchinson," which include many documents omitted from the published collection.

A community study such as the present work requires a line-by-line perusal of the extant records and a continuing compilation and comparison of data. Thus, for example, the material presented and the conclusions drawn as to the enrichment of Boston as a result of its being the capital of the commonwealth are based upon a compilation of the officers of the commonwealth and county situated in the town and the amount of their compensation, together with the known payments to officers, witnesses, jurymen and so forth to meet their expenses at Boston's inns and rooming houses. The conclusions about the independent institutional development of the town are founded upon a compilation of the commonwealth laws and actions regarding the town, and a comparison with the known activities of the community. Moreover, a community study of this nature requires that the author become familiar with as many individuals within the town as possible. A student of a twentieth-century community could do this by sending questionnaires to every householder and businessman; a student of the seventeenth century can do much the same thing, but he must fill out the questionnaires himself, painstakingly recording the answers as they reveal themselves in the course of his research. In the present case, biographical data for approximately 1,500 male residents of the town during the years covered has been amassed from the records and supplemented by such works as James Savage's *A Genealogical Dictionary of New England*, 4 vols. (Boston, 1860-62); Oliver Ayer Roberts, *History of the Military Company of Massachusetts, Now Called the Ancient and Honorable Artillery*, 4 vols. (Boston, 1895-1901); Robert F. Seybolt, *The Town Officials of Colonial Boston, 1634-1775* (Cambridge, Mass., 1929); the work of Charles Edward Banks, notably *The Planters of the Commonwealth, 1620-1640* (Boston, 1930); and the prodigious labors of New England's genealogists as reflected in the *New England Historical and Genealogical Register* and other journals. Wherever possible information has been compiled as to the date of arrival of each adult male; place of origin; dates of temporary and permanent departures and destinations; occupations (plural inasmuch as some Bostonians tended to change vocations frequently); property (including valuations, dates acquired, and, where applicable, disposition); investments and commercial transactions; dates of inhabitantship; freemanship; names of wives and dates of marriages; origins of wives; church status of husband and wife, together with the dates of affiliation; the names, birthdates, church affiliations (including dates of baptisms and church memberships if applicable) of children; church and secular discipline; church, town, and commonwealth offices; the extent of participation in church, town, and commonwealth affairs. The data so gathered is the backbone of the conclusions relative to the numbers and relationships to one another and the community as a whole of the inhabitants, church members, freemen, and sojourners, the nature of the town's gentry and its hold upon the community, landholding, economic activity —indeed, the data is an integral part of almost every line of the work.

With regard to population figures given here and there in the text and particularly in the chart of "Estimated Population of the Commonwealth and Town, 1630-50" in chap. 7, the fact should be noted that all such figures are no more than calculated guesses based upon careful computations and the comparison of figures arrived at by various computing methods. Figures for the commonwealth population are occasionally given in the sources and, with some few exceptions, are cited in Evarts B. Greene and Virginia D. Harrington, comps., *American Population Before the Federal Census of 1790* (N. Y., 1932) or Franklin B. Dexter, comp., *Estimates of Population in the American Colonies* (Worcester, 1887). Greater refinement can be obtained by establishing a figure for January 1631—the Winthrop fleet's 700, plus old settlers and other arrivals, less departures and deaths—and adding to this figure a calculated annual increase based upon the number of ship arrivals to 1643 (approximately 200 in all), the average number of passengers carried computed from extant passenger lists (80 in the years through 1636 and 154 thereafter, the difference being accounted for by the lighter freight carried in the later ships), plus an estimated natural increase, less estimated numbers to account for deaths, those returning to England, and those moving on from the Bay to settlements in Connecticut or Rhode Island. The increase from 1643 through 1650 can be established by computing natural increase, plus an estimated number of new arrivals, less deaths and departures.

With regard to Boston, the present author has used three basic methods of computation, arriving at a final figure by comparing the results. The first was based upon the number of known property owners in the town at a given moment as compiled by Samuel C. Clough in his "Remarks on the Compilation of the Boston Book of Possessions," Col. Soc. Mass., *Publications*, 27 (1932) and Charles Lamb in *Series of Plans of Boston Showing Existing Ways and Owners of Property 1630-1635–1640-1645* (Boston, 1905), both being revised in the light of the author's own listing of property owners on and off—the latter a factor neglected by both Lamb and Clough—Shawmut. The second was based upon tax and militia assessments laid upon the town by the General Court, using the formula

$$\frac{\text{Boston Assessments}}{\text{Total Assessments}} \quad \text{as} \quad \frac{\text{Boston Population}}{\text{Total Population}}$$

This method was particularly useful for the early 1630's when specific levies were frequently assessed and the town's proportion was determined largely on the basis of population. Still a third method was to calculate upon the basis of families and single persons identifiable as residents of the town at any given moment.

On the whole, secondary material, though often illuminating, has contributed little to the conclusions reached on any major point, its use with regard to the English scene and (in chap. 1 particularly) prevalent English assumptions as to the nature of the state and church being the exception. In this regard, mention should be made of Charles H. and Katherine George's very refreshing *The Protestant Mind of the English Reformation,*

1570-1640 (Princeton, 1961), a study which stands in sharp contrast to those which, following a long tradition, work backward from the events of the English Civil War and in New England to find a unique Puritan strand in English thought.

Certain general studies dealing with New England and Massachusetts have contributed to the broad framework of the present study. Of older works, the most useful was John Gorham Palfrey's *History of New England During the Stuart Dynasty,* 3 vols. (Boston, 1859-64). Among more recent works those of Edmund S. Morgan stand out—*The Puritan Dilemma: The Story of John Winthrop* (Boston and Toronto, 1958), *The Puritan Family: Essays on Religion and Domestic Relations in Seventeenth Century New England* (Boston, 1944), and his very excellent *Visible Saints: The History of a Puritan Idea* (N. Y., 1963)—as do those of Perry Miller, his *The New England Mind,* vol. I, *The Seventeenth Century* (N. Y., 1939), and vol. II, *From Colony to Province* (Cambridge, Mass., 1953), together with *Orthodoxy in Massachusetts, 1630-1650* (Cambridge, Mass., 1933); Samuel Eliot Morison, *The Puritan Pronaos: Studies in the Intellectual Life of New England in the Seventeenth Century* (N. Y., 1946), and particularly his *The Founding of Harvard College* (Cambridge, Mass., 1935); Charles M. Andrews, *The Colonial Period of American History: The Settlements,* 3 vols. (New Haven, 1934-37); George Lee Haskins, *Law and Authority in Early Massachusetts . . .* (N. Y., 1960); Bernard Bailyn, *The New England Merchants in the Seventeenth Century* (Cambridge, Mass., 1955); Emery Battis, *Saints and Sectaries: Anne Hutchinson and the Antinomian Controversy in the Massachusetts Bay Colony* (Chapel Hill, 1962); Larzer Ziff, *The Career of John Cotton: Puritanism and the American Experience* (Princeton, 1962).

Works dealing with Boston alone are many, although almost invariably antiquarian in outlook. The best are Arthur A. Ellis, *History of the First Church in Boston* (Boston, 1881); Justin Winsor's monumental *Memorial History of Boston, Including Suffolk County, Massachusetts,* vol. I, *The Early and Colonial Periods* (Boston, 1882); Nathaniel B. Shurtleff's older *A Topographical and Historical Description of Boston* (Boston, 1871);

Walter Muir Whitehill, *Boston: A Topographical History* (Cambridge, Mass., 1959)—invaluable in tracing the geographical changes of over three centuries; and the pertinent sections of Carl Bridenbaugh's *Cities in the Wilderness: The First Century of Urban Life in America, 1625-1742* (N. Y., 1938).

Although the present writer does not agree completely with any of these authors, he is indebted to all of them in some way. A peculiar debt is owed to B. Katherine Brown, whose articles on "The Puritan Concept of Aristocracy" and "Freemanship in Massachusetts" in the *Mississippi Valley Historical Review*, 61 (1954-55), and *American Historical Review*, 59 (1954), first led him to doubt the long-standing shibboleths about New England.

INDEX